© Canetti Erben Zürich / Carl Hanser Ver[...]

Elias Canetti

I Want to Keep Smashing Myself Until I Am Whole

Edited and with an Introduction by Joshua Cohen

Elias Canetti was born in 1905 into a Sephardic Jewish family in Ruse, Bulgaria. He moved to Vienna in 1924, where he became involved in literary circles while studying for a degree in chemistry. He remained in Vienna until the Anschluss, when he immigrated to England and later to Switzerland, where he died in 1994. In 1981, Canetti was awarded the Nobel Prize in Literature for "writings marked by a broad outlook, a wealth of ideas and artistic power."

Joshua Cohen is the author of six novels, including *Witz*, *Book of Numbers*, and, most recently, *The Netanyahus*, which won the 2022 Pulitzer Prize for Fiction and the 2021 National Jewish Book Award for Fiction. His writing has appeared in *Harper's Magazine*, the *London Review of Books*, *n+1*, and *The Paris Review*, among other publications. Called "a major American writer" by *The New York Times* and "an extraordinary prose stylist, surely one of the most prodigious at work in American fiction today" by *The New Yorker*, Cohen was awarded Israel's 2013 Matanel Prize, and in 2017 was named one of *Granta*'s Best of Young American Novelists. He lives in New York City.

Also by Elias Canetti

Notes from Hampstead

The Agony of Flies

The Secret Heart of the Clock

Essays in Honor of Elias Canetti

The Play of the Eyes

The Conscience of Words

Comedy of Vanity and *Life-Terms*

The Torch in My Ear

The Tongue Set Free

Earwitness: Fifty Characters

The Human Province

The Voices of Marrakesh

Crowds and Power

Auto-da-Fé

I Want
to Keep
Smashing
Myself
Until I
Am
####### Whole

I Want
to Keep
Smashing
Myself
Until I
Am
Whole

An Elias Canetti Reader

Edited and with an Introduction by
Joshua Cohen

Picador   New York

Picador
120 Broadway, New York 10271

Library of Congress Cataloging-in-Publication Data
Names: Canetti, Elias, 1905–1994, author. | Cohen, Joshua, 1980– editor, writer of
    introduction.
Title: I want to keep smashing myself until I am whole : an Elias Canetti reader /
    Elias Canetti ; edited and with an introduction by Joshua Cohen.
Description: First edition. | New York : Picador, 2022.
Identifiers: LCCN 2022018468 | ISBN 9780374298425 (paperback)
Subjects: LCSH: Canetti, Elias, 1905–1994—Translations into English. | LCGFT: Essays.
Classification: LCC PT2605.A58 I33 2022 | DDC 834/.912—dc23/eng/20220415
LC record available at https://lccn.loc.gov/2022018468

Designed by Gretchen Achilles

Our books may be purchased in bulk for promotional,
educational, or business use. Please contact your local bookseller
or the Macmillan Corporate and Premium Sales Department at
1-800-221-7945, extension 5442, or by email at
MacmillanSpecialMarkets@macmillan.com.

For book club information, please visit facebook.com/picadorbookclub
or email marketing@picadorusa.com.

picadorusa.com • instagram.com/picador
twitter.com/picadorusa • facebook.com/picadorusa

10 9 8 7 6 5 4 3 2 1

Contents

Introduction

By Joshua Cohen

How to biographize Elias Canetti, one of the world's great *auto*biographers? What account would be useful? What usefulness could also be made beautiful? What should be the relationship between his own version of himself—his own multiple versions—and this? On the one hand, it would be wasteful to spend this introduction previewing the very same information that will be encountered again, in better prose, in the pages to come (and in the hundreds and hundreds of Canetti's pages that I didn't include, many of which struck me on certain days as just as worthy of inclusion). On the other hand, to be too unfaithful to Canetti's memoirs would be a betrayal: it would be pointless if not merely uncharitable to make a survey of the author's omissions, obscurations, mutilations, and straight-up falsifications, because my purpose here is to introduce Canetti the Major Writer You Should Read and not to vouch for the character of Canetti the Friend (not a very good friend), or Canetti the Husband (not a very good husband), or Canetti the Lover or Brother or Father or Son (it's all pretty messy, to be honest).

I might take counsel from Canetti's wife Veza, herself a novelist of high accomplishment, who once wrote in a letter to Canetti's brother Georg: "No document that gives access to Canetti's inmost being must be allowed to survive."

Or I might take counsel from Georg, who, when Veza asked him to destroy that letter—to destroy all her letters—did not.

And that, I'm realizing, is the best approach: to address myself to the destructions that did happen, to address myself to the burnings.

The First Austrian Republic in which Canetti came of age was the fractious remnant of a lost empire, a struggling democracy rived between an entrenched rightist nationalism aligned with industry and the Catholic Church and a diffuse coalition of socialist/communist/generally leftist labor organizations. Each camp maintained its own paramilitaries composed primarily of veterans of the First World War. In the winter of 1927, a rightist paramilitary called the Frontkämpfervereinigung held a rally in Schattendorf, near the Hungarian border, which was considered the territory of a leftist paramilitary called the Schutzbund. The two groups clashed outside the Schattendorf train station and two affiliates of the Schutzbund were shot dead: Matthias Csmarits—a Croatian who'd lost an eye fighting for the dual monarchy—and Josef Grössing, a schoolboy, age eight. Three Frontkämpfer were charged with murder in the Vienna courts, but they pleaded self-defense and in midsummer were acquitted. The day of the verdict was July 15, the day after Bastille Day. The workers of Vienna called for strikes and a street protest turned into a riot. Agitators descended on the Palace of Justice, just off the Ringstraße, shattered its windows, smashed its furnishings, and set its archives on fire. Firefighters arrived, but the rioters cut their hoses. The police responded with bullets, which left nearly ninety people dead and nearly six hundred people wounded.

Among the witnesses to the carnage was Elias Canetti, whose chronicle of the event appears here on page 303, and includes the statement that July 15, 1927, "may have been the most crucial day of my life after my father's death."

At the time, Canetti was a twenty-one-year-old student desultorily pursing a medical education at the University of Vienna. He had already lived in five countries (Ottoman Bulgaria, England, Switzerland, Germany, Austria), acquired five languages (Ladino, Bulgarian, English, French, German), and weathered one world war.

What made July 15, 1927, especially "crucial" (only the English has the implication of excruciation and martyrdom) was that it provided Canetti with the scenes and themes—of fires, of crowds—for the two major books of his career.

Die Blendung (The Blinding) is Canetti's only novel, published in 1935. It concerns a reclusive Viennese bibliophile and Sinologist who, at erotic and professional loose ends, or merely channeling the society that surrounds him, ends up torching his own vast library, and in the process immolates himself. Canetti derived the character from an unidentified man in the crowd who, in the throes of the July 15 unrest, was yelling, "The files are burning! All the files!" The question of what would motivate a man to mourn the death of archives amid the deaths of fellow humans was to preoccupy Canetti through the advent of the Nazi book pyres. *Die Blendung* was translated into English as *Auto-da-Fé*—the preferred ordeal of the Inquisition, which displaced Canetti's Sephardic Jewish ancestors from Spain—though Canetti's original suggestion for the translated title was *Holocaust*.

Masse und Macht (*Crowds and Power*) is a nonfiction treatise that Canetti claimed to have begun even before he began the novel, though he published it only in 1960. Its few hundred dense pages of anthropology, sociology, comparative religion, and incomparable metaphysics mine its author's memories of July 15 to forge a prototype and study of "the crowd," that amorphous and often arsonous body that Canetti regarded as the ultimate political symbol of his era—a symbol that was also a process, by which individuals become consolidated and absorbed into a mass: "In the crowd the individual feels that he is transcending the limits of his own person." Note how this transcendence is just a feeling, however, a promise that when unfulfilled causes a reaction of base physicality, of craven violence, which doesn't always ebb as the crowd disperses: "So long as the fleeing crowd does not disintegrate into individuals worried only about themselves, about their own persons, then the crowd still exists, although fleeing."

Canetti's milieu might have been the last in world history to still *believe*—to accept as a substitute for the belief in God a belief in the attainability of Enlightenment synthesis. Novelists Hermann Broch and Robert Musil were producing books that tried simultaneously to document reality—which was being changed by innovations of mass communication, or media—and to arrange it according to the principles of realism; their writing was founded on this paradox, in which fiction was responsible both for reporting the facts and for making their chaos conform to aesthetic order. Writers of nonfiction, meanwhile, worked toward theories, systems, rationalistic or at least self-rationalizing methodologies of explanation. Think of the Frankfurt School, for example, which erected itself atop the ruins of Freud and Marx. Canetti tried his hand at the epic novel and concluded its pages in flames. He tried his hand at the grand unifying theory of crowds and wound up alone and lonely, claiming he never wanted or needed the followers he never even had. It was only in the memoirs that he achieved the dream of novelistic fluency and programmatic amplitude, though even that series went unfinished. Of the five planned volumes, each to be titled after an organ of sense, only three—*The Tongue Set Free*, *The Torch in My Ear*, and *The Play of the Eyes*—were completed and published. The third volume ends with its hero at his mother's deathbed in Paris, on June 15, 1937. The author himself went on to London after the Anschluss and never wrote the fourth, a volume dedicated to the olfactory: the smoke of the Blitz might've been too acrid. (*Party in the Blitz*, an abandoned manuscript that never appeared in Canetti's lifetime, presents the author's chronicle of the Germanophone émigré scene in wartime Hampstead, and, aside from vibrant sketches of Arthur Waley and Franz Boas, is most notable for its pungent treatment of Iris Murdoch. As for a fifth volume dedicated to touch: the cheek-by-jowl masses of *Crowds and Power* must suffice.)

The more distance Canetti had from Mitteleuropa, the less interest he evinced in a totalizing prose project, which he came to associate with totalitarianism. It was as if the book that had once aspired to contain the world had now become the book that could only confine it and chain the author to his desk, his chair, his first-person singular pronoun and its convictions. Where once certainty had obtained, mistrust and doubt were setting in, which might explain why, when the Swedes awarded him the Nobel Prize in Literature in 1981 "for writings marked by a broad outlook, a wealth of ideas and artistic power," Canetti accepted mutely: he gave the Stockholm crowd no lecture.

Canetti's late-life writing, both before and after the Nobel, consists almost exclusively of *Aufzeichnungen*, a bureaucratic, even clinical word that can be translated as "records," or "re-

cordings," or "briefs," or "notes," which Canetti applied to a
diverse array of texts—traditional aphorisms, feuilletonesque
caricatures, mock-Socratic dialogues—that all had their origins
in his notebooks. Canetti's daily dedication to these notebooks
turned them into the realest of his memoirs, almost a real-time
diary of his thoughts, with hardly any autobiographical content. Faced with the prospect, or with the dread, of publication,
Canetti would often merely cull from these notebooks, making
various selections: *The Human Province*, for example, contains
Aufzeichnungen from 1942 to 1972, while *Notes from Hampstead* contains *Aufzeichnungen* from 1954 to 1971, though
the volumes have scant overlapping material. At other times,
Canetti would take one or more of his *Aufzeichnungen* as the
basis of a theme, to guide his further writing in the development of standalone volumes, such as *Earwitness*, a miscellany
of character types, and *The Voices of Marrakesh*, a travelogue.
It was in the *Aufzeichnungen*, and through his reading of clas-
sical Chinese philosophy, and of Kafka, that Canetti finally
came to terms with the principle of incompletion, and to understand it not as a failure of the artist, but as a triumph of art—
specifically, as a triumph of art over death, because the aura cast
by incompletion made that art into a mystery for the future.
To make something unfinished—to set out to make something
unfinished—was to enlist the imagination of the generations to
come, should they be up to the task, should they even comprehend the task. Canetti's final book, the posthumously published
The Book Against Death, excerpts of which appear here for the
first time in English, is the epitome of that challenge.

Almost three decades after Canetti's passing (Zurich, 1994),
here he is again, in America, a country he alternately ignored
and derided. I can't help but wonder which favor America will

return on this occasion. I accepted the honor of putting Canetti between fresh covers because I, like pretty much everyone else during the past two years of pandemic-caused lockdown and crowd avoidance, became interested in "freedom"—rather, I became interested in why I'm often ashamed to speak that word, and why I'm often ashamed to admit that I'm ashamed to speak it, and so on. Perhaps my reaction has to do with the clunk of the verbiage itself—I can't help but regard that "-dom" slapped onto the end as vaguely sadomasochistically sexual—or perhaps it's the hint of sanctimony or sham piety with which it tends to be employed. In Canetti's youth, peoples—entire ethnicities, entire races—yearned and fought for collective freedoms and self-determined governance. Consider the innocence of early Zionism, or the patriotic fervor of Ottoman- and Habsburg-era Bulgarians, Romanians, Slovenes, Croats, and Poles. But sometime after the Second World War, in which Germany failed to re-create by force a perverse version of the empires that crumbled in the First, these notions of autonomy suffered a contraction, especially in America: now the entity seeking freedom was doing so not in an imperial but in a national context and was more likely to be the subgroup (female, gay, black), or the individual subsumed into multiple groups at the intersections of depersonalized identity.

It might be that my discomfort with the word "freedom" is only my discomfort with the exclusionary politics of those who abuse it (in much the same way, I'm disturbed by the exemptionary politics of those who abuse "liberty"). But then it might also have to do with the fact that I was born in 1980 and so grew up in an America that was still cheering the collapse of the Soviet Union when it was attacked by religious fundamentalists and reacted by declaring war on the world—an endless technologized jihad of surveillance and control that by now has lasted half my lifetime. Whatever the cause of my word-aversion, the fact remains: as I became an adult, I found it harder and harder to write the word "free" without irony and to read the word "free" without thinking that it referred to something that cost nothing. As a writer—not just as a writer in a free society, but as a writer period—it sometimes feels as if I possess, or would be able to possess, every freedom except one, which is the freedom to be unpolitical, the freedom not to have my every sentence be judged by the terms of my identity, as construed by each of my readers.

Canetti, exile, cosmopole, polyglot, was among the first modern voices who refused this—among the first modern voices who refused identity and politics and their conflation in what's now called "identity politics," which his Viennese experience told him was the primary sign, or symptom, of the individual's absorption by the crowd, or of the crowd's co-option of selfhood and independent conscience. Canetti's scorning of this crowd-consumed human was akin to his scorning of Freudian orthodoxy and of the fashionable Marxist, or Marxish, Frankfurt thought of Adorno, Horkheimer, Marcuse, and Habermas: he abhorred the former's tendency to relate all behavior and ideation to trauma, just as he abhorred the latter's tendency to relate all behavior and ideation to capital. "I want to keep smashing myself until I am whole," this indefinable, unassimilable Spanish-Jewish, Ottoman-Balkan, Viennese, British, Swiss world citizen wrote in one of his *Aufzeichnungen* from the start of the 1950s, when Europe had been smashed and wholeness was no longer the property of crowds but the ambition of the information-crowded individual.

Canetti's destructive-creative act takes the violence he witnessed in Vienna and turns it inward: the smashing that he's advocating is one in which we individually shatter our superficial vocabularies and politicized identities of false belonging and go sifting through the rubble for the common thoughts and emotions that underlie them and connect us with others and enable us to imagine and inhabit other lives.

It's this Ovidian ideal of mutual imagination and inhabitation that inspired another of the texts that makes its English-language debut here, "The Profession of the Poet," an essay-manifesto in which Canetti declares:

> A poet should try, no matter the cost, to preserve a gift that once was inherent but now has atrophied, and he should do so in order to keep open the doors between people—himself and others. He must be capable of becoming everyone: the smallest, the most naive, the most powerless. But this desire to experience others from within can never be determined by the goals that compose what we call our normal or official lives. This desire would have to be completely free from any hope of success or achievement; it would have to constitute its own desire: the desire for metamorphosis.

Whether an "inherent" poetic gift granted by the gods, or an "atrophied" speech freedom guaranteed by the state, this metamorphic ability to "becom[e] everyone," this protean desire "to experience others from within," remains unrealized for most of us—writers very much included—unwilling as we are to step from the crowd and perform its destruction on ourselves.

A Note on the Contents

In the hopes of emphasizing the scope and variety of Canetti's writing, I have chosen to intersperse my selections of the *Aufzeichnungen* between excerpts of the memoirs, *Auto-da-Fé*, *Crowds and Power*, and other volumes. While the *Aufzeichnungen* are drawn from collections published throughout Canetti's career, I've decided to arrange them by theme and not chronology, whereas the memoir excerpts are presented in chronological order, or at least in the order in which they originally appeared. Throughout, my intention was to create a book that, like its author, trusted its existence to mutability.

One omission I regret is Canetti's book about Kafka, *Kafka's Other Trial: The Letters to Felice*, a brief masterpiece of criticism I found unexcerptable, though fortunately it's still in print, where it begs to be read in its entirety. Another omission has to do with Canetti's correspondence, much of which is not publicly available, or reproducible, according to the terms of Canetti's will and the wishes of the Canetti estate. I made my selections not from the materials I had, but from the materials I could publish. All the texts in this volume were previously published in books by Farrar, Straus and Giroux, save the excerpts from *The Book Against Death*, translated for this volume by Peter Filkins, and "The Profession of the Poet," translated for this volume by Lucas Zwirner. I would like to thank Peter and Lucas, as well as my editors Jeremy Davies and Ian Van Wye, and finally to honor the memory of the translators and editors who came before them, especially Ralph Manheim, Joachim Neugroschel, Carol Stewart, and C. V. Wedgwood.

I

Notes and
Memoirs

1.

From *Notes from Hampstead: The Writer's Notes, 1954–1971*

Translated by John Hargraves

He wavers uncertainly between his descendants and his forebears. Which are more reliable? Who offer him more?

No sooner does the mere possibility of success appear on the horizon, than he tries to escape. His mistrust of success has become so great that he wants only to want it, not to have it.

I should like to contain everything within myself yet stay quite simple. That is hard. For I don't want to lose this variety, much as I wish to be simple.

The mystic's nature is not mine; it seems to me the mystic sacrifices too much for his happiness.

It all depends on this: *with whom we confuse ourselves.*

This tenderness toward everything we have seen before, and this revulsion toward so much we are seeing now.

———

His fear of all his endless little notebooks! By now they are mounting into the hundreds, every page covered, and he never opens a one of them! This prolific writer of nothing, what is so important for him to tell no one?

2.

From *The Tongue Set Free*

Part I: "Ruschuk, 1905–1911"

Translated by Joachim Neugroschel

My Earliest Memory

My earliest memory is dipped in red. I come out of a door on the arm of a maid, the floor in front of me is red, and to the left a staircase goes down, equally red. Across from us, at the same height, a door opens, and a smiling man steps forth, walking toward me in a friendly way. He steps right up close to me, halts, and says: "Show me your tongue." I stick out my tongue, he reaches into his pocket, pulls out a jackknife, opens it, and brings the blade all the way to my tongue. He says: "Now we'll cut off his tongue." I don't dare pull back my tongue, he comes closer and closer, the blade will touch me any second. In the last moment, he pulls back the knife, saying: "Not today, tomorrow." He snaps the knife shut again and puts it back in his pocket.

Every morning, we step out of the door and into the red hallway, the door opens, and the smiling man appears. I know what he's going to say and I wait for the command to show my tongue. I know he's going to cut it off, and I get more and more scared each time. That's how the day starts, and it happens very often.

I kept it to myself and asked my mother about it only much later. She could tell by the ubiquitous red that it was the guesthouse in Carlsbad, where she had spent the summer of 1907 with my father and me. To take care of the two-year-old baby, she had brought along a nanny from Bulgaria, a girl who wasn't even fifteen. Every morning at the crack of dawn, the girl went out holding the child on her arm; she spoke only Bulgarian, but got along fine in the lively town, and was always back punctually with the child. Once, she was seen on the street with an unknown young man, she couldn't say anything about him, a chance acquaintance. A few weeks later, it turned out that the young man lived in the room right across from us, on the other side of the corridor. At night, the girl sometimes went to his room quickly. My parents felt responsible for her and sent her back to Bulgaria immediately.

Both of them, the maid and the young man, had always left the house very early in the morning, that's how they must have met, that's the way it must have started. The threat with the knife worked, the child quite literally held his tongue for ten years.

Family Pride

Ruschuk, on the lower Danube, where I came into the world, was a marvelous city for a child, and if I say that Ruschuk is in Bulgaria, then I am giving an inadequate picture of it. For people of the most varied backgrounds lived there, on any one day you could hear seven or eight languages. Aside from the Bulgarians, who often came from the countryside, there were many Turks, who lived in their own neighborhood, and next to it was the neighborhood of the Sephardim, the Spanish Jews—our neighborhood. There were Greeks, Albanians, Armenians, Gypsies. From the opposite side of the Danube came Rumanians; my wet nurse, whom I no longer remember, was Rumanian. There were also Russians here and there.

As a child, I had no real grasp of this variety, but I never stopped feeling its effects. Some people have stuck in my memory only because they belonged to a particular ethnic group and wore a different costume from the others. Among the servants that we had in our home during the course of six years, there was once a Circassian and later on an Armenian. My mother's best friend was Olga, a Russian woman. Once every week, Gypsies came into our courtyard, so many that they seemed like an entire nation; the terrors they struck in me will be discussed below.

Ruschuk was an old port on the Danube, which made it fairly significant. As a port, it had attracted people from all over, and the Danube was a constant topic of discussion. There were stories about the extraordinary years when the Danube froze over; about sleigh rides all the way across the ice to Rumania; about starving wolves at the heels of the sleigh horses.

Wolves were the first wild animals I heard about. In the fairy tales that the Bulgarian peasant girls told me, there were werewolves, and one night, my father terrorized me with a wolf mask on his face.

It would be hard to give a full picture of the colorful time of those early years in Ruschuk, the passions and the terrors. Anything I subsequently experienced had already happened in Ruschuk. There, the rest of the world was known as "Europe," and if someone sailed up the Danube to Vienna, people said he

was going to Europe. Europe began where the Turkish Empire
had once ended. Most of the Sephardim were still Turkish sub-
jects. Life had always been good for them under the Turks, better than for the Christian Slavs in the Balkans. But since many
Sephardim were well-to-do merchants, the new Bulgarian re-
gime maintained good relations with them, and King Ferdinand,
who ruled for a long time, was said to be a friend of the Jews.

The loyalties of the Sephardim were fairly complicated.
They were pious Jews, for whom the life of their religious community was rather important. But they considered themselves
a special brand of Jews, and that was because of their Spanish
background. Through the centuries since their expulsion from
Spain, the Spanish they spoke with one another had changed
little. A few Turkish words had been absorbed, but they were
recognizable as Turkish, and there were nearly always Spanish
words for them. The first children's songs I heard were Spanish, I heard old Spanish *romances*; but the thing that was most
powerful, and irresistible for a child, was a Spanish attitude.
With naive arrogance, the Sephardim looked down on other
Jews; a word always charged with scorn was *Todesco*, meaning
a German or Ashkenazi Jew. It would have been unthinkable
to marry a *Todesca*, a Jewish woman of that background, and
among the many families that I heard about or knew as a child
in Ruschuk, I cannot recall a single case of such a mixed marriage. I wasn't even six years old when my grandfather warned
me against such a misalliance in the future. But this general
discrimination wasn't all. Among the Sephardim themselves,
there were the "good families," which meant the ones that had
been rich since way back. The proudest words one could hear
about a person were: "*Es de buena famiglia*—he's from a good
family." How often and *ad nauseam* did I hear that from my
mother. When she enthused about the Viennese *Burgtheater*

and read Shakespeare with me, even later on, when she spoke about Strindberg, who became her favorite author, she had no scruples whatsoever about telling that she came from a good family, there was no better family around. Although the literatures of the civilized languages she knew became the true substance of her life, she never felt any contradiction between this passionate universality and the haughty family pride that she never stopped nourishing.

Even back in the period when I was utterly her thrall (she opened all the doors of the intellect for me, and I followed her, blind and enthusiastic), I nevertheless noticed this contradiction, which tormented and bewildered me, and in countless conversations during that time of my adolescence I discussed the matter with her and reproached her, but it didn't make the slightest impression. Her pride had found its channels at an early point, moving through them steadfastly; but while I was still quite young, that narrowmindedness, which I never understood in her, biased me against any arrogance of background. I cannot take people seriously if they have any sort of caste pride, I regard them as exotic but rather ludicrous animals. I catch myself having reverse prejudices against people who plume themselves on their lofty origin. The few times that I was friendly with aristocrats, I had to overlook their talking about it, and had they sensed what efforts this cost me, they would have forgone my friendship. All prejudices are caused by other prejudices, and the most frequent are those deriving from their opposites.

Furthermore, the caste in which my mother ranked herself was a caste of Spanish descent and also of money. In my family, and especially in hers, I saw what money does to people. I felt that those who were most willingly devoted to money were the worst. I got to know all the shades, from money-grubbing to paranoia. I saw brothers whose greed had led them to destroy one another in years of litigation, and who kept on litigating when there was no money left. They came from the same "good" family that my mother was so proud of. She witnessed all those things too, we often spoke about it. Her mind was penetrating; her knowledge of human nature had been schooled in the great works of world literature as well as in the experiences of her own life. She recognized the motives of the lunatic self-butchery her family was involved in; she could easily have penned a novel about it; but her pride in this same family remained unshaken. Had it been love, I could have readily understood it. But she didn't even love many of the protagonists, she was indignant at some, she had scorn for others, yet for the family as a whole, she felt nothing but pride.

Much later, I came to realize that I, translated to the greater dimensions of mankind, am exactly as she was. I have spent the best part of my life figuring out the wiles of man as he appears in the historical civilizations. I have examined and analyzed power as ruthlessly as my mother her family's litigations. There is almost nothing bad that I couldn't say about humans and humankind. And yet my pride in them is so great that there is only one thing I really hate: their enemy, death.

Kako la Gallinica
Wolves and Werewolves

An eager and yet tender word that I often heard was *la butica*. That was what they called the store, the business, where my grandfather and his sons usually spent the day. I was rarely taken there because I was too little. The store was located on a steep road running from the height of the wealthier districts of Ruschuk straight down to the harbor. All the major stores were on this street; my grandfather's *butica* was in a three-story building that struck me as high and stately because the residential houses up on the rise had only one story. The *butica* dealt in wholesale groceries, it was a roomy place and it smelled wonderful. Huge, open sacks stood on the floor, containing various kinds of cereals, there was millet, barley, and rice. If my hands were clean, I was allowed to reach into the sacks and touch the grains. That was a pleasant sensation, I filled my hand, lifted it up, smelled the grains, and let them slowly run back down again; I did this often, and though there were many other strange things in the store, I liked doing that best, and it was hard to get me away from the sacks. There was tea and coffee and especially chocolate. There were huge quantities of everything, and it was always beautifully packed, it wasn't sold in small amounts as in ordinary shops. I also especially liked the open sacks on the floor because they weren't too high for me and because when I reached in, I could feel the many grains, which meant so much to me.

Most of the things in the store were edible, but not all. There were matches, soaps, and candles. There were also knives, scissors, whetstones, sickles, and scythes. The peasants who came from the villages to shop used to stand in front of the instruments for a long time, testing the keenness with their fingers. I watched them, curious and a bit fearful; I was not allowed to touch the blades. Once, a peasant, who was probably amused by my face, took hold of my thumb, put it next to his, and showed me how hard his skin was. But I never received a gift of chocolate; my grandfather, who sat in an office in the back, ruled with an iron hand, and everything was wholesale. At home, he showed me his love because I had his full name, even his first name. But he didn't much care to see me in the store, and I wasn't allowed to stay long. When he gave an order, the employee who got the order dashed off, and sometimes an employee would leave the *butica* with packages. My favorite was a skinny, poorly dressed, middle-aged man, who always smiled absently. He had indefinite movements and jumped when my grandfather said anything. He appeared to be dreaming and was altogether different from the other people I saw in the store. He always had a friendly word for me; he spoke so vaguely that I could never understand him, but I sensed that he was well disposed toward me. His name was Chelebon, and since he was a poor and hopelessly incapable relative, my grandfather hired him out of pity. My grandfather always called to Chelebon as if he were a servant; that was how I remembered him, and I found out only much later that he was a brother of my grandfather's.

The street running past the huge gate of our courtyard was dusty and drowsy. If it rained hard, the street turned into mud, and the droshkeys left deep tracks. I wasn't allowed to play in the street, there was more than enough room in our big courtyard, and it was safe. But sometimes I heard a violent clucking from outside, it would get louder and louder and more excited. Then, before long, a man in black, tattered clothes, clucking and trembling in fear, would burst through the gate, fleeing the street children. They were all after him, shouting "*Kako! Kako!*" and clucking like hens. He was afraid of chickens, and that was why they harassed him. He was a few steps ahead of them and, right before my eyes, he changed into a hen. He clucked violently, but in desperate fear, and made fluttering motions with his arms. He breathlessly dashed up the steps to my grandfather's house, but never dared to enter; he jumped down on the other side and remained lying motionless. The children halted at the gate, clucking, they weren't allowed into the courtyard. When he lay there as if dead, they were a bit scared and ran away. But then they promptly launched into their victory chant: "*Kako la galli-nica! Kako la gallinica!*—Kako the chicken! Kako the chicken!" No sooner were they out of earshot than he got to his feet, felt himself all over, peered about cautiously, listened anxiously for a while, and then stole out of the courtyard, hunched, but utterly silent. Now he was no longer a chicken, he didn't flutter or cluck, and he was once again the exhausted neighborhood idiot.

Sometimes, if the children were lurking not too far away in the street, the sinister game started all over again. Usually, it moved to another street, and I couldn't see anything more. Maybe I felt sorry for Kako, I was always scared when he jumped, but what I couldn't get enough of, what I always watched in the same excitement, was his metamorphosis into a gigantic black hen. I couldn't understand why the children ran after him, and when he lay motionless on the ground after his leap, I was afraid he would never get up again and turn into a chicken again.

The Danube is very wide in its Bulgarian lower reaches. Giurgiu, the city on the other bank, was Rumanian. From there, I was told, my wet nurse came, my wet nurse, who fed me her milk. She had supposedly been a strong, healthy peasant woman and also nursed her own baby, whom she brought along. I always heard her praises, and even though I can't remember her, the word "Rumanian" has always had a warm sound for me because of her.

In rare winters, the Danube froze over, and people told exciting stories about it. In her youth, Mother had often ridden a sleigh all the way over to Rumania, she showed me the warm furs she had been bundled in. When it was very cold, wolves came down from the mountains and ravenously pounced on the horses in front of the sleighs. The coachman tried to drive them away with his whip, but it was useless, and someone had to fire at them. Once, during such a sleigh ride, it turned out that they hadn't taken anything to shoot with. An armed Circassian, who lived in the house as a servant, was supposed to come along, but he had been gone, and the coachman had started without him. They had a terrible time keeping the wolves at bay and were in great danger. If a sleigh with two men hadn't happened to come along from the opposite direction, things might have ended very badly, but the two men shot and killed one wolf and drove the others away. My mother had been terribly afraid; she described the red tongues of the wolves, which had come so close that she still dreamed about them in later years.

I often begged her to tell me this story, and she enjoyed telling it to me. Thus wolves became the first wild beasts to fill my imagination. My terror of them was nourished by the fairy tales I heard from the Bulgarian peasant girls. Five or six of them always lived in our home. They were quite young, perhaps ten or twelve years old, and had been brought by their families from the villages to the city, where they were hired out as serving maids in middle-class homes. They ran around barefoot in the house and were always in a high mettle; they didn't have much to do, they did everything together, and they became my earliest playmates.

In the evening, when my parents went out, I stayed at home with the girls. Low Turkish divans ran all the way along the walls of the huge living room. Aside from the carpets everywhere and a few small tables, they were the only constant furnishing that I can remember in that room. When it grew dark, the girls got scared. We all huddled together on one of the divans, right by the window; they took me into their midst, and now they began their stories about werewolves and vampires. No sooner was one story finished than they began the next; it was scary, and yet, squeezing against the girls on all sides, I felt good. We were so frightened that no one dared to stand up, and when my parents came home, they found us all wobbling in a heap.

Of the fairy tales I heard, only the ones about werewolves and vampires have lodged in my memory. Perhaps no other kinds were told. I can't pick up a book of Balkan fairy tales without instantly recognizing some of them. Every detail of them is present to my mind, but not in the language I heard them in. I heard them in Bulgarian, but I know them in German; this mysterious translation is perhaps the oddest thing that I have to tell about my youth, and since the language history of most children runs differently, perhaps I ought to say more about it.

To each other, my parents spoke German, which I was not allowed to understand. To us children and to all relatives and friends, they spoke Ladino. That was the true vernacular, albeit an ancient Spanish, I often heard it later on and I've never forgotten it. The peasant girls at home knew only Bulgarian, and I must have learned it with them. But since I never went to a Bulgarian school, leaving Ruschuk at six years of age, I very soon forgot Bulgarian completely. All events of those first few years were in Ladino or Bulgarian. It wasn't until much later that most of them were rendered into German within me. Only especially dramatic events, murder and manslaughter so to speak, and the worst terrors have been retained by me in their Ladino wording, and very precisely and indestructibly at that. Everything else, that is, most things, and especially anything Bulgarian, like the fairy tales, I carry around in German.

I cannot say exactly how this happened. I don't know at what point in time, on what occasion, this or that translated itself. I never probed into the matter; perhaps I was afraid to destroy my most precious memories with a methodical examination based on rigorous principles. I can say only one thing with certainty: The events of those years are present to my mind in all their

strength and freshness (I've fed on them for over sixty years),
but the vast majority are tied to words that I did not know at
that time. It seems natural to me to write them down now; I
don't have the feeling that I am changing or warping anything.
It is not like the literary translation of a book from one language
to another, it is a translation that happened of its own accord
in my unconscious, and since I ordinarily avoid this word like
the plague, a word that has become meaningless from overuse, I
apologize for employing it in this one and only case.

The Armenian's Ax
The Gypsies

The delight in topographical drawing, which Stendhal so deftly
indulges in throughout his *Henri Brulard*, is beyond me, and, to
my sorrow, I was always a poor draftsman. So I have to describe
the layout of the residential buildings around our courtyard
garden in Ruschuk.

When you stepped through the large gate from the street
into the courtyard, Grandfather Canetti's house stood immediately to the right. It looked statelier than the other houses, it
was also higher. But I can't say whether it had an upper floor in
contrast to the other single-story houses. It appeared taller in
any event because there were more steps leading up to it. It was
also brighter than the other houses, it may have been painted a
light color.

Opposite, to the left of the courtyard gate, stood the house
where my father's eldest sister, Aunt Sophie, lived with her
husband, Uncle Nathan. His family name was Eliakim, a name
I never cared for; perhaps it disturbed me because it didn't
sound Spanish like all the other names. They had three chil-

dren, Régine, Jacques, and Laurica. This last child, the youngest, was four years older than I, an age difference that played a baleful part.

Next to this house, in the same line, also on the left side of the courtyard, stood our house, which looked just like my uncle's. A few steps ran up to the two houses, ending in a porch the width of both together.

The garden courtyard between these three houses was very large; the draw well for water stood facing us, not in the center, but a little off to the side. It didn't yield enough, and most of the water came in gigantic barrels that were drawn by mules from the Danube. The Danube water couldn't be used without first being boiled, and it stood then in huge caldrons, cooling off on the porch in front of the house.

Behind the draw well and separated from the courtyard by a hedge, there was the orchard. It wasn't especially attractive, it was too regular, and perhaps not old enough; my mother's relatives had far more beautiful orchards.

It was through the narrow side of our house that you came in from the large courtyard. The house then stretched out far into the back, and even though it had only that one floor, it is very spacious in my memory. On the further side of the courtyard, you could walk all the way around the house, past the long side, and then enter a smaller yard, into which the kitchen opened. Here there was wood to be chopped, geese and chickens scurried about, there was always a hustle and bustle in the kitchen, the cook carried things out or in, and the half dozen little girls jumped about and were busy.

In this kitchen yard, there was often a servant chopping wood, and the one I remember best was my friend, the sad Armenian. While chopping, he sang songs, which I couldn't understand, but which tore my heart. When I asked my mother why he was so sad, she said bad people had wanted to kill all the Armenians in Istanbul, and he had lost his entire family. He had watched from a hiding place when they had killed his sister. Then he had fled to Bulgaria, and my father had felt sorry for him and taken him into the house. When he chopped wood now, he always had to think of his little sister, and that was why he sang those sad songs.

I developed a deep love for him. Whenever he chopped wood, I stood up on the divan at the end of the long living room, by the window facing the kitchen yard. Then I leaned out the window to watch him, and when he sang, I thought of his sister—and then I would always wish for a little sister myself. He had a long black mustache and pitch-black hair, and he seemed very huge, perhaps because I saw him when he lifted his arm up high with the ax. I loved him even more than the store employee Chelebon, whom I saw very infrequently after all. The Armenian and I exchanged a few words, but very few, and I don't know what the language was. But he waited for me before he started chopping. The instant he saw me, he smiled slightly and raised the ax, and it was terrible to watch his rage as he smashed into the wood. He became gloomy then and sang his songs. When he put the ax down, he smiled at me again, and I waited for his smile just as he waited for me, he, the first refugee in my life.

Every Friday, the Gypsies came. On Friday, the Jewish homes prepared everything for the Sabbath. The house was cleaned from top to bottom, the Bulgarian girls scooted all over the place, the kitchen hummed with activity, no one had time for me. I was all alone and waiting for the Gypsies, my face pressed against the garden window of the gigantic living room. I lived in panic fear of them. I assume it was the girls who also told me about Gypsies during the long evenings in the darkness. I thought about their stealing children and was convinced that they were after me.

But despite my fear, I wouldn't have missed seeing them; it was a splendid sight they offered. The courtyard gate had been opened wide for them, for they needed space. They came like an entire tribe: in the middle, tall and erect, a blind patriarch, the great-grandfather, as I was told, a handsome, white-haired old man; he walked very slowly, leaning on two grown grand-daughters right and left and wearing colorful rags. Around him, thronging densely, there were Gypsies of all ages, very few men, almost nothing but women, and countless children, the infants in their mother's arms; the rest sprang about, but never moved very far from the proud old man, who always remained the center. The whole procession had something strangely dense about it, I never otherwise saw so many people huddling so close together as they moved along; and in this very colorful city, they were the most colorful sight. The rags they had pieced together for their clothing shone in all colors, but the one that stood out sharpest was red. Sacks dangled from many of the shoulders, and I couldn't look at those sacks without imagining that they contained stolen children.

The Gypsies struck me as something without number, yet when I now try to estimate their number in my image of them, I would think that they were no more than thirty or forty. But still, I had never seen so many people in the big courtyard, and since they moved so slowly because of the old man, they seemed to fill the courtyard endlessly. They didn't stay there, however, they moved around the house and into the smaller courtyard by the kitchen, where the wood also lay in stacks, and that was where they settled.

I used to wait for the moment when they first appeared at

the entrance gate, and no sooner had I spotted the blind old man than I dashed, yelling "*Zinganas! Zinganas!*" through the long living room and the even longer corridor that connected the living room with the kitchen in back. My mother stood there, giving instructions for the Sabbath dishes; certain special delicacies she prepared herself. I ignored the little girls, whom I often met on the way; I kept yelling and yelling, until I stood next to my mother, who said something calming to me. But instead of remaining with her, I ran the whole long way back, glanced through the window at the progress of the Gypsies, who were a bit further by now, and then I promptly reported on them in the kitchen again. I wanted to see them, I was obsessed with them, but the instant I saw them I was again seized with fear that they were after me, and I ran away screaming. For a whole while, I kept dashing back and forth like that, and that's why, I believe, I retained such an intense feeling for the wide range of the house between the two courtyards.

As soon as they had all arrived at their destination by the kitchen, the old man settled down, the others grouped around him, the sacks opened, and the women accepted all the gifts without fighting for them. They got big pieces of wood from the pile, they seemed particularly keen on them; they got many foods. They got something of everything that was already prepared, by no means were leftovers fobbed off on them. I was relieved when I saw that they had no children in the sacks, and under my mother's protection I walked among them, studying them carefully but making sure I didn't get too close to the women, who wanted to caress me. The blind old man ate slowly from a bowl, resting and taking his time. The others didn't touch any of the food stuffs, everything vanished in the big sacks and only the children were allowed to nibble on the sweet things they had been given. I was amazed at how friendly they were to their children, not at all like nasty child-snatchers. But that changed nothing in my terror of them. After what seemed like a very long while, they started off again, the procession moved somewhat faster than upon entering; it went around the house and through the courtyard. I watched them from the same window as they vanished through the gate. Then I ran to the kitchen one last time to announce: "The Gypsies are gone!" Our servant took me by the hand, led me to the gate, and locked it up, saying: "Now they won't come back." The courtyard gate normally stayed open in the daytime, but on Fridays it was locked, so that any further group of Gypsies coming along afterward would know their people had been here already and would move on.

My Brother's Birth

At a very early time, when I was still in a highchair, the floor seemed very far away, and I was scared of falling out. Uncle Bucco, my father's eldest brother, visited us, picked me up, and placed me on the floor. Then he made a solemn face, put his palm on my head, and spoke: "*Yo ti bendigo, Eliachicu, Amen!*" (I bless thee, little Elias, Amen!) He said it very emphatically, I liked the solemn tone; I believe I felt bigger when he blessed me. But he was a joker and laughed too soon; I sensed he was making fun of me, and the great moment of benediction, which I was always taken in by, ended in embarrassment.

This uncle endlessly repeated everything he did. He taught me lots of ditties, never resting until I could sing them myself. When he came again, he asked about them, patiently training me to perform for the adults. I would wait for his blessing, even though he always promptly destroyed it, and had he been more restrained, he would have been my favorite uncle. He lived in

Varna, where he managed a branch of Grandfather's business, and he came to Ruschuk for the holidays and special occasions. The family spoke respectfully about him because he was the *Bucco*, which was the honorary title for the firstborn son in a family. I learned early on how important it was to be a firstborn son, and had I remained in Ruschuk, I would also have become a *Bucco*.

For four years, I remained the only child, and all that time, I wore little dresses like a girl. I wanted to wear trousers like a boy, and was always put off until later. Then my brother Nissim was born, and on this occasion I was allowed to wear my first pants. Everything that happened then I experienced in my trousers with great pride, and that is why I have retained every detail.

There were lots of people in the house, and I saw anxious faces. I was not allowed to go to my mother in the bedroom, where my crib was too; I wandered around by the door, to catch a glimpse of her whenever someone went in. But they always shut the door so quickly that I never laid eyes on her. I heard a wailing voice, which I didn't recognize, and when I asked who that was, I was told: "Go away!" I had never seen the grown-ups so anxious, and no one paid any attention to me, which I wasn't used to. (As I found out later, it was a long and hard labor, and they feared for my mother's life.) Dr. Menakhemoff was there, the physician with the long, black beard, and he too—who was otherwise so friendly and had me sing little ditties, for which he praised me—he neither looked at me nor spoke to me, and glared when I wouldn't go away from the door. The wailing grew louder, I heard "*Madre mia querida! Madre mia querida!*" I pressed my head against the door; when it opened, the moaning was so loud that I was horror-stricken. Suddenly I realized it came from my mother, and it was so eerie that I didn't want to see her anymore.

Finally, I was allowed into the bedroom, everyone was smiling, my father was laughing, and they showed me a little brother. Mother lay white and motionless in bed. Dr. Menakhemoff said: "She needs rest!" But the place wasn't at all restful. Strange women were going about the room; now I was there again for everyone, I was cheered up, and Grandmother Arditti, who seldom came into the house, said: "She's better." Mother said nothing. I was afraid of her and ran out and didn't hang around the door either. For a long while after that, my mother was alien to me, and it took months for me to regain confidence in her.

The next thing I can see is the Feast of Circumcision. Many more people came into the house. I was allowed to watch during the circumcision. I have the impression that they deliberately let me look. All doors were open, even the house door, a long covered table for the guests stood in the living room, and in another room, facing the bedroom, the circumcision took place. It was witnessed only by men, all standing. My tiny brother was held over a basin, I saw the knife, and particularly I saw a lot of blood dripping into the basin.

My brother was named after my mother's father, Nissim, and they explained that I was the eldest and was therefore named after my paternal grandfather. The position of the eldest son was so greatly emphasized that I remained conscious of it from that moment of the circumcision on and never lost my pride in it.

People then made merry at the table; I paraded around in my pants. I didn't rest until each of the guests had noticed them, and when new visitors came, I ran to greet them at the door and remained expectantly in front of them. There was a lot of coming and going; when everyone was there, they still missed Cousin Jacques from the neighboring house. "He's gone off on his bicycle," somebody said, and his behavior was disapproved of. After the meal, he arrived, covered with dust. I saw him jumping off the bicycle in front of the house; he was eight years older than I and wore the uniform of a Gymnasium student. He explained about the glorious new thing, he had only just been given the bicycle. Then he tried to sneak inconspicuously into the party, but I blurted out that I wanted a bike too. Aunt Sophie, his mother, swooped upon him and hauled him over the coals. He threatened me with his finger and vanished again.

On that day, I also realized that one has to keep one's mouth closed when eating. Régine, the sister of the bicycle owner, put nuts into her mouth, I stood before her spellbound, watching her chew with her mouth closed. It took a long time, and when she was done, she declared that I would have to eat like that too, otherwise they would stick me back into skirts. I must have learned fast, for I would not give up my trousers for anything in the world.

The Turk's House
The Two Grandfathers

Sometimes, when Grandfather Canetti was in the store, I was taken over to his house to pay respects to my grandmother. She sat on the Turkish divan, smoking and drinking strong coffee. She always stayed home, she never went out; I can't recall ever seeing her outside the house. Her name was Laura and, like Grandfather, she came from Adrianople. He called her "*Oro*," which actually means "gold," I never understood her name. Of all the relatives, she was the one that remained most Turkish. She never got up from her divan, I don't even know how she ever got there, for I never saw her walking, and she would sigh from time to time and drink another cup of coffee and smoke. She would greet me with a lamenting tone and, having said nothing to me, she let me go, lamenting. She had a few wailing sentences for whoever brought me. Perhaps she thought she was ill, perhaps she really was, but she was certainly lazy in an Oriental way, and she must have suffered under Grandfather, who was fiendishly lively.

Wherever he appeared, he was always instantly the center, which I didn't realize at the time; he was feared in his family, a tyrant who could weep hot tears if he wanted to. He felt most comfortable with his grandsons, who bore his name. Among friends and acquaintances, indeed throughout the Sephardic community, he was popular for his beautiful voice, which women particularly succumbed to. Whenever he was invited anywhere, he never took Grandmother along; he couldn't stand her stupidity and her continuous wailing. He was instantly surrounded by a big circle of people, told stories in which he played many parts, and on special occasions, he yielded to entreaties to sing.

Aside from Grandmother, there was a lot in Ruschuk that was Turkish. The first children's song I learned—"*Manzanicas coloradas, las que vienen de Stambol*," "Little apples, red, red apples, those that come from Istanbul"—ended with the name of the Turkish capital, and I heard how gigantic it was, and I soon connected it with the Turks we saw in our city. Edirne (Turkish for Adrianople, the city from which both Canetti grandparents came) was often mentioned. Grandfather sang never-ending Turkish songs, the point being to dwell on certain high notes for a very long time; I much preferred the fiercer and faster Spanish songs.

Not far from us, the well-to-do Turks had their homes; you could recognize them by the narrow-set bars on the windows for guarding the women. The first murder I ever heard about

was when a Turk killed someone out of jealousy. On the way
to Grandfather Arditti's home, my mother took me past one
of those houses; she showed me a high grating, saying a Turkish woman had stood there and looked at a Bulgarian passing
by. The Turk, her husband, then came and stabbed her. I don't
believe that I had previously really grasped what a dead person
was. But I learned what it meant during this promenade with
my mother. I asked her whether the Turkish woman, who had
been found in a pool of blood on the floor, had gotten up again.
"Never!" she said. "Never! She was dead, do you understand?"
I heard, but I didn't understand, and I asked again, forcing her
to repeat her answer several times, until she lost patience and
spoke about something else. It was not just the dead woman in
the pool of blood that impressed me in this story, but also the
man's jealousy, which had led to the murder. Something about
it appealed to me, and much as I balked at the woman's being
definitively dead, I accepted the jealousy without resisting.

I experienced jealousy personally when we arrived at Grandfather Arditti's home. We used to visit him once a week, every
Saturday. He lived in a spacious, reddish mansion. You entered
through a side gate, to the left of the house, into an old garden,
which was far more beautiful than ours. A huge mulberry tree
stood there, with low branches and easy to climb. I was not allowed to climb it, but Mother never passed it without showing
me a branch at the top; it was her hiding place, where she used
to sit as a young girl when she wanted to read undisturbed. She
would steal up there with her book and sit there as quiet as a
mouse, and she did it so cleverly that they couldn't see her from
below, and when they called her, she didn't hear, because she
liked the book so much; she read all her books up there. Not far
from the mulberry tree, steps led up to the house; the residential

rooms were higher than in our house, but the corridors were dark. We would walk through many rooms until the last room, where Grandfather sat in an armchair, a small, pale man, always warmly bundled in scarves and tartans; he was sickly.

"*Li beso las manos, Señor Padre!*" said Mother. "I kiss your hands, Señor Father!" Then she pushed me ahead; I didn't like him and I had to kiss his hand. He was never funny or angry or tender or severe like the other grandfather, whose name I bore; he was always the same, he sat in an armchair and never budged, he never spoke to me, never gave me anything, and merely exchanged a few phrases with my mother. Then came the end of the visit, and I hated it, it was always the same. He would eye me with a sly smirk and ask in a low voice: "Whom do you like better, Grandfather Arditti or Grandfather Canetti?" He knew the answer, everyone, old and young, was bewitched by Grandfather Canetti, and no one liked Grandfather Arditti. But he wanted to force the truth out of me, and he placed me in a horribly embarrassing predicament, which he enjoyed, for it happened again every Saturday. At first I said nothing, gazing at him helplessly, he asked his question again, until I found the strength to lie and said: "Both!" He would then raise his finger threateningly and yell—it was the only loud sound I ever heard from him: "*Fálsu!*" (False child!) And he drawled out the ac-cented *a*; the word sounded both ominous and plaintive, I can still hear it as though I had visited him only yesterday.

Walking out through the many rooms and corridors, I felt guilty for lying and I was very low-spirited. My mother, though unshakably attached to her family and unwilling ever to give up this ritual of a visit, must have also felt a bit guilty for al-ways reexposing me to this accusation, which was really meant for the other grandfather but struck only me. As a solace, she took me to the *bagtché*, the orchard and rose garden behind the house. There she showed me all her favorite flowers from her girlhood, and inhaled their fragrances deeply, she had wide nostrils which always quivered. She lifted me up so that I too could smell the roses, and if any fruits were ripe, she would pick some, but Grandfather was not supposed to know because it was the Sabbath. It was the most wonderful garden that I can remember, not too well kept, a bit overgrown; and the fact that Grandfather was not to know about this Sabbath fruit, the fact that Mother herself did a prohibited thing for my sake, must have relieved my feeling of guilt, for on the way home I was quite cheerful and kept asking questions again.

At home, I learned from Cousin Laurica that this grandfather was jealous because all his grandchildren liked their other grandfather more, and she confided the reason to me in utmost secrecy: He was *mizquin*, avaricious, but I mustn't tell my mother.

Purim; The Comet

The holiday that we children felt most strongly, even though, being very small, we couldn't take part in it, was Purim. It was a joyous festival, commemorating the salvation of the Jews from Haman, the wicked persecutor. Haman was a well-known figure, and his name had entered the language. Before I ever found out that he was a man who had once lived and concocted horrible things, I knew his name as an insult. If I tormented adults with too many questions or didn't want to go to bed or refused to do something they wanted me to do, there would be a deep sigh: "*Hamán!*" Then I knew that they were in no mood for jokes, that I had played out. "*Hamán*" was the final word, a deep sigh, but also a vituperation. I was utterly amazed when I was told later on that Haman had been a wicked man who wanted to kill all the Jews. But thanks to Mordecai and Queen Esther, he failed, and, to show their joy, the Jews celebrated Purim.

The adults disguised themselves and went out, there was noise in the street, masks appeared in the house, I didn't know who they were, it was like a fairy tale; my parents stayed out till late at night. The general excitement affected us children; I lay awake in my crib and listened. Sometimes our parents would show up in masks, which they then took off; that was great fun, but I preferred not knowing it was they.

One night, when I had dozed off, I was awakened by a giant wolf leaning over my bed. A long, red tongue dangled from his mouth, and he snarled fearfully. I screamed as loud as I could: "A wolf! A wolf!" No one heard me, no one came; I shrieked and yelled louder and louder and cried. Then a hand slipped out, grabbed the wolf's ears, and pulled his head down. My father was behind it, laughing. I kept shouting: "A wolf! A wolf!" I wanted my father to drive it away. He showed me the wolf mask in his hand; I didn't believe him, he kept saying: "Don't you see? It was me, that was no real wolf." But I wouldn't calm down, I kept sobbing and crying.

The story of the werewolf had thus come true. My father couldn't have known what the little girls always told me when we huddled together in the dark. Mother reproached herself for her sleigh story but scolded him for his uncontrollable pleasure in masquerading. There was nothing he liked better than play-acting. When he had gone to school in Vienna, he only wanted to be an actor. But in Ruschuk, he was mercilessly thrust into his father's business. The town did have an amateur theater, where he performed with Mother, but what was it measured by his earlier dreams in Vienna? He was truly unleashed, said

Mother, during the Purim festival: He would change his masks several times in a row, surprising and terrifying all their friends with the most bizarre scenes.

My wolf panic held on for a long time; night after night I had bad dreams, very often waking my parents, in whose room I slept. Father tried to calm me down until I fell asleep again, but then the wolf reappeared in my dreams; we didn't get rid of him all that soon. From that time on, I was considered a jeopardized child whose imagination must not be overstimulated, and the result was that for many months I heard only dull stories, all of which I've forgotten.

The next event was the big comet, and since I have never thought about one event without the other, there must be some connection between them. I believe that the appearance of the comet freed me from the wolf; my childhood terror merged into the universal terror of those days, for I have never seen people so excited as during the time of the comet. Also, both of them, the wolf and the comet, appeared at night, one more reason why they came together in my memory.

Everyone talked about the comet before I saw it, and I heard that the end of the world was at hand. I couldn't picture what that was, but I did notice that people changed and started whispering whenever I came near, and they gazed at me full of pity. The Bulgarian girls didn't whisper, they said it straight out in their unabashed way: The end of the world had come. It was the general belief in town, and it must have prevailed for quite a while since it left such a deep stamp on me without my fearing anything specific. I can't say to what extent my parents, as educated people, were infected with that belief. But I'm sure they didn't oppose the general view. Otherwise, after our earlier experience, they would have done something to enlighten me, only they didn't.

One night, people said the comet was now here and would now fall upon the earth. I was not sent to bed; I heard someone say it made no sense, the children ought to come into the garden too. A lot of people were standing around in the courtyard. I had never seen so many there; all the children from our houses and the neighboring houses were among them, and everyone, adults and children, kept staring up at the sky, where the comet loomed gigantic and radiant. I can see it spreading across half the heavens. I still feel the tension in the back of my neck as I tried to view its entire length. Maybe it got longer in my memory, maybe it didn't occupy half, but only a smaller part of the sky. I must leave the answer to that question to others, who were grown up then and not afraid. But it was bright outdoors, almost like during the day, and I knew very well that it actually ought to be night, for that was the first time I hadn't been put to bed at that hour, and that was the real event for me. Everyone stood in the garden, peering at the heavens and waiting. The grown-ups scarcely walked back and forth; it was oddly quiet, voices were low, at most the children moved, but the grown-ups barely heeded them. In this expectation, I must have felt something of the anxiety filling everyone else, for in order to relieve me, somebody gave me a twig of cherries. I had put one cherry into my mouth and was craning my neck, trying to follow the gigantic comet with my eyes, and the strain, and perhaps also the wondrous beauty of the comet made me forget the cherry, so that I swallowed the pit.

It took a long time; no one grew tired of it, and people kept standing around in a dense throng. I can't see Father or Mother among them, I can't see any of the individual people who made up my life. I only see them all together, and if I hadn't used the word so frequently later on, I would say that I see them as a mass, a crowd: a stagnating crowd of expectation.

The Magic Language
The Fire

The biggest cleaning in the house came before *Pesach*, Passover.
Everything was moved topsy-turvy, nothing stayed in the same
place, and since the cleaning began early—lasting about two
weeks, I believe—this was the period of the greatest disorder.
Nobody had time for you, you were always underfoot and were
pushed aside or sent away, and as for the kitchen, where the
most interesting things were being prepared, you could at best
sneak a glance inside. Most of all, I loved the brown eggs, which
were boiled in coffee for days and days.

On the seder evening, the long table was put up and set in
the dining room; and perhaps the room had to be so long, for
on this occasion the table had to seat very many guests. The
whole family gathered for the seder, which was celebrated in
our home. It was customary to pull in two or three strangers
off the street; they were seated at the feast and participated in
everything.

Grandfather sat at the head of the table, reading the Hagga-
dah, the story of the exodus of the Jews from Egypt. It was his
proudest moment: Not only was he placed above his sons and
sons-in-law, who honored him and followed all his directions,
but he, the eldest, with his sharp face like a bird of prey, was also
the most fiery of all; nothing eluded him. As he chanted in sing-
song, he noticed the least motion, the slightest occurrence at the
table, and his glance or a light movement of his hand would set
it aright. Everything was very warm and close, the atmosphere
of an ancient tale in which everything was precisely marked
out and had its place. On seder evenings, I greatly admired my
grandfather; and even his sons, who didn't have an easy time
with him, seemed elevated and cheerful.

As the youngest male, I had my own, not unimportant function; I had to ask the *Ma-nishtanah*. The story of the exodus is presented as a series of questions and answers about the reasons for the holiday. The youngest of the participants asks right at the start what all these preparations signify: the unleavened bread, the bitter herbs, and the other unusual things on the table. The narrator, in this case my grandfather, replies with the detailed story of the exodus from Egypt. Without my question, which I recited by heart, holding the book and pretending to read, the story could not begin. The details were familiar to me, they had been explained often enough; but throughout the reading I never lost the sense that my grandfather was answering me personally. So it was a great evening for me too, I felt important, downright indispensable; I was lucky there was no younger cousin to usurp my place.

But although following every word and every gesture of my grandfather's, I looked forward to the end throughout the narrative. For then came the nicest part: The men suddenly all stood up and jigged around a little, singing together as they danced: "*Had gadya, had gadya!*"—"A kid! A kid!" It was a merry song, and I was already quite familiar with it, but it was part of the ritual for an uncle to call me over when it was done and to translate every line of it into Ladino.

When my father came home from the store, he would instantly speak to my mother. They were very much in love at that time and had their own language, which I didn't understand; they spoke German, the language of their happy schooldays in Vienna. Most of all, they talked about the *Burgtheater*; before ever meeting, they had seen the same plays and the same actors there and they never exhausted their memories of it. Later I found out that they had fallen in love during such conversations, and

while neither of them had managed to make their dream of the
theater come true—both had passionately wanted to act—they
did succeed in getting married despite a great deal of opposition.

Grandfather Arditti, from one of the oldest and most pros-
perous Sephardic families in Bulgaria, was against letting his
youngest, and favorite, daughter marry the son of an upstart
from Adrianople. Grandfather Canetti had pulled himself up by
his bootstraps; an orphan, cheated, turned out of doors while
young, he had worked his way up to prosperity; but in the eyes
of the other grandfather, he remained a playactor and a liar. "*Es
mentiroso* (He's a liar)," I heard Grandfather Arditti once say
when he didn't realize I was listening. Grandfather Canetti, however, was indignant about the pride of the Ardittis, who looked
down on him. His son could marry any girl, and it struck him as
a superfluous humiliation that he wanted to marry the daughter
of that Arditti of all people. So my parents at first kept their love
a secret, and it was only gradually, very tenaciously, and with the
active help of their older brothers and sisters and well-disposed
relatives, that they succeeded in getting closer to making their
wish come true. At last, both fathers gave in, but a tension always
remained between them, and they couldn't stand each other. In
the secret period, the two young people had fed their love incessantly with German conversations, and one can imagine how
many loving couples of the stage played their part here.

So I had good reason to feel excluded when my parents began their conversations. They became very lively and merry, and
I associated this transformation, which I noted keenly, with the
sound of the German language. I would listen with utter intensity
and then ask them what this or that meant. They laughed, saying it was too early for me, those were things I would understand only later. It was already a great deal for them to give in on
the word "Vienna," the only one they revealed to me. I believed

they were talking about wondrous things that could be spoken of only in that language. After begging and begging to no avail, I ran away angrily into another room, which was seldom used, and I repeated to myself the sentences I had heard from them, in their precise intonation, like magic formulas; I practiced them often to myself, and as soon as I was alone, I reeled off all the sentences or individual words I had practiced—reeled them off so rapidly that no one could possibly have understood me. But I made sure never to let my parents notice, responding to their secrecy with my own.

I found out that my father had a name for my mother which he used only when they spoke German. Her name was Mathilde, and he called her Mädi. Once, when I was in the garden, I concealed my voice as well as I could, and called loudly into the house: "Mädi! Mädi!" That was how my father called to her from the courtyard whenever he came home. Then I dashed off around the house and appeared only after a while with an innocent mien. My mother stood there perplexed and asked me whether I had seen Father. It was a triumph for me that she had mistaken my voice for his, and I had the strength to keep my secret, while she told him about the incomprehensible event as soon as he came home.

It never dawned on them to suspect me, but among the many intense wishes of that period, the most intense was my desire to understand their secret language. I cannot explain why I didn't really hold it against my father. I did nurture a deep resentment toward my mother, and it vanished only years later, after his death, when she herself began teaching me German.

One day, the courtyard was filled with smoke; a few of our girls ran out into the street and promptly came back with the excited news that a neighborhood house was on fire. It was already all in flames and about to burn up. Instantly, the three houses around our courtyard emptied, and except for my grandmother, who never rose from her divan, all the tenants ran out toward the blaze. It happened so fast that they forgot all about me. I was a little scared to be all alone like that; also I felt like going out, perhaps to the fire, perhaps even more in the direction I saw them all running in. So I ran through the open courtyard gate out into the street, which I was not allowed to do, and I wound up in the racing torrent of people. Luckily, I soon caught sight of two of our older girls, and since they wouldn't have changed directions for anything in the world, they thrust me between themselves and hastily pulled me along. They halted at some distance from the conflagration, perhaps so as not to endanger me, and thus, for the first time in my life, I saw a burning house. It was already far gone; beams were collapsing and sparks were flying. The evening was gathering, it slowly became dark, and the fire shone brighter and brighter. But what made an even greater impact on me than the blazing house was the people moving around it. They looked small and dark from that distance; there were very many of them, and they were scrambling all over the place. Some remained near the house, some moved off, and the latter were all carrying something on their backs. "Thieves!" said the girls. "Those are thieves! They're carrying things away from the house before anyone can catch them!" They were no less excited about the thieves than about the fire, and as they kept shouting "Thieves!" their excitement infected me. They were indefatigable, those tiny black figures, deeply bowed, they fanned out in all directions. Some had flung bundles on their shoulders, others ran stooped under the burden of angular objects, which I couldn't recognize, and when I asked what they were carrying, the girls merely kept repeating: "Thieves! They're thieves!"

This scene, which has remained unforgettable for me, later merged into the works of a painter, so that I no longer could say what was original and what was added by those paintings. I was nineteen, in Vienna, when I stood before Brueghel's pictures. I instantly recognized the many little people of that fire in my childhood. The pictures were as familiar to me as if I had always moved among them. I felt a tremendous attraction to them and came over every day. That part of my life which had commenced with the fire continued immediately in these paintings, as though fifteen years had not gone by in between. Brueghel became the most important painter for me; but I did not absorb him, as so many later things, by contemplation and reflection. I found him present within me as though, certain that I would have to come to him, he had been awaiting me for a long time.

Adders and Letters

An early memory takes place on a lake. I see the lake, which is vast, I see it through tears. We are standing by a boat on the shore, my parents and a girl who holds me by the hand. My parents say they want to take the boat out on the lake. I try to tear loose and climb into the boat, I want to go along, I want to go along, but my parents say I can't, I have to stay behind with the girl who's holding my hand. I cry, they talk to me, I keep crying. This takes a long time, they are unrelenting, the girl won't let me go, so I bite her hand. My parents are angry and leave me behind with her, but now to punish me. They vanish in the boat, I yell after them at the top of my lungs, now they're far away, the lake grows bigger and bigger, everything melts in tears.

It was Lake Wörther, in Austria; I was three years old, they told me so a long time afterward. In Kronstadt, Transylvania, where we spent the next summer, I see forests and a mountain, a castle and houses on all sides of the castle hill; I myself do not appear in this picture, but I remember stories my father told me about serpents. Before coming to Vienna, he had been to boarding school in Kronstadt. There were a lot of adders in the area, and the farmers wanted to get rid of them. The boys learned how to catch them, and received two kreuzers for every sack of dead adders. Father showed me how to grab an adder, right behind the head, so that it can't do anything to you, and how to kill it then. It's easy, he said, once you know how, and it's not the least bit dangerous. I greatly admired him and wanted to know if they were really quite dead in the sack. I was scared that they would pretend to be dead and suddenly shoot out of the sack. The sack was tightly bound up, he said, and they had to be dead, otherwise you couldn't have gotten the two kreuzers. I didn't believe that something could be really fully dead.

Thus we spent three summer vacations in a row in parts of the old Austro-Hungarian monarchy: Carlsbad, Lake Wörther, and Kronstadt. A triangle connecting these three remote points contained a good portion of the old empire.

There would be a great deal to say about the Austrian influence on us even in that early Ruschuk period. Not only had both my parents gone to school in Vienna, not only did they speak German to each other, but my father read the liberal Viennese newspaper *Neue Freie Presse* every day; it was a grand moment when he slowly unfolded it. As soon as he began reading it, he no longer had an eye for me, I knew he wouldn't answer anything no matter what; Mother herself wouldn't ask him anything, not even in German. I tried to find out what it was that fascinated him in the newspaper, at first I thought it was the smell; and when I was alone and nobody saw me, I would climb up on the chair and greedily smell the newsprint. But then I noticed he was moving his head along the page, and I imitated that behind his back without having the page in front of me, while he held it in both hands on the table and I played on the floor behind him. Once, a visitor who had entered the room called to him; he turned around and caught me performing my imaginary reading motions. He then spoke to me even before focusing on the visitor and explained that the important thing was the letters, many tiny letters, on which he knocked his fingers. Soon I would learn them myself, he said, arousing within me an unquenchable yearning for letters.

I knew that the newspaper came from Vienna, this city was far away, it took four days to get there on the Danube. They often spoke of relatives who went to Vienna to consult famous physicians. The names of the great specialists of those days were the very first celebrities that I heard about as a child. When I came to Vienna subsequently, I was amazed that all these names—Lorenz, Schlesinger, Schnitzler, Neumann, Hajek, Halban—really existed as people. I had never tried to picture them physically; what they consisted of was their pronouncements, and these pronouncements had such a weight, the journey to them was so long, the changes their pronouncements effected in the people around me were so cataclysmic, that the names took on something of spirits that one fears and appeals to for help. When someone came back from them, he could eat only certain things, while other things were prohibited for him. I imagined the physicians speaking in a language of their own, which nobody else understood and which one had to guess. It never crossed my mind that this was the same language that I heard from my parents and practiced for myself, secretly, without understanding it.

People often talked about languages; seven or eight different tongues were spoken in our city alone, everyone understood something of each language. Only the little girls, who came from villages, spoke just Bulgarian and were therefore considered stupid. Each person counted up the languages he knew; it was important to master several, knowing them could save one's own life or the lives of other people.

In earlier years, when merchants went traveling, they carried all their cash in money belts slung around their abdomens. They wore them on the Danube steamers too, and that was dangerous. Once, when my mother's grandfather got on deck and pretended to sleep, he overheard two men discussing a murder plan in Greek. As soon as the steamer approached the next town, they wanted to mug and kill a merchant in his stateroom, steal his heavy money belt, throw the body into the Danube through a porthole, and then, when the steamer docked, leave the ship immediately. My great-grandfather went to the captain and told him what he had heard in Greek. The merchant was warned, a member of the crew concealed himself in the stateroom, others were stationed outside, and when the two cutthroats went to carry out their plan, they were seized, clapped into chains, and handed over to the police in the very harbor where they had intended to make off with their booty. This happy end came from understanding Greek, and there were many other edifying language stories.

The Murder Attempt

My cousin Laurica and I were inseparable playmates. She was the youngest daughter of Aunt Sophie in the next house, but four years my senior. The courtyard was our domain. Laurica made sure I didn't run out into the street, but the courtyard was big, and there I was allowed to go anywhere, only I couldn't climb up on the edge of the draw well; a child had once fallen in and drowned. We had a lot of games and got on very well; it was as if the age difference between us didn't exist. We had joint hiding places, which we revealed to no one, and we mutually collected little objects there, and whatever one of us had belonged to the other as well. Whenever I got a present, I promptly ran off with it, saying: "I have to show it to Laurica!" We then conferred about what hiding place to put it in, and we never argued. I did whatever she wanted, she did whatever I wanted, we loved each other so much that we always wanted the same thing. I never let her feel that she was only a girl and a youngest child. Since my brother's birth, when I had started wearing pants, I had been keenly aware of my dignity as the eldest son. Perhaps that helped to make up for the age difference between us.

Then Laurica started school and remained away all morning. I missed her terribly. I played all alone, waiting for her, and when she came home, I caught her right at the gate and asked her all about what she had done in school. She told me about it, I pictured it and longed to go to school in order to be with her. After a time, she came back with a notebook; she was learning how to read and write. She solemnly opened the notebook in front of me; it contained letters of the alphabet in blue ink, they fascinated me more than anything I had ever laid eyes on. But when I tried to touch them, she suddenly grew earnest. She said I wasn't allowed to, only she could touch it, she was not permitted to part with it. I was deeply hurt by this first refusal. But all I could get from her with my tender pleading was that I could point my fingers at letters without touching them, and I asked what the letters meant. This one time, she answered, giving me information, but I realized she was shaky and contradicted herself, and since I was hurt about her holding back the note-book, I said: "You don't even know! You're a bad pupil!"

After that, she always kept the notebooks away from me. She soon had lots of them; I envied her for each one of those note-books. She knew very well that I did, and a terrible game began. She changed altogether toward me, letting me feel how small I was. Day after day, she let me beg for the notebooks; day after day, she refused to give them to me. She knew how to tantalize me and prolong the torture. I am not surprised that things came to a catastrophe, even if no one foresaw the form it took.

On the day that no one in the family ever forgot, I stood at the gate as usual, waiting for her. "Let me see the writing," I begged the instant she appeared. She said nothing; I realized everything was about to happen again, and no one could have separated us at that moment. She slowly put down the school-bag, slowly took out the notebooks, slowly leafed around in them, and then held them in front of my nose lightning-fast. I grabbed at them, she pulled them back, and leaped away. From afar, she held an open notebook out at me and shouted: "You're too little! You're too little! You can't read yet!"

I tried to catch her, running after her all over the place, I begged, I pleaded for the notebooks. Sometimes she let me come very near so that I thought I had my hands on the note-books, and then she snatched them away and pulled away in the last moment. Through skillful maneuvers, I succeeded in chas-ing her into the shadow of a not very high wall, where she could no longer escape me. Now I had her and I screamed in utmost excitement: "Give them to me! Give them to me! Give them to me!"—by which I meant both the notebooks and the writing, they were one and the same for me. She lifted her arms with the notebooks far over her head, she was much bigger than I, and she put the notebooks up on the wall. I couldn't get at them, I was too little, I jumped and jumped and yelped, it was no use, she stood next to the wall, laughing scornfully. All at once, I left her there and walked the long way around the house to the kitchen yard, to get the Armenian's ax and kill her with it.

The wood lay there, chopped up, stacked up, the ax lay next to it, the Armenian wasn't there. I raised the ax high and, holding it straight in front of me, I marched back over the long path into the courtyard with a murderous chant on my lips, repeating incessantly: "*Agora vo matar a Laurica! Agora vo matar a Laurica!*" — "Now I'm going to kill Laurica! Now I'm going to kill Laurica!"

When I came back and she saw me holding the ax out with both hands, she ran off screeching. She screeched at the top of her lungs, as though the ax had already swung and hit her. She screeched without pausing even once, easily drowning my battle chant, which I kept repeating to myself, incessantly, resolutely, but not especially loud: "*Agora vo matar a Laurica!*"

Grandfather dashed out of the house, armed with a cane; he ran toward me, snatched the ax from my hand, and barked at me furiously. Now all three houses around the courtyard came alive, people emerged from all of them; my father was out of town, but my mother was there. They assembled for a family council and discussed the homicidal child. I could plead all I liked that Laurica had tortured me bloody; the fact that I, at the age of five, had reached for the ax to kill her—indeed, the very fact that I had been able to carry the heavy ax in front of me—was incomprehensible to everyone. I think they understood that the "writing," the "script," had been so important to me; they were Jews, and "Scripture" meant a great deal to all of them, but there had to be something very bad and dangerous in me to get me to the point of wanting to murder my playmate.

I was severely punished, but Mother, who was herself very

frightened, did comfort me after all, saying: "Soon you'll learn how to read and write yourself. You don't have to wait till you're in school. You can learn before then."

No one recognized the connection between my murderous goal and the fate of the Armenian. I loved him, his sad songs and words. I loved the ax with which he chopped wood.

A Curse on the Voyage

My relationship to Laurica, however, did not break off fully. She distrusted me and avoided me when she came back from school, and she made sure not to unpack her schoolbag in front of me. I was no longer interested in her writing. After the murder attempt, I was perfectly convinced that she was a bad pupil and was ashamed to show her wrong letters. Perhaps I could save my pride only by telling myself that.

She took a terrible revenge on me, although stubbornly denying it then and later. All I could admit in her favor is that she may not have known what she did.

Most of the water used in the houses was brought in gigantic barrels from the Danube. A mule hauled the barrel, which was installed in a special kind of vehicle, and a "water carrier," who, however, carried nothing, trudged alongside in front, holding a whip. The water was sold at the courtyard gate for very little, unloaded, and put in huge caldrons, where it was boiled. The caldrons of boiling water were then placed in front of the house, on a fairly long terrace, where they stood for a good while to cool off.

Laurica and I were getting on again at least well enough to play tag occasionally. Once, the caldrons of hot water were standing there; we ran in between them, much too close, and when Laurica caught me right next to one, she gave me a shove, and I fell into the hot water. I was scalded all over my body, except for my head. Aunt Sophie, upon hearing the shriek, pulled me out and tore off my clothes, my whole skin went along with them, the family feared for my life, and for many weeks I lay abed in awful pains.

My father was in England at the time, and that was the worst thing of all for me. I thought I was going to die and kept calling out for him, I wailed that I would never see him again; that was worse than the pains. I cannot remember the pains, I no longer feel them, but I still feel the desperate longing for my father. I thought he didn't know what had happened to me, and when they assured me he did know, I cried: "Why doesn't he come? Why doesn't he come? I want to see him!" Perhaps they really were hesitant; he had only just arrived in Manchester a few days earlier to prepare for our moving there. Perhaps they thought my condition would improve by itself and he didn't have to return on the spot. But even if he did learn about it immediately and started back without delay, the journey was long, and he couldn't get here all that soon. They put me off from day to day and, when my condition got worse, from hour to hour. One night, when they thought I had finally fallen asleep, I jumped out of bed and yanked everything off me. Instead of moaning in pain, I shouted for him: "*Cuando viene? Cuando viene?*" (When is he coming? When is he coming?) Mother, the doctor, all the others taking care of me, didn't matter; I can't see them, I don't know what they did, they must have done many careful things for me in those days. I didn't register them, I had only one thought, it was more than a thought, it was the wound in which everything went: my father.

Then I heard his voice, he came to me from behind, I was lying on my belly, he softly called my name, he walked around the bed, I saw him, he lightly put his hand on my hair, it was father, and I had no pains.

Everything that happened from then on I know only from what I was told. The wound became a wonder, the recovery began, he promised not to go away any more and he stayed during the next few weeks. The doctor was positive I would have died if my father hadn't come and remained. The doctor had already given me up but insisted on my father's return, his only, not very sure hope. He was the physician who had brought all three of us into the world, and later on he used to say that of all the births he had ever known this *re*birth had been the hardest.

A few months earlier, in January 1911, my youngest brother had come into the world. The delivery had been easy, and my mother felt strong enough to nurse him herself. It was quite different from the previous time; little ado was made over this birth, perhaps because it had gone so easily, and it remained a center of attention only briefly.

I did sense, however, that great events were in the offing. My parents' conversations had a different tone, they sounded resolute and earnest, they didn't always speak German in front of me, and they often mentioned England. I learned that my little brother was named George, after the new king of England. I liked that because it was unexpected, but my grandfather cared less for it, he wanted a biblical name and insisted on one, and I heard my parents say they wouldn't give in, it was their child, and they would give it the name they wanted to give it.

The rebellion against the grandfather had probably been going on for a while; the choice of this name was an open declaration of war. Two brothers of my mother's had started a business in Manchester, it had flourished quickly, one of them had suddenly died, the other offered my father a partnership if he came to England. For my parents, this was a desirable opportunity to free themselves from Ruschuk, which was too confining and too Oriental for them, and from the far more confining tyranny of the grandfather. They immediately agreed to the partnership, but it was easier said than done, for now a fierce battle commenced between them and my grandfather, who refused to give up one of his sons for anything in the world. I did not know the details of this battle, which lasted for six months, but I sensed the changed atmosphere in the house and especially in the courtyard, where the members of the family had to meet.

Grandfather grabbed me in the courtyard at every opportunity, hugging and kissing me, and, when someone could see, weeping hot tears. I didn't care at all for the continual wetness on my cheeks, although he always proclaimed that I was his dearest grandchild and he could not live without me. My parents realized he was trying to bias me against England and, counteracting that, they told me how wonderful it would be. "There all the people are honest," said my father. "When a man says something, he does it, he doesn't even have to shake hands on it." I was on his side, how else could I have been, he didn't have to promise me that I would start school immediately in England and learn how to read and write.

Grandfather behaved differently to him, and especially to my mother—differently than to me. He regarded her as the author of the emigration project, and when she once said to him, "Yes! We can't stand this life in Ruschuk anymore! We both want to get away from here!" he turned his back to her and never spoke to her again; during the remaining months he treated her like air. As for Father, however, who still had to go to the store, he assaulted him with his anger, which was terrible and became more and more terrible from week to week. Then he saw there was nothing he could do, and a few days before the departure, he cursed his son solemnly in the courtyard, in front of the relatives who were present and who listened in horror. I heard them speaking about it: Nothing, they said, was more dreadful than a father cursing his son.

3.

From *Notes from Hampstead*

Telling stories to anyone who will hear them as stories, who doesn't know you, who doesn't expect literature. Life as a wandering storyteller would be nice. Someone says the word, and you tell the story. You never stop, day or night, you go blind, you lose the use of your limbs. But your mouth still serves its function, and you speak whatever is in your head. You have no possessions, only an infinite, ever-growing number of stories.

Nicest of all would be if you could live on words alone and did not even need to eat.

His life, in which nothing, absolutely nothing, happened. He embarked on no adventures, he was in no war. He was never in prison, he never killed anyone. He neither won nor lost a fortune. All he ever did was live in this century. But that alone was enough to give his life *dimension*, both of feeling and of thought.

To mangle a sentence into a landscape.

Every forgotten idea crops up again on the other side of the world.

His greatest satisfaction, which he constantly denies himself, is putting things in context.

He doesn't want to describe something, he wants to *be* that something. If he can't be it, he wants to sing its praises. If he can't praise it, then he wants to divine it.

Your original sin: you opened your mouth. As long as you listen, you are innocent.

His sentences rub against and so erase each other. This drives him to despair. So he makes of every sentence its own cage.

Interpreting a statement's meaning—all that remains of the tradition of consulting oracles. But since this takes place outside the scope of fear, not even that is left.

To say the most horrible thing such that it is no longer horrible; it gives one hope because it was said out loud.

Diaries which are too accurate are the end of freedom. Thus we should keep them only intermittently, so that the "empty" intervals become the fullest entries.

A labyrinth made of all the paths one has taken.

It's against his nature to be a critic—he is too grateful.

Probably all satirists are one and the same person.

———

The fate of the man who hated the idea of surviving: he made sure that *he* was survived.

An enemy you have to lend teeth to.

Those who maintain their simplicity while avoiding mere cleverness will find justification in the eyes of history. Those who cultivate their cleverness till they attain all that is due to the simple, posterity will view as scum.

A person wounds himself to see blood flow. A person kills himself to kill.

Look for someone to make you *slow*.

Six days in Vienna make us false for six years.

A god who could be any animal but never like a man.

He has withdrawn from everything new and now lives off his own saliva.

The Jews' obedience to God, that which has preserved them over the centuries, irritates me. In their wisest, most wonderful stories, there is always this obedience. How I love their *readers*, who remain poor because they read but who are nonetheless accorded the highest respect! How I love the sense of justice Jews demand of people, their patience, often their kindness! But their obedience to the never-ending threat of God disgusts me. I know in this I am a child of my time. I have been a witness to too much obedience. And one need hardly still say it: those against God were the most obedient, but their obedience was a model and the brutes would settle for nothing less. The constant bowing I saw as a child was repeated for the visible rulers of the world to horrific effect.

Can we stand up against a visible lord if we have no invisible lord? A trying question.

A little more concision, and I can say I am writing Chinese.

4.

From *The Tongue Set Free*

Part II: "Manchester, 1911–1913"

Wallpaper and Books
Strolls Along the Mersey

For a few months after his death, I slept in my father's bed. It was dangerous leaving Mother alone. I don't know who it was who thought of making me the guardian of her life. She wept a great deal, and I listened to her weeping. I couldn't console her, she was inconsolable. But when she got up and stationed herself at the window, I leaped up and stood next to her. I put my arms around her and wouldn't let go. We did not speak, these scenes did not take place with words. I held her very tight, and if she had jumped out the window, she would have had to take me along. She didn't have the strength to kill me along with herself. I felt her body yield when the tension waned, and she turned to me from the despair of her decision. She pressed my head to her body and sobbed louder. She had thought I was asleep, and strove to weep quietly, so that I wouldn't awake. She was so absorbed in her sorrow that she didn't notice that I was secretly awake, and when she got up very quietly and stole to the window, she was certain that I was fast asleep. Years later, when we spoke about that period, she admitted that she was always surprised each time I stood next to her right away and threw my arms around her. She couldn't escape me, I wouldn't give her up. She let me hold her back, but I sensed that my watchfulness was burdensome to her. She never tried it more than once in any night. After the excitement, we both fell asleep, exhausted. Gradually, she developed something like respect for me and she began treating me like an adult in many ways.

After a few months, we moved from the house on Burton Road, where my father had died, to her older brother's home on Palatine Road. This was a large mansion with many people, and the acute danger was past.

However, the period before that in Burton Road was not just made up of those dreadful nightly scenes. The days were calm and subdued. Toward evening, Mother and I dined at a small card table in the yellow salon. The table, brought in specially (it didn't really belong in the salon), was set for the two of us. There was a cold snack consisting of lots of little delicacies, it was always the same: white sheep's cheese, cucumbers, and olives, as in Bulgaria. I was seven, Mother was twenty-seven. We had an earnest, civilized conversation, the house was very still, there was no noise as in the nursery, my mother said to me: "You are my big son," and she inspired me with the responsibility I felt for her at night. All day long, I yearned for these suppers. I served myself, taking very little on my plate, like her; everything proceeded in gentle movements like clockwork, but as much as I recall the motions of my fingers, I no longer know what we talked about; I have forgotten everything but the one, frequently reiterated sentence: "You are my big son." I see my mother's faint smile when she leaned toward me, the movements of her mouth when she spoke, not passionately as usual, but with restraint; I think that I never felt any sorrow in her during these meals, perhaps it was dulled by my sympathetic presence. Once she explained something about olives to me.

Previously, Mother hadn't meant very much to me. I never saw her alone. We were in a governess's care and always played upstairs in the nursery. My brothers were four and five and one-half years my junior. George, the youngest, had a small playpen. Nissim, the middle son, was notorious for his pranks. No sooner was he left by himself than he got into mischief. He turned on the faucet in the bathroom, and water was already running down the stairs to the ground floor by the time anyone noticed; or he unrolled the toilet paper until the upstairs corridor was covered with it. He kept devising new and worse pranks, and since nothing could stop him, he was dubbed "the naughty boy."

I was the only one going to school, to Miss Lancashire's in Barlowmore Road; I will tell about this school later on.

At home in the nursery, I usually played alone. Actually, I seldom played, I spoke to the wallpaper. The many dark circles in the pattern of the wallpaper seemed like people to me. I made up stories in which they appeared, either I told them the stories or they played with me, I never got tired of the wallpaper people and I could talk to them for hours. When the governess went out with my two younger brothers, I made a point of staying alone with the wallpaper. I preferred its company to anyone else's, at least to that of my little brothers; with them there was nothing but silly excitement and trouble, like Nissim's pranks. When my brothers were nearby, I merely whispered to the wallpaper people; if the governess was present, I simply thought out my stories, not even moving my lips to them. But then everyone left the room, I waited a bit, and then started talking undisturbed. Soon my words were loud and agitated; I only remember that I tried to persuade the wallpaper people to do bold deeds, and when they refused, I let them feel my scorn. I heartened them, I railed at them; when alone, I was always a bit scared, and whatever I felt myself, I ascribed to them, *they* were the cowards. But they also performed and uttered their own lines. A circle in a highly conspicuous place opposed me with its own eloquence, and it was no small triumph when I succeeded in convincing it. I was involved in such an argument with it when the governess returned earlier than expected and heard voices in the nursery. She quickly entered and caught me in the act, my secret was out, from then on I was always taken along on strolls; it was considered unhealthy to leave me alone so much. The loud wallpaper fun was over, but I was tenacious and I got used to articulating my stories quietly, even when my little brothers were in the room. I managed to play with them while also dealing with the wallpaper people. Only the governess, who had set herself the task of weaning me fully from these unhealthy tendencies, paralyzed me; in her presence the wallpaper was mute.

However, my finest conversations in that period were with my real-life father. Every morning, before leaving for his office, he came to the nursery and had special, cogent words for each one of us. He was cheery and merry and always hit upon new antics. In the morning they didn't last long; it was before breakfast, which he had with Mother downstairs in the dining room, and he hadn't read the newspaper yet. But in the evening, he arrived with presents; he brought something for everyone, on no day did he come home without bearing gifts for us. Then he stayed in the nursery for a longer time and did gymnastics with us. His main feat was to put all three of us on his outstretched arm. He held the two little brothers fast, I had to learn to stand free, and even though I loved him like no one else in the world, I was always a bit scared of this part of the exercises.

A few months after I started school, a thing solemn and exciting happened, which determined my entire life after that. Father brought home a book for me. He took me alone into a back room, where we children slept, and explained it to me. It was *The Arabian Nights*, in an edition for children. There was a colorful picture on the cover, I think it was Aladdin and his magic lamp. My father spoke very earnestly and encouragingly to me and told me how nice it would be to read. He read me a story, saying that all the other stories in the book were as lovely as this one, and that I should try to read them and then in the evening always tell him what I had read. Once I'd finished the book, he'd bring me another. I didn't have to be told twice, and even though I had only just learned how to read in school, I pitched right into the wondrous book and had something to report to him every evening. He kept his promise, there was always a new book there; I never had to skip a single day of reading.

The books were a series for children, all in the same square format. They differed only in the colorful picture on the cover. The letters were the same size in all volumes, it was like reading the same book on and on. But what a series that was, it has never had its peer. I can remember all the titles. After *The Arabian Nights* came Grimm's fairy tales, *Robinson Crusoe*, *Gulliver's Travels*, *Tales from Shakespeare*, *Don Quixote*, Dante, *William Tell*. I wonder how it was possible to adapt Dante for children. Every volume had several gaudy pictures, but I didn't like them, the stories were a lot more beautiful; I don't even know whether I would recognize the pictures today. It would be easy to show that almost everything that I consisted of later on was already in these books, which I read for my father in the seventh year of my life. Of the characters who never stopped haunting me after that, only Odysseus was missing.

I spoke about each book to my father after reading it. Sometimes I was so excited that he had to calm me down. But he never told me, as adults will, that fairy tales are untrue; I am particularly grateful to him for that, perhaps I still consider them true today. I noticed, of course, that Robinson Crusoe was different from Sinbad the Sailor, but it never occurred to me to think less of one of these stories than the other. However, I did have bad dreams about Dante's Inferno. When I heard my mother say to him, "Jacques, you shouldn't have given him that, it's too early for him," I was afraid he wouldn't bring me any more books, and I learned to keep my dreams a secret. I also believe—but I'm not quite certain—that my mother connected my frequent conversations with the wallpaper people to the books. That was the period when I liked my mother least. I was cunning enough to whiff danger, and perhaps I wouldn't have given up my loud wallpaper conversations so willingly and hypocritically if the books and my conversations about them with my father hadn't become the most important thing in the world for me.

But he stuck to his purpose and tried *William Tell* after Dante. It was here that I first heard the word "freedom." He said something to me about it, which I have forgotten. But he added something about England: That was why we had moved to England, he said, because people were free here. I knew how much he loved England, while my mother doted on Vienna. He made an effort to learn the language properly, and once each week a woman came by to give him lessons. I noticed that he pronounced his English sentences differently from German, which he was fluent in since his youth and usually spoke with

Mother. Sometimes I heard him pronounce and repeat single sentences. He uttered them slowly, like something very beautiful, they gave him pleasure and he uttered them again. He always spoke English to us children now; Ladino, which had been my language until then, receded into the background, and I only heard it from others, particularly older relatives.

When I reported to him on the books I read, it had to be in English. I think that this passionate reading helped me to make very rapid progress. He was delighted that my reports were so fluent. What *he* had to say, however, had a special weight, for he thought it out very carefully to make absolutely sure there was no error, and he spoke almost as if he were reading to me. I have a solemn memory of these hours, he was altogether different than when he played with us in the nursery and incessantly kept inventing new antics.

The last book I received from him was about Napoleon. It was written from a British point of view, and Napoleon appeared as an evil tyrant, who wanted to gain control of all countries, especially England. I was reading this book when my father died. My distaste for Napoleon has been unshakable ever since. I had started telling my father about the book, but I hadn't gotten very far. He had given it to me right after *William Tell*, and it was a small experiment for him after the conversation on freedom. When I soon talked excitedly to him about Napoleon, he said: "Just wait, it's too soon. You have to keep reading. It's going to turn out quite different." I know for sure that Napoleon hadn't been crowned emperor yet. Maybe it was a test, maybe he wanted to see if I could resist the imperial splendor. I then finished it after his death, I reread it countless times like all the books I'd gotten from him. I had had little experience with power. My first notion of it stemmed from this book, and I have never been able to hear Napoleon's name without connecting it

to my father's sudden death. Of all of Napoleon's murders, the
greatest and most dreadful was of my father.

On Sundays, he sometimes took me strolling alone. Not far from
our house, the little Mersey River flowed by. On the left side,
it was edged by a reddish wall; on the other side, a path wound
through a luxuriant meadow full of flowers and high grass. He
had told me the English word "meadow," and he asked me for it
during every stroll. He felt it was an especially beautiful word;
it has remained the most beautiful word in the English language
for me. Another favorite word of his was "island." It must have
been very important to him that England was an island; perhaps
he thought of it as an Isle of the Blest. He also explained it to
me, much to my astonishment, over and over again, even when
I'd known it for a long time. On our last stroll through the
meadow by the Mersey River, he spoke altogether differently
than I was accustomed to hearing. He asked me very urgently
what I wanted to be, and I said without thinking: "A doctor!"

"You will be what you want to be," he said with so much
tenderness that both of us stopped in our tracks. "You don't
have to become a businessman like me and the uncles. You will
go to the university and you will be what you want most."

I always regarded that conversation as his last wish. But at the
time, I didn't know why he was so different when he uttered it.
It was only when finding out more about his life that I realized
he had been thinking about himself. During his schooldays in
Vienna, he had passionately frequented the *Burgtheater*, and his
greatest desire was to become an actor. Sonnenthal was his idol,
and young as he was, he managed to get in to see him and tell him
of his desire. Sonnenthal told him he was too short for the stage,
an actor couldn't be so short. From Grandfather, who was an actor in every utterance of his life, Father had inherited a theatrical

gift, but Sonnenthal's pronouncement was devastating for him, and he buried his dreams. He was musical, he had a good voice and he loved his violin above everything. Grandfather, who ruled his children as a ruthless patriarch, thrust each of his sons into the business very early; he wanted to have a branch, managed by one of the sons, in every major city in Bulgaria. When Father spent too many hours with his violin, it was taken away from him, and he came right into the business against his will. He didn't like it at all; nothing interested him less than what was to his advantage. But he was a lot weaker than Grandfather and gave in. He was twenty-nine by the time he finally succeeded, with Mother's help, in fleeing Bulgaria and settling in Manchester. By then, he had a family with three children, whom he had to take care of, so he remained a businessman. It was already a victory for him to have escaped his father's tyranny and left Bulgaria. He had, of course, parted with him on bad terms and he bore his father's curse; but he was free in England and he was determined to treat his own sons differently.

I don't believe my father was very well-read. Music and theater meant more to him than books. A piano stood downstairs in the dining room, and every Saturday and Sunday, when Father wasn't in the office, my parents would make music there. He sang, and Mother accompanied him on the keyboard. It was always German lieder, usually Schubert and Loewe. One lied—it was called "The Grave on the Heath," and I don't know who it was by—swept me off my feet. Whenever I heard it, I would open the nursery door upstairs, sneak down the steps, and hide behind the door to the dining room. I didn't understand German at that time, but the song was heartrending. I was discovered behind the door, and from then on I had the right to listen inside the dining room. I was brought down especially for this lied and I didn't have to steal downstairs anymore. The text was explained to me, I had indeed often heard German in Bulgaria and secretly repeated it to myself without understanding it; but this was the first time something was translated for me, the first German words I mastered came from "The Grave on the Heath." The song was about a deserter who gets caught and is standing in front of his comrades, who are supposed to shoot him. He sings about what enticed him to flee, I think it was a song from his homeland that he heard. The lyrics end with the verse: "Farewell, you brothers, here's my chest!" Then comes a shot, and finally, there are roses on the grave in the heath.

I waited all atremble for the shot, it was an excitement that never faded. I wanted to hear it over and over again and I tormented my father, who sang it for me two or three times in a row. Every Saturday, when he came home, I asked him, even before he had unpacked our gifts, whether he would sing "The Grave on the Heath." He said: "Maybe," but he was actually undecided, because my obsession with this song began to trouble him. I refused to believe that the deserter was really dead; I hoped he'd be saved, and when they had sung it several times and he wasn't saved, I was devastated and bewildered. At night in bed, he came to my mind, and I brooded about him. I couldn't grasp that his comrades had shot him. He had explained everything so well, after all; I certainly wouldn't have fired at him. His death was incomprehensible to me, it was the first death that I mourned.

Father's Death
The Final Version

We had been in England for about a year when Mother fell ill. Supposedly, the English air didn't agree with her. The doctor prescribed a cure at Bad Reichenhall; in the summertime, it may have been August 1912, she went. I didn't pay much attention, I didn't miss her, but Father asked me about her, and I had to say something. Perhaps he was worried that her absence wouldn't be good for us children, and he wanted to catch the first signs of change in us on the spot. After a couple of weeks, he asked me whether I would mind if Mother stayed away longer. If we were patient, he added, she would keep improving and would come home to us in full health. The first few times, I had pretended to miss her; I sensed that he expected me to. Now, I was all the more honest in agreeing that she should have a longer treatment. Sometimes he came into the nursery with a letter from her, pointing to it and saying she had written. But he wasn't himself in this period, his thoughts were with her, and he was concerned. In the last week of her absence, he spoke little and never mentioned her name to me; he didn't listen to me very long, never laughed, and devised no pranks. When I wanted to tell him about the latest book he had given me, *The Life of Napoleon*, he was absentminded and impatient, and cut me off; I thought I had said something foolish and I was ashamed. The very next day, he came to us as merry and exuberant as usual and announced that Mother was arriving tomorrow. I was glad because he was glad; and Miss Bray told Edith something I didn't understand: She said it was *proper* for the mistress to come home. "Why is it proper?" I asked, but she shook her head: "You wouldn't understand. It is *proper*!" When I eventually asked Mother about it in detail—there were so many obscure things, leaving me no peace—I learned that she had been gone for six weeks and wanted to stay on. Father had lost patience and wired her to come back immediately.

The day of her arrival, I didn't see him, he didn't come to the nursery that evening. But he reappeared the very next morning and got my little brother to talk. "Georgie," he said; "Canetti," said the boy; "Two," said Father; "Three," said the boy; "Four," said Father; "Burton," said the boy; "Road," said Father; "West," said the boy; "Didsbury," said Father; "Manchester," said the boy; "England," said Father; and I, in the end, very loudly and superfluously, said, "Europe." So our address was together again. There are no words that I have retained more sharply, they were my father's last words.

He went down to breakfast as usual. Before long, we heard loud yells. The governess dashed down the stairs, I at her heels. By the open door to the dining room, I saw my father lying on the floor. He was stretched out full length, between the table and the fireplace, very close to the fireplace, his face was white, he had foam on his mouth, Mother knelt at his side, crying: "Jacques, speak to me, speak to me, Jacques, Jacques, speak to me!" She kept shouting it over and over again, people came, our neighbors the Brockbanks, a Quaker couple, strangers walked in off the street. I stood by the door, Mother grabbed her head, tore hair out, and kept shouting. I took a timid step into the room, toward my father, I didn't understand, I wanted to ask him, then I heard someone say: "Take the child away." The Brockbanks gently took my arm, led me out into the street, and into their front yard.

Here, their son Alan welcomed me, he was much older than I and spoke to me as if nothing had happened. He asked me about the latest cricket match at school, I answered him, he wanted to know every detail about it and kept asking until I had nothing more to say. Then he wanted to know if I was a good climber, I said yes, he showed me a tree standing there, bending somewhat toward our own front yard. "But I bet you can't climb that one," he said, "I bet you can't. It's too hard for you. You wouldn't dare." I took the challenge, looked at the tree, had my doubts, but didn't show them, and said: "I can too. I can too!" I strode over to the tree, touched the bark, threw my arms around the trunk, and was about to swing up, when a window in our dining room opened. Mother leaned way out, saw me standing at the tree with Alan, and yelled: "My son, you're playing, and your father is dead! You're playing, you're playing, and your father is dead! Your father is dead! Your father is dead! You're playing, your father is dead!"

She yelled it out into the street, she kept yelling louder and louder, they yanked her back into the room by force, she resisted, I heard her shouting after I no longer saw her, I heard her shouting for a long time. Her shouts pushed Father's death into me, and it has never left me since.

I wasn't allowed to see Mother. I was taken to the Florentins, who lived halfway to school, in Barlowmore Road. Arthur, their son, was already something of a friend to me, and in the coming days we became inseparable. Mr. Florentin and Nelly, his wife, two kindhearted people, never took their eyes off me for an instant, they were afraid I might run off to my mother. She was very sick, I was told, no one could see her, she would soon be fully well again, and then I could go back to her. But they were wrong, I didn't want to go to her at all, I wanted to go to my father. They spoke little about him. The day of his funeral, which was not kept from me, I resolutely declared that I wanted to go along to the cemetery. Arthur had picture books about foreign countries, he had stamps and many games. He was occupied with me day and night; I slept in the same room, and he was so friendly and inventive and earnest and funny that I have a warm feeling even now when I think about him. But on the day of the funeral, nothing helped; when I noticed he wanted to keep me from going to the funeral, I lost my temper and struck out at him. The whole family tried to help me, they locked all doors for safety's sake. I raged and threatened to smash them down, which may not have been beyond me on that day. Finally, they had a fortunate idea, which gradually calmed me down. They promised that I could *watch* the funeral procession. It could be seen from the nursery, they said, if I leaned out, but only from afar.

I believed them and didn't think about how far it would be. When the time came, I leaned way out of the nursery window, so far out that I had to be held fast from behind. I was told that the procession was just turning the corner of Burton Road into Barlowmore Road and then moving away from us toward the cemetery. I peered my eyes out and saw nothing. But they so clearly depicted what could be seen that I finally perceived a light fog in the given direction. That was it, they said, that was it. I was exhausted from the long struggle and I accepted the situation.

I was seven years old when my father died, and he wasn't even thirty-one. There was a lot of discussion about it, he was supposed to have been in perfect health, he smoked a lot, but that was really all they could blame his sudden heart attack on. The English physician who examined him after his death found nothing. But the family didn't much care for English doctors. It was the great age of Viennese medicine, and everyone had consulted a Viennese professor at some point or other. I was unaffected by these conversations, I *could* not recognize any cause for his death, and so it was better for me if none were found.

But, as the years went by, I kept questioning my mother about it. What I learned from her changed every few years; as I gradually got older, new things were added, and an earlier version proved to have been "solicitous" of my youth. Since nothing preoccupied me so much as this death, I lived full of trust at various stages. I finally settled into my mother's last version, making myself at home in it, cleaving to every detail as though it came from a Bible, referring anything that happened in my environment to that version, simply everything that I read or thought. My father's death was at the center of every world I found myself in. When I learned something new a few years later, the earlier world collapsed around me like a stage set, nothing held anymore, all conclusions were false, it was as though someone were wrenching me away from a faith, but the lies that this someone demonstrated and demolished were lies that he himself had told me with a clear conscience, in order to protect my youth. My mother always smiled when she suddenly said: "I only told you that at the time because you were too young. You couldn't have understood." I feared that smile, it was different from her usual smile, which I loved for its haughtiness, but also for its intelligence. She realized she was smashing me to bits when she told me anything new about my father's death. She was cruel and she liked doing it, thereby getting back at me for the jealousy with which I made her life difficult.

My memory has stored up all the versions of that account, I can't think of anything I have retained more faithfully. Perhaps someday I can write them all down completely. They would make a book, an entire book, but now I am following other trails.

I want to record what I heard at the time and also the final version, which I still believe today.

The Florentins spoke about a war having broken out, the Balkan War. It may not have been so important for the British; but I lived among people who all came from Balkan countries, for them it was a domestic war. Mr. Florentin, an earnest, thoughtful man, avoided talking about Father with me, but he did say one thing when we were alone. He said it as though it were something very important, I had the feeling he was confiding in me, because the women, there being several in the household, were not present. He told me that Father had been reading the newspaper at his last breakfast, and the headline had said that Montenegro had declared war on Turkey; he realized that this spelled the outbreak of the Balkan War and that many people would now have to die, and this news, said Mr. Florentin, had killed him. I recalled seeing the *Manchester Guardian* next to him on the floor. Whenever I found a newspaper anywhere in the house, he allowed me to read him the headlines, and now and then, if it wasn't too difficult, he explained what they meant.

Mr. Florentin said there was nothing worse than war, and Father had shared this opinion, they had often spoken about it. In England, all the people were against war, he went on, and there would never be another war here.

His words sank into me as though Father had spoken them personally. I kept them to myself, just as they had been spoken between us, as though they were a dangerous secret. In later years, whenever people spoke about how Father, who had been very young, in perfect health, with no disease, had suddenly died as though struck by lightning, I knew—and nothing could ever have gotten me to change my mind—that the lightning had been that dreadful news, the news about the outbreak of the war. There has been warfare in the world since then, and each war, wherever it was, and perhaps scarcely present in the consciousness of the people around me, has hit me with the force of that early loss, absorbing me as the most *personal* thing that could happen to me.

For my mother, however, the picture was quite different, and from her final and definitive version, which she revealed to me twenty-three years later under the impact of my first book, I learned that Father had not exchanged a word with her since the previous evening. She had felt very good in Reichenhall, where she had moved among her own kind, people with serious intellectual interests. Her physician spoke with her about Strindberg, and she began reading him too, she never stopped reading Strindberg after that. The physician asked her about these books, their conversations became more and more interesting, she started realizing that life in Manchester, among the semieducated Sephardim, was not enough for her, perhaps that was her illness. She confessed this to the doctor, and he confessed his love for her. He proposed that she separate from my father and become his wife. Nothing, except in words, happened between them, nothing that she could reproach herself for, and she never for an instant thought seriously of leaving my father. But the conversations with the doctor meant more and more to her, and she did her best to prolong her stay in Reichenhall. She felt her health rapidly improving, which gave her a not dishonest reason for asking my father to let her continue her cure. But since she was very proud and didn't care to lie, her letters also mentioned the fascinating conversations with the physician. Ultimately, she was grateful to Father when he forced her, by telegraph, to return immediately. She herself might not have had the strength to leave Reichenhall. She arrived in Manchester radiant and happy, and in order to placate my father and perhaps also a bit out of vanity, she told him the whole story and about rejecting the doctor's offer to stay with him. Father couldn't understand how the situation could have reached that point, he interrogated her, and every answer he received added to his jealousy. He insisted that she had made herself culpable, he refused to believe her and saw her answers as lies. Finally, he became so furious that he threatened not to speak another word with her until she confessed the whole truth. He spent the entire evening and the night in silence and without sleeping. She felt utterly sorry for him, even though he was tormenting her, but, unlike him, she was convinced that she had proved her love by returning, and she was not aware of having done anything wrong. She hadn't even allowed the doctor to kiss her goodbye. She did all she could to get Father to talk, but since her hours of effort were to no avail, she grew angry and gave up, lapsing into silence herself.

In the morning, coming down to breakfast, he took his place at the table wordlessly and picked up the newspaper. When he collapsed, under the impact of the stroke, he hadn't spoken a single word to her. First she thought he was trying to frighten her and punish her some more. She knelt down next to him on the floor and begged him, pleaded with him, more and more desperately, to talk to her. When she realized he was dead, she thought he had died because of his disappointment in her.

I know that Mother told me the truth that final time, the truth as she saw it. There had been long, heavy struggles between us, and she had often been on the verge of disowning me forever. But now, she said, she understood the struggle that I had waged for my freedom, now she acknowledged my right to this freedom, despite the great unhappiness that this struggle had brought upon her. The book, which she had read, was flesh of her flesh, she said, she recognized herself in me, she had always viewed people the way I depicted them, that was exactly how she would have wanted to write herself. Her forgiveness was not enough, she went on, she was bowing to me, she acknowledged me doubly as her son, I had become what she had most wanted me to be. She lived in Paris at this time, and she had written a similar letter to me in Vienna, before I visited her. I was very frightened by this letter; even in the days of our bitterest enmity, I had admired her most for her pride. The thought of her bowing to me because of this novel—important as the book may have been to me—was unendurable (her not bowing to anything made up my image of her). When I saw her again, she may have felt my shame, embarrassment, and disappointment, and to convince me that she was in earnest, she let herself go and finally told me the whole truth about my father's death.

Despite her earlier versions, I had occasionally sensed the facts, but then always reproached myself that the distrust which I had inherited from her was leading me astray. To put my mind at ease, I had always repeated my father's last words in the nursery. They were not the words of an angry or despairing man. Perhaps one may infer that after a dreadful and sleepless night, he was about to soften, and perhaps he would have spoken to her after all in the dining room, when his shock at the outbreak of war interfered and struck him down.

German on Lake Geneva

By May 1913, everything had been prepared for moving to Vienna, and we left Manchester. The journey took place in stages; for the first time, I grazed cities that would eventually expand into the measureless centers of my life. In London, we stayed, I believe, only for a few hours. But we drove through the town from one railroad station to the other, and I stared in sheer delight at the high, red busses and begged my mother to let me ride in one on the upper deck. There wasn't much time, and my excitement at the jammed streets, which I have retained as endlessly long black whirls, merged into my excitement at Victoria Station, where countless people ran around without bumping into one another.

I have no recollection of the voyage across the Channel, but the arrival in Paris was all the more impressive. A newlywed couple was waiting for us at the station, David, my mother's plainest and youngest brother, a gentle mouse, and, at his side, a sparkling young wife with pitch-black hair and rouged cheeks. There they were again, the red cheeks, but so red that Mother warned me they were artificial when I refused to kiss my new aunt on any other spot. Her name was Esther and she was fresh out of Salonika, which had the largest Sephardic community, so that young men who wanted to marry would get their brides from there. In their apartment, the rooms were so small that I impudently called them doll's rooms. Uncle David wasn't offended, he always smiled and said nothing, the exact opposite of his powerful brother in Manchester, who had scornfully rejected him as a business partner. David was at the peak of his young bliss, they had married a week ago. He was proud that I was instantly enamored of my sparkling aunt, and he kept telling me to kiss her. He didn't know, the poor man, what lay ahead; she soon turned out to be a tenacious and insatiable fury.

We stayed awhile in the apartment with the tiny rooms, and I was glad. I was curious and my aunt allowed me to watch her put on her makeup. She explained to me that all women in Paris used makeup, otherwise the men wouldn't like them. "But Uncle David likes you," I said; she didn't answer. She applied some perfume and asked whether it smelled good. I was leery of perfumes; Miss Bray, our governess, said they were "wicked." So I evaded Aunt Esther's question, saying: "Your hair smells best!" Then she seated herself, let down her hair, which was even blacker than my brother's much-admired curls; while she dressed I was allowed to sit next to her and admire her. All this took place openly, right in front of Miss Bray, who was unhappy about it, and I heard her tell Mother that this Paris was bad for the children.

Our journey continued into Switzerland, to Lausanne, where

Mother planned to spend a few months. She rented an apartment at the top of the city, with a radiant view of the lake and the sailboats sailing on it. We often climbed down to Ouchy, strolling along the shores of the lake and listening to the band that played in the park. Everything was very bright, there was always a soft breeze, I loved the water, the wind, and the sails, and when the band played, I was so happy that I asked Mother: "Why don't we stay here, it's nicest here."

"You have to learn German now," she said, "you'll attend school in Vienna." And although she never spoke the word "Vienna" without ardor, it never enticed me as long as we were in Lausanne. For when I asked her if Vienna had a lake, she said: "No, but it's got the Danube," and instead of the mountains in Savoy across from us, she added, Vienna had woods and hills. Now I had known the Danube since my infancy, and since the water that had scalded me came from the Danube, I bore a grudge against it. But here there was this wonderful lake, and mountains were something new. I stubbornly resisted Vienna, and that may have been one slight reason why we stayed in Lausanne somewhat longer than planned.

But the real reason was that I had to learn German first. I was eight years old, I was to attend school in Vienna, and my age would put me in the third grade of elementary school there. My mother could not bear the thought of my perhaps not being accepted into this grade because of my ignorance of the language, and she was resolved to teach me German in a jiffy.

Not very long after our arrival, we went to a bookshop; she asked for an English-German grammar, bought the first book they showed her, took me home immediately, and began instruction. How can I depict that instruction believably? I know how it went—how could I forget?—but I still can't believe it myself.

We sat at the big table in the dining room, I on the narrower side, with a view of the lake and the sails. She sat around the corner to my left and held the textbook in such a way that I couldn't look in. She always kept it far from me. "You don't need it," she said, "you can't understand it yet anyway." But despite this explanation, I felt she was withholding the book like a secret. She read a German sentence to me and had me repeat it. Disliking my accent, she made me repeat the sentence several times, until it struck her as tolerable. But this didn't occur often, for she derided me for my accent, and since I couldn't stand her derision for anything in the world, I made an effort and soon pronounced the sentence correctly. Only then did she tell me what the sentence meant in English. But this she never repeated, I had to note it instantly and for all time. Then she quickly went on to the next sentence and followed the same procedure; as soon as I pronounced it correctly, she translated it, eyed me imperiously to make me note it, and was already on the next sentence. I don't know how many sentences she expected to drill me in the first time; let us conservatively say a few; I fear it was many. She let me go, saying: "Repeat it all to yourself. You must not forget a single sentence. Not a single one. Tomorrow, we shall continue." She kept the book, and I was left to myself, perplexed.

I had no help, Miss Bray spoke only English, and during the rest of the day Mother refused to pronounce the sentences for me. The next day, I sat at the same place again, the open window in front of me, the lake and the sails. She took up yesterday's sentences, had me repeat one and asked what it meant. To my misfortune, I had noted the meaning, and she said in satisfaction: "I see this is working!" But then came the catastrophe, and that was all I knew; except for the first, I hadn't retained a single sentence. I repeated them after her, she looked at me expectantly, I stuttered and lapsed into silence. When this happened with several sentences, she grew angry and said: "You remembered the first one, so you must be able to do it right. You don't want to. You want to remain in Lausanne. I'll leave you alone in Lausanne. I'm going to Vienna, and I'll take Miss Bray and the babies along. You can stay in Lausanne by yourself!"

I believe I feared that less than her derision. For when she became particularly impatient, she threw her hands together over her head and shouted: "My son's an idiot! I didn't realize that my son's an idiot!" Or: "Your father knew German too, what would your father say!"

I fell into an awful despair, and to hide it, I looked at the sails, hoping for help from the sails, which couldn't help me. Something happened that I still don't understand today. I became as attentive as the devil and learned how to retain the meanings of the sentences on the spot. If I knew three or four of them correctly, she did not praise me; instead, she wanted the others, she wanted me to retain all the sentences each time. But since this never happened, she never praised me once and was always gloomy and dissatisfied whenever she let me go during those weeks.

I now lived in terror of her derision, and during the day, wherever I was, I kept repeating the sentences. On walks with the governess, I was sullen and untalkative. I no longer felt the wind, I didn't hear the music, I always had my German sentences and their English meanings in my head. Whenever I could, I sneaked off to the side and practiced them aloud by myself, sometimes drilling a mistake as obsessively as the correct sentences. After all, I had no book to check myself in; she stubbornly and mercilessly refused to let me have it, though knowing what friendship I felt for books and how much easier it would all have been for me with a book. But she had the notion that one shouldn't make things easy for oneself; that books are bad for learning languages; that one must learn them orally, and that a book is harmless only when one knows something of the language. She didn't notice that I ate little because of my distress. She regarded the terror I lived in as pedagogical.

On some days, I succeeded in remembering all the sentences and their meanings, aside from one or two. Then I looked for signs of satisfaction in her face. But I never found them, and the most I could attain was her not deriding me. On other days, it went less well, and then I trembled, awaiting the "idiot" she had brought into the world; that affected me the worst. As soon as the "idiot" came, I was demolished, and she failed to hit the target only with her remark about Father. His affection comforted me, never had I gotten an unfriendly word from him, and whatever I said to him, he enjoyed it and let me be.

I hardly spoke to my little brothers now and gruffly pushed them away, like my mother. Miss Bray, whose favorite was the youngest, but who liked all three of us very much, sensed the dangerous state I was in, and when she caught me drilling all my German sentences, she became vexed and said it was enough, I ought to stop, I already knew too much for a boy of my age; she said she had never learned a foreign language and got along just as well in her life. There were people all over the world who understood English. Her sympathy did me a lot of good, but the substance of her words meant nothing to me; my mother had trapped me in a dreadful hypnosis, and she was the only one who could release me.

Of course, I listened when Miss Bray said to Mother: "The boy is unhappy. He says Madame considers him an idiot!"

"But he *is* one!" she was told. "Otherwise I wouldn't say so!" That was very bitter, it was the word on which everything hinged for me. I thought of my cousin Elsie in Palatine Road, she was retarded and couldn't speak properly. The adults had said pityingly: "She's going to remain an idiot."

Miss Bray must have had a good and tenacious heart, for ultimately it was she who saved me. One afternoon, when we had just settled down for the lesson, Mother suddenly said: "Miss Bray says you would like to learn the Gothic script. Is that so?" Perhaps I had said it once, perhaps she had hit upon the idea herself. But since Mother, while saying these words, gazed at the book in her hand, I grabbed the opportunity and said: "Yes, I would like to. I'll need it at school in Vienna." So I finally got the book in order to study the angular letters. But teaching me the script was something for which Mother had no patience at all. She threw her principles overboard, and I kept the book.

The worst sufferings, which may have lasted for a month, were past. "But only for the writing," Mother had said when entrusting me with the book. "We shall still continue drilling the sentences orally." She couldn't prevent me from reading the sentences too. I had learned a great deal from her already, and there *was* something to it, in the emphatic and compelling way she pronounced the sentences for me. Anything new I kept learning from her as before. But whatever I heard I could subsequently strengthen by reading, thus making a better showing in front of her. She had no more grounds for calling me an "idiot" and was relieved about it herself. She had been seriously worried about me, she said afterward; perhaps I was the only one in the huge clan who was not good at languages. Now she was convinced of the reverse, and our afternoons turned into sheer pleasure. It could even happen that I astounded her, and sometimes, against her will, words of praise escaped her, and she said: "You are my son, after all."

It was a sublime period that commenced. Mother began speaking German to me outside the lessons. I sensed that I was close to her again, as in those weeks after Father's death. It was only later that I realized it hadn't just been for my sake when she instructed me in German with derision and torment. She herself had a profound need to use German with me, it was the language of her intimacy. The dreadful cut into her life, when, at twenty-seven, she lost my father, was expressed most sensitively for her in the fact that their loving conversations in German were stopped. Her true marriage had taken place in that language. She didn't know what to do, she felt lost without him, and tried as fast as possible to put me in his place. She expected a great deal from this and found it hard to bear when I threatened to fail at the start of her enterprise. So, in a very short time, she forced me to achieve something beyond the strength of any child, and the fact that she succeeded determined the deeper nature of my German; it was a belated mother tongue, implanted in true pain. The pain was not all, it was promptly followed by a period of happiness, and that tied me indissolubly to that language. It must have fed my propensity for writing at an early moment, for I had won the book from her in order to learn how to write, and the sudden change for the better actually began with my learning how to write Gothic letters.

She certainly did not tolerate my giving up the other languages; education, for her, was the literature of all the languages she knew, but the language of our love—and what a love it was!—became German.

She now took just me along on visits to friends and family in Lausanne, and it is not surprising that the two visits that have stuck in my memory were connected with her situation as a young widow. One of her brothers had died in Manchester even before we moved there; his widow Linda and her two children were now living in Lausanne. It may have been because of her that my mother stopped over in Lausanne. She was invited to dinner at Linda's and took me along, explaining that Aunt Linda had been born and bred in Vienna and spoke a particularly beautiful German. I had already made enough progress, she said, to show what I knew. I was ecstatic about going; I was burning to wipe out all traces of my recent derision forever and always. I was so excited that I couldn't sleep the night before, and I talked to myself in long German conversations that always ended in triumph. When the time for the visit came, Mother explained to me that a gentleman would be present, he came to Aunt Linda's for dinner every day. His name was Monsieur Cottier, he was a dignified gentleman, no longer young, and a highly prominent official. I asked whether he was my aunt's husband and I heard my mother saying, hesitant and a bit absent: "He may be someday. Now Aunt Linda is still thinking of her two children. She wouldn't like to hurt their feelings by marrying so quickly, even though it would be a great support for her." I instantly sniffed danger and said: "You've got three children, but I'm your support." She laughed. "What are you thinking!" she said in her arrogant way. "I'm not like Aunt Linda. I have no Monsieur Cottier."

So German became less important and I had to stand my ground in two ways. Monsieur Cottier was a large, corpulent man with a Vandyke and a belly, who greatly enjoyed the meal at my aunt's. He spoke slowly, pondering every sentence, and gazed with delight at my mother. He was already old and he struck me as treating her like a child. He talked only to her, he said nothing to Aunt Linda, but she kept filling up his plate; he acted as if he didn't notice and kept on eating calmly.

"Aunt Linda's beautiful!" I said enthusiastically on the way home. She had a dark skin and wonderfully large, black eyes. "She smells so good," I added; she had kissed me and smelled even better than my aunt in Paris. "Goodness," said Mother, "she has a gigantic nose and elephant's legs. But the way to a man's heart is through his stomach." She had already said that once during the meal, sarcastically eyeing Monsieur Cottier. I was surprised at her repeating it and asked her what it meant. She explained, very harshly, that Monsieur Cottier liked to eat well, and Aunt Linda kept a fine cuisine. That was why he came every day. I asked if that was why she smelled so good. "That's her perfume," said Mother, "she's always used too much perfume." I sensed that Mother disapproved of her, and though she had acted very friendly to Monsieur Cottier and made him laugh, she didn't seem to think very highly of him.

"No one's going to come to our house to eat," I said suddenly, as though grown up, and Mother smiled and encouraged me further: "You won't allow it, will you, you'll watch out."

The second visit, to Monsieur Aftalion, was a very different matter. Of all the Sephardim that Mother knew, he was the richest. "He's a millionaire," she said, "and still young." When I asked if he was a lot richer than Uncle Solomon, and she assured me he was, I was instantly won over to him. He looked very different too, she told me, he was a good dancer and a cavalier. Everyone lionized him, he was so noble, she said, that he could live at a royal court. "We don't have such people among us anymore," she said, "we were like that in the old days, when we lived in Spain." Then she confided that Monsieur Aftalion had once wanted to marry her, but she had already been secretly engaged to my father. "Otherwise, I might have married him," she said. He had been very sad after that, she told me, and had not wanted any other woman for years. He had only gotten married very recently, and was spending his honeymoon in Lausanne with his wife Frieda, a renowned beauty. He lived in the most elegant hotel, she said, and that was where we would visit him.

I was interested in him because she put him above my uncle.

I despised my uncle so much that Monsieur Aftalion's marriage proposal had no special effect on me. I was anxious to see him, merely to have that Napoleon shrink down to a wretched nothing next to him. "Too bad Uncle Solomon won't come along!" I said.

"He's in England," she said. "He can't possibly come along."

"But it would be nice if he came along, so he could see what a real Sephardi is like."

My mother did not resent my hatred of her brother. Although admiring his efficiency, she found it right for me to rebel against him. Perhaps she realized how important it was for me not to have him replace Father as my model, perhaps she regarded this early, indelible hatred as "character," and "character" was more important to her than anything else in the world.

We entered a palace of a hotel, I had never seen anything like it, I even believe it was called "Lausanne Palace." Monsieur Aftalion lived in a suite of gigantic, luxuriously appointed rooms; I felt as if I were in *The Arabian Nights*, and I thought scornfully about my uncle's mansion in Palatine Road, which had so deeply impressed me a year ago. A double door opened, and Monsieur Aftalion appeared in a dark-blue suit and white spats; with his face wreathed in smiles, he walked toward my mother and kissed her hand. "You've grown even more beautiful, Mathilde," he said; she was dressed in black.

"And you have the most beautiful wife," said Mother, she was never at a loss for words. "Where is she? Isn't Frieda here? I haven't seen her since the institute in Vienna. I've told my son so much about her, I brought him along because he absolutely wanted to see her."

"She'll be along in a moment. She hasn't quite finished dressing yet. You two will have to put up with something less beautiful for the moment." Everything was very elegant and

refined, in accordance with the grand rooms. He asked what
Mother's plans were, listening very attentively but still smiling, and he approved of her settling in Vienna, approved it with
fairy-tale words: "You belong in Vienna, Mathilde," he said,
"the city loves you, you were always most alive and most beautiful in Vienna."

I wasn't the least bit jealous, not of him, not of Vienna. I
found out something that I didn't know and that wasn't written
in any of my books, the idea that a city can love a human being, and I liked the idea. Then Frieda came in, and she was the
greatest surprise. I had never seen such a beautiful woman, she
was as radiant as the lake and splendidly attired and she treated
Mother as though *she* were the princess. Culling the loveliest
roses from the vases, she gave them to Monsieur Aftalion, and
he handed them to Mother with a bow. It wasn't a very long
visit, nor did I understand everything that was said; the conversation alternated between French and German, and I wasn't all
that good yet in either language, especially French. I also felt
that some things that I was not supposed to understand were
said in French; but whereas I normally was outraged at such a
secret tongue of the adults, I would have cheerfully accepted
much worse things from this victor over Napoleon and from his
marvelously beautiful wife.

When we left the palace, my mother struck me as slightly
confused. "I nearly married him," she said, looking at me suddenly and adding a sentence that frightened me: "But then you
wouldn't exist today!" I couldn't imagine that, how could I not
exist; I was walking next to her. "But I *am* your son," I said
defiantly. She may have regretted speaking to me like that, for
she paused and hugged me tight, together with the roses she was
carrying, and then she praised Frieda: "That was noble of her.
She has character!" She very rarely said that, and simply never

about a woman. I was glad that she too liked Frieda. When we talked about this visit in later years, she said she had left with the feeling that everything we saw, all that splendor, actually belonged to her, and she had been surprised that she didn't resent or envy Frieda, granting her what she would never have granted any other woman.

We spent three months in Lausanne, and I sometimes think that no other time in my life has been as momentous. But one often thinks that when focusing seriously on a period, and it is possible that each period is the most important and each contains everything. Nevertheless, in Lausanne, where I heard French all around me, picking it up casually and without dramatic complications, I was reborn under my mother's influence to the German language, and the spasm of that birth produced the passion tying me to both, the language and my mother. Without these two, basically one and the same, the further course of my life would have been senseless and incomprehensible.

In August, we set out for Vienna, stopping in Zurich for several hours. Mother left the little brothers in Miss Bray's care in the waiting room and took me up Mount Zurich in a cable car. We got out at a place called Rigiblick. It was a radiant day, and I saw the city spread out vast before me, it looked enormous, I couldn't understand how a city could be so big. That was something utterly new for me, and it was a bit eerie. I asked whether Vienna was this big, and upon hearing that it was "a great deal bigger," I wouldn't believe it and thought Mother was joking. The lake and the mountains were off to the side, not as in Lausanne, where I always had them right before my eyes; there they were in the center, the actual substance of any view. There weren't so many houses to be seen in Lausanne, and here it was the huge number of houses that amazed me, they ran up the slopes of Mount Zurich, where we were standing, and I made no attempt whatsoever to count the uncountable, although I usually enjoyed doing it. I was astonished and perhaps frightened too; I said to Mother reproachfully: "We'll never find them again," and I felt we should never have left the "children"—as we called them in private—alone with the governess, who didn't know a word of any other language. So my first grand view of a city was tinged by a sense of being lost, and the memory of that first look at Zurich, which eventually became the paradise of my youth, has never left me.

We must have found the children and Miss Bray again, for I can see us on the next day, the eighteenth of August, traveling through Austria. All the places we rode through were hung with flags, and when the flags took no end, Mother allowed herself a joke, saying the flags were in honor of our arrival. But she herself didn't know what they were for, and Miss Bray, accustomed to her Union Jack, was getting more and more wrought up and gave us no peace until Mother asked some other passengers. It was the Kaiser's birthday. Franz Joseph, whom Mother had known as the old Kaiser twenty years earlier during her youth in Vienna, was still alive, and all the villages and towns seemed delighted. "Like Queen Victoria," said Miss Bray, and through the many hours of our train ride to Vienna, I heard stories from her about the long-dead queen—stories that bored me a little— and, by way of variety, stories from Mother about Franz Joseph, who was still alive.

II

Auto-da-Fé

5.

From *Auto-da-Fé*

Part I: "A Head Without a World"

Translated by C. V. Wedgwood

Chapter I: The Morning Walk

"What are you doing here, my little man?"

"Nothing."

"Then why are you standing here?"

"Just because."

"Can you read?"

"Oh, yes."

"How old are you?"

"Nine and a bit."

"Which would you prefer, a piece of chocolate or a book?"

"A book."

"Indeed? Splendid! So that's your reason for standing here?"

"Yes."

"Why didn't you say so before?"

"Father scolds me."

"Oh. And who is your father?"

"Franz Metzger."

"Would you like to travel to a foreign country?"

"Yes. To India. They have tigers there."

"And where else?"

"To China. They've got a huge wall there."

"You'd like to scramble over it, wouldn't you?"

"It's much too thick and too high. Nobody can get over it. That's why they built it."

"What a lot you know! You must have read a great deal already?"

"Yes. I read all the time. Father takes my books away. I'd like to go to a Chinese school. They have forty thousand letters in their alphabet. You couldn't get them all into one book."

"That's only what you think."

"I've worked it out."

"All the same it isn't true. Never mind the books in the window. They're of no value. I've got something much better here. Wait. I'll show you. Do you know what kind of writing that is?"

"Chinese! Chinese!"

"Well, you're a clever little fellow. Had you seen a Chinese book before?"

"No, I guessed it."

"These two characters stand for Meng Tse, the philosopher Mencius. He was a great man in China. He lived 2,250 years ago and his works are still being read. Will you remember that?"

"Yes. I must go to school now."

"Aha, so you look into the bookshop windows on your way to school? What is your name?"

"Franz Metzger, like my father."

"And where do you live?"

"Twenty-four Ehrlich Strasse."

"I live there too. I don't remember you."

"You always look the other way when anyone passes you on the stairs. I've known you for ages. You're Professor Kien, but

you haven't a school. Mother says you aren't a real Professor.
But I think you are—you've got a library. Our Marie says, you
wouldn't believe your eyes. She's our maid. When I'm grown
up I'm going to have a library. With all the books there are,
in every language. A Chinese one too, like yours. Now I must
run."

"Who wrote this book? Can you remember?"

"Meng Tse, the philosopher Mencius. Exactly 2,250 years
ago."

"Excellent. You shall come and see my library one day. Tell
my housekeeper I've given you permission. I can show you pictures from India and China."

"Oh good! I'll come! Of course I'll come! This afternoon?"

"No, no, little man. I must work this afternoon. In a week
at the earliest."

Professor Peter Kien, a tall, emaciated figure, man of learning and specialist in sinology, replaced the Chinese book in the
tightly packed briefcase which he carried under his arm, carefully closed it, and watched the clever little boy out of sight.
By nature morose and sparing of his words, he was already
reproaching himself for a conversation into which he had entered for no compelling reason.

It was his custom on his morning walk, between seven and
eight o'clock, to look into the windows of every bookshop
which he passed. He was thus able to assure himself, with a kind
of pleasure, that smut and trash were daily gaining ground. He
himself was the owner of the most important private library in
the whole of this great city. He carried a minute portion of it
with him wherever he went. His passion for it, the only one
which he had permitted himself during a life of austere and ex-
acting study, moved him to take special precautions. Books,
even bad ones, tempted him easily into making a purchase.

Fortunately the greater number of the bookshops did not open until after eight o'clock. Sometimes an apprentice, anxious to earn his chief's approbation, would come earlier and wait on the doorstep for the first employee, whom he would ceremoniously relieve of the latch key. "I've been waiting since seven o'clock," he would exclaim, or "I can't get in!" So much zeal communicated itself all too easily to Kien; with an effort he would master the impulse to follow the apprentice immediately into the shop. Among the proprietors of smaller shops there were one or two early risers, who might be seen busying themselves behind their open doors from half past seven onward. Defying these temptations, Kien tapped his own well-filled briefcase. He clasped it tightly to him, in a very particular manner which he had himself thought out, so that the greatest possible area of his body was always in contact with it. Even his ribs could feel its presence through his cheap, thin suit. His upper arm covered the whole side elevation; it fitted exactly. The lower portion of his arm supported the case from below. His outstretched fingers splayed out over every part of the flat surface to which they yearned. He privately excused himself for this exaggerated care because of the value of the contents. Should the briefcase by any mischance fall to the ground, or should the lock, which he tested every morning before setting out, spring open at precisely that perilous moment, ruin would come to his priceless volumes. There was nothing he loathed more intensely than battered books.

Today, when he was standing in front of a bookshop on his way home, a little boy had stepped suddenly between him and the window. Kien felt affronted by the impertinence. True, there was room enough between him and the window. He always stood about three feet away from the glass; but he could easily read every letter behind it. His eyes functioned to his entire satisfaction: a fact notable enough in a man of forty who sat, day in, day out, over books and manuscripts. Morning after morning his eyes informed him how well they did. By keeping his distance from these venal and common books, he showed his contempt for them, contempt which, when he compared them with the dry and ponderous tomes of his library, they richly deserved. The boy was quite small, Kien exceptionally tall. He could easily see over his head. All the same he felt he had a right to greater respect. Before administering a reprimand, however, he drew to one side in order to observe him further. The child stared hard at the titles of the books and moved his lips slowly and in silence. Without a stop his eyes slipped from one volume to the next. Every minute or two he looked back over his shoulder. On the opposite side of the street, over a watchmaker's shop, hung a gigantic clock. It was twenty minutes to eight. Evidently the little fellow was afraid of missing something important. He took no notice whatever of the gentleman standing behind him. Perhaps he was practicing his reading. Perhaps he was learning the names of the books by heart. He devoted equal attention to each in turn. You could see at once when anything held up his reading for a second.

Kien felt sorry for him. Here was he, spoiling with this depraved fare an eager spiritual appetite, perhaps already hungry for the written word. How many a worthless book might he not come to read in later life for no better reason than an early familiarity with its title? By what means is the suggestibility of these early years to be reduced? No sooner can a child walk and make out his letters than he is surrendered at mercy to the hard pavement of any ill-built street, and to the wares of any wretched tradesman who, the devil knows why, has set himself up as a dealer in books. Young children ought to be brought up in some important private library. Daily conversation with none

but serious minds, an atmosphere at once dim, hushed, and intellectual, a relentless training in the most careful ordering both
of time and of space—what surroundings could be more suitable to assist these delicate creatures through the years of childhood? But the only person in this town who possessed a library
which could be taken at all seriously was he, Kien, himself. He
could not admit children. His work allowed him no such di-
versions. Children make a noise. They have to be constantly
looked after. Their welfare demands the services of a woman.
For cooking, an ordinary housekeeper is good enough. For
children, it would be necessary to engage a mother. If a mother
could be content to be nothing but a mother: but where would
you find one who would be satisfied with that particular part
alone? Each is a specialist first and foremost as a woman, and
would make demands which an honest man of learning would
not even dream of fulfilling. Kien repudiated the idea of a wife.
Women had been a matter of indifference to him until this moment; a matter of indifference they would remain. The boy with
the fixed eyes and the moving head would be the loser.

Pity had moved him to break his usual custom and speak to
him. He would gladly have bought himself free of the prickings
of his pedagogic conscience with the gift of a piece of chocolate.
Then it appeared that there are nine-year-old children who prefer a book to a piece of chocolate. What followed surprised him
even more. The child was interested in China. He read against his
father's will. The stories of the difficulties of the Chinese alphabet fascinated instead of frightening him. He recognized the language at first sight, without having seen it before. He had passed
an intelligence test with distinction. When shown the book, he
had not tried to touch it. Perhaps he was ashamed of his dirty
hands. Kien had looked at them: they were clean. Another boy
would have snatched the book, even with dirty ones. He was

in a hurry—school began at eight—yet he had stayed until the last possible minute. He had fallen upon that invitation like one starving; his father must be a great torment to him. He would have liked best to come on that very afternoon, in the middle of the working day. After all, he lived in the same house.

Kien forgave himself for the conversation. The exception which he had permitted seemed worthwhile. In his thoughts he saluted the child—now already out of sight—as a rising sinologist. Who indeed took an interest in these remote branches of knowledge? Boys played football, adults went to work; they wasted their leisure hours in love. So as to sleep for eight hours and waste eight hours, they were willing to devote themselves for the rest of their time to hateful work. Not only their bellies, their whole bodies had become their gods. The sky God of the Chinese was sterner and more dignified. Even if the little fellow did not come next week, unlikely though that was, he would have a name in his head which he would not easily forget: the philosopher Meng. Occasional collisions unexpectedly encountered determine the direction of a lifetime.

Smiling, Kien continued on his way home. He smiled rarely. Rarely, after all, is it the dearest wish of a man to be the owner of a library. As a child of nine he had longed for a bookshop. Yet the idea that he would walk up and down in it as its proprietor had seemed to him even then blasphemous. A bookseller is a king, and a king cannot be a bookseller. But he was still too little to be a salesman. As for an errand boy—errand boys were always being sent out of the shop. What pleasure would he have of the books, if he was only allowed to carry them as parcels under his arm? For a long while he sought for some way out of the difficulty. One day he did not come home after school. He went into the biggest bookstore in the town, six great show windows all full of books, and began to howl at the top of his voice. "I want to leave the room, quick, I'm going to have an accident!" he blubbered. They showed him the way at once. He took careful note of it. When he came out again he thanked them and asked if he could not do something to help. His beaming face made them laugh. Only a few moments before it had been screwed up into such comic anguish. They drew him out in conversation; he knew a great deal about books. They thought him sharp for his age. Toward the evening they sent him away with a heavy parcel. He traveled there and back on the tram. He had saved enough pocket money to afford it. Just as the shop was closing—it was already growing dark—he announced that he had completed his errand and put down the receipt on the counter. Someone gave him an acid drop for a reward. While the staff were pulling on their coats he glided noiselessly into the back regions to his lavatory hideout and bolted himself in. Nobody noticed it; they were all thinking of the free evening before them. He waited a long time. Only after many hours, late at night, did he dare to come out. It was dark in the shop. He felt about for a switch. He had not thought of that by daylight. But when he found it and his hand had already closed over it, he was afraid to turn on the light. Perhaps someone would see him from the street and haul him off home.

His eyes grew accustomed to the darkness. But he could not read; that was a great pity. He pulled down one volume after another, turned over the pages, contrived to make out many of the names. Later on he scrambled up onto the ladder. He wanted to know if the upper shelves had any secrets to hide. He tumbled off it and said: I haven't hurt myself! The floor is hard. The books are soft. In a bookshop one falls on books. He could have made a castle of books, but he regarded disorder as vulgar and, as he took out each new volume, he replaced the one before. His back hurt. Perhaps he was only tired. At home he would have been asleep long ago. Not here, excitement kept him awake. But his eyes could not even make out the largest titles anymore and that annoyed him. He worked out how many years he would be able to spend reading in this shop without ever going out into the street or to that silly school. Why could he not stay here always? He could easily save up to buy himself a small bed. His mother would be afraid. So was he, but only a little, because it was so very quiet. The gas lamps in the street went out. Shadows crept along the walls. So there *were* ghosts. During the night they came flying here and crouched over the books. Then they read. They needed no light, they had such big eyes. Now he would not touch a single book on the upper shelves, nor on the lower ones either. He crept under the counter and his teeth chattered. Ten thousand books and a ghost crouching over each one. That was why it was so quiet. Sometimes he heard them turn over a page. They read as fast as he did himself. He might have grown used to them, but there were ten thousand of them and perhaps one of them would bite. Ghosts get cross if you brush against them, they think you are making fun of them. He made himself as small as possible; they flew over him without touching him. Morning came only after many long nights. Then he fell asleep. He did not hear the assistants opening up the shop. They found him under the counter and shook him awake. First he pretended that he was still asleep, then he suddenly burst out howling. They had locked him in last night, he was afraid of his mother, she must have been looking for him everywhere. The proprietor cross-questioned him and as soon as he had found out his name, sent him off home with one of the shopwalkers. He sent his sincerest apologies to the lady. The little boy had been locked in by mistake, but he seemed to be safe and sound. He assured her of his respectful attention. His mother believed it all and was delighted to have him safely home again. Today the little liar of yesterday was the owner of a famous library and a name no less famous.

Kien abhorred falsehood; from his earliest childhood he had held fast to the truth. He could remember no other falsehood except this. And even this one was hateful to him. Only the conversation with the schoolboy, who had seemed to him the image of his own childhood, had recalled it to him. Forget it, he thought, it is nearly eight o'clock. Punctually at eight his work began, his service for truth. Knowledge and truth were for him identical terms. You draw closer to truth by shutting yourself off from mankind. Daily life was a superficial clatter of lies. Every passerby was a liar. For that reason he never looked at them. Who among all these bad actors, who made up the mob, had a face to arrest his attention. They changed their faces with every moment; not for one single day did they stick to the same part. He had always known this, experience was superfluous. *His* ambition was to persist stubbornly in the same manner of existence. Not for a mere month, not for a year, but for the whole of his life, he would be true to himself. Character, if you had a character, determined your outward appearance. Ever since he had been able to think, he had been tall and too thin. He knew his face only casually, from its reflection in bookshop windows. He had no mirror in his house, there was no room for it among the books. But he knew that his face was narrow, stern, and bony; that was enough.

Since he felt not the slightest desire to notice anyone, he kept his eyes lowered or raised above their heads. He sensed where the bookshops were without looking. He simply relied on instinct. The same force which guides a horse home to the stable, served as well for him. He went out walking to breathe the air of alien books, they aroused his antagonism, they stimulated him. In his library everything went by clockwork. But between

seven and eight he allowed himself a few of those liberties which
constitute the entire life of other beings.

Although he savored this hour to the full, he did all by rote.
Before crossing a busy street, he hesitated a little. He preferred
to walk at a regular pace; so as not to hasten his steps, he waited
for a favorable moment to cross. Suddenly he heard someone
shouting loudly at someone else: "Can you tell me where Mut
Strasse is?" There was no reply. Kien was surprised: so there
were other silent people besides himself to be found in the busy
streets. Without looking up he listened for more. How would
the questioner behave in the face of this silence? "Excuse me
please, could you perhaps tell me where Mut Strasse is?" So;
he grew more polite; he had no better luck. The other man still
made no reply. "I don't think you heard me. I'm asking you the
way. Will you be so kind as to tell me how I get to Mut Strasse?"
Kien's appetite for knowledge was whetted; idle curiosity he did
not know. He decided to observe this silent man, on condition
of course that he still remained silent. Not a doubt of it, the
man was deep in thought and determined to avoid any interruption. Still he said nothing. Kien applauded him. Here was one
among thousands, a man whose character was proof against all
chances. "Here, are you deaf?" shouted the first man. Now he
will have to answer back, thought Kien, and began to lose his
pleasure in his protégé. Who can control his tongue when he is
insulted? He turned toward the street; the favorable moment
for crossing it had come. Astonished at the continued silence,
he hesitated. Still the second man said nothing. All the more
violent would be the outburst of anger to come. Kien hoped for
a fight. If the second man appeared after all to be a mere vulgar-
ian, Kien would be confirmed in his own estimation of himself
as the sole and only person of character walking in this street.
He was already considering whether he should look round. The

incident was taking place on his right hand. The first man was
now yelling: "You've no manners! I spoke to you civil. Who
do you think you are? You lout. Are you dumb?" The second
man was still silent. "I demand an apology! Do you hear?" The
other did not hear. He rose even higher in the estimation of the
listener. "I'll fetch the police! What do you take me for! You rag
and bone man! Call yourself a gentleman! Where did you get
those clothes? Out of the rag bag? That's what they look like!
What have you got under your arm! I'll show you! Go and boil
your head! Who do you think you are?"

Then Kien felt a nasty jolt. Someone had grabbed his briefcase and was pulling at it. With a movement far exceeding his
usual effort, he liberated the books from the alien clutch and
turned sharply to the right. His glance was directed to his briefcase, but it fell instead on a small fat man who was bawling up
at him. "You lout! You lout! You lout!" The other man, the
silent one, the man of character, who controlled his tongue even
in anger, was Kien himself. Calmly he turned his back on the
gesticulating illiterate. With this small knife, he sliced his clamor
in two. A loutish creature whose courtesy changed in so many
seconds to insolence had no power to hurt him. Nevertheless he
walked along the streets a little faster than was his usual custom.
A man who carries books with him must seek to avoid physical
violence. He always had books with him.

There is after all no obligation to answer every passing
fool according to his folly. The greatest danger which threatens a man of learning, is to lose himself in talk. Kien preferred
to express himself in the written rather than the spoken word.
He knew more than a dozen Oriental languages. A few of the
Western ones did not even need to be learned. No branch of
human literature was unfamiliar to him. He thought in quotations and wrote in carefully considered sentences. Countless

texts owed their restoration to him. When he came to misreadings or imperfections in ancient Chinese, Indian, or Japanese manuscripts, as many alternative readings suggested themselves for his selection as he could wish. Other textual critics envied him; he for his part had to guard against a superfluity of ideas. Meticulously cautious, he weighed up the alternatives month after month, was slow to the point of exasperation; applying his severest standards to his own conclusions, he took no decision, on a single letter, a word, or an entire sentence, until he was convinced that it was unassailable. The papers which he had hitherto published, few in number, yet each one the starting point for a hundred others, had gained for him the reputation of being the greatest living authority on sinology. They were known in every detail to his colleagues, indeed almost word for word. A sentence once set down by him was decisive and binding. In controversial questions he was the ultimate appeal, the leading authority even in related branches of knowledge. A few only he honored with his letters. That man, however, whom he chose so to honor would receive in a single letter enough stimuli to set him off on years of study, the results of which—in the view of the mind whence they had sprung—were foregone conclusions. Personally he had no dealings with anyone. He refused all invitations. Whenever any chair of Oriental philology fell vacant, it was offered first to him. Polite but contemptuous, he invariably declined.

He had not, he averred, been born to be an orator. Payment for his work would give him a distaste for it. In his own humble opinion, those unproductive popularizers to whom instruction in the grammar schools was entrusted, should occupy the university chairs also; then genuine, creative research workers would be able to devote themselves exclusively to their own work. As it was there was no shortage of mediocre intelligences.

Should he give lectures, the high demands which he would nec-
essarily make upon an audience would naturally very much reduce its numbers. As for examinations, not a single candidate, as
far as he could see, would be able to pass them. He would make
it a point of honor to fail these young immature students at least
until their thirtieth year, by which time, either through very
boredom or through a dawning of real seriousness, they must
have learned something, if only a very little. He regarded the
acceptance of candidates whose memories had not been most
carefully tested in the lecture halls of the faculty as a totally useless, if not indeed a questionable, practice. Ten students, selected
by the most strenuous preliminary tests, would, provided they
remained together, achieve far more than they could do when
permitted to mingle with a hundred beer-swilling dullards, the
general run of university students. His doubts were therefore
of the most serious and fundamental nature. He could only request the faculty to withdraw an offer which, although intended
no doubt to show the high esteem in which they held him, was
not one which he could accept in that spirit.

At scholastic conferences, where there is usually a great deal
of talk, Kien was a much-discussed personality. The learned
gentlemen, who for the greater part of their lives were silent,
timid, and myopic mice, on these occasions, every two years
or so, came right out of themselves; they welcomed each other,
stuck the most inapposite heads together, whispered nonsense
in corners, and toasted each other clumsily at the dinner table.
Deeply moved and profoundly gratified, they raised aloft the
banner of learning and upheld the integrity of their aims. Over
and over again in all languages they repeated their vows. They
would have kept them even without taking them. In the intervals they made bets. Would Kien really come this time? He was
more spoken of than a merely famous colleague; his behavior

excited curiosity. But he would not trade on his fame; for the last ten years he had stubbornly refused invitations to banquets and congresses where, in spite of his youth, he would have been warmly acclaimed; he announced for every conference an important paper, which was then read for him from his own manuscript by another scholar: all this his colleagues regarded as mere postponement. The time would come—perhaps this was the time—when he would suddenly make his appearance, would graciously accept the applause which his long retirement had made only the more vociferous, and would permit himself to be acclaimed president of the assembly, an office which was only his due, and which indeed he arrogated to himself after his own fashion even by his absence. But his learned colleagues were mistaken. Kien did not appear. The more credulous of them lost their bets.

At the last minute he refused. Sending the paper he had written to a privileged person, he would add some ironical expressions of regret. In the event of his colleagues finding time for serious study in the intervals of a program so rich in entertainment—an eventuality which in the interests of their general satisfaction he could hardly desire—he asked leave to lay before the conference this small contribution to knowledge, the result of two years' work. He would carefully save up any new and surprising conclusions to which his researches might have brought him for moments such as these. Their effects and the discussions to which they gave rise, he would follow from a distance, suspiciously and in detail, as though probing their textual accuracy. The gatherings were ready enough to accept his contempt. Eighty out of every hundred present relied entirely on his judgment. His services to science were inestimable. Long might he live. To most of them indeed his death would have been a severe shock.

Those few who had known him in his earlier years had forgotten what his face was like. Repeatedly he received letters asking for his photograph. He had none, he would answer, nor did
he intend to have one taken. Both statements were true. But
he had willingly agreed to a different sort of concession. As a
young man of thirty he had, without however making any other
testamentary dispositions, bequeathed his skull with all its contents to an institute for cranial research. He justified this step by
considering the advantage to be gained if it could be scientifi-
cally proved that his truly phenomenal memory was the result
of a particular structure, or perhaps even a heavier weight, of
brain. Not indeed that he considered—so he wrote to the head
of the institute—that memory and genius were the same thing,
a theory all too widely accepted of recent years. He himself was
no genius. Yet it would be unscholarly to deny that the almost
terrifying memory at his disposal had been remarkably useful in
his learned researches. He did indeed carry in his head a library
as well-provided and as reliable as his actual library, which he
understood was so much discussed. He could sit at his writing desk and sketch out a treatise down to the minutest detail
without turning over a single page, except in his head. Naturally
he would check quotations and sources later out of the books
themselves; but only because he was a man of conscience. He
could not remember any single occasion on which his memory
had been found at fault. His very dreams were more precisely
defined than those of most people. Blurred images without form
or color were unknown in any of the dreams which he had hitherto recollected. In his case night had no power to turn things
topsy-turvy; the noises he heard could be exactly referred to their
cause of origin; conversations into which he entered were entirely reasonable; everything retained its normal meaning. It was

outside his sphere to examine the probable connection between the accuracy of his memory and the lucidity of his dreams. In all humility he drew attention to the facts alone, and hoped that the personal data which he had taken the liberty of recording would be regarded as a sign neither of pretentiousness nor garrulity.

Kien called to mind one or two more facts from his daily life, which showed his retiring, untalkative, and wholly unpresumptuous nature in its true light. But his irritation at the insolent and insufferable fellow who had first asked him the way and then abused him, grew greater with every step. There is nothing else I can do, he said at last; he stepped aside into the porch of a house, looked round—nobody was watching him—and drew a long narrow notebook from his pocket. On the title page, in tall, angular letters was written the word: STUPIDITIES. His eyes rested at first on this. Then he turned over the pages; more than half the notebook was full. Everything he would have preferred to forget he put down in this book. Date, time, and place came first. Then followed the incident which was supposed to illustrate the stupidity of mankind. An apt quotation, a new one for each occasion, formed the conclusion. He never read these collected examples of stupidity; a glance at the title page sufficed. Later on he thought of publishing them under the title "Morning Walks of a Sinologist."

He drew out a sharply pointed pencil and wrote down on the first empty page: "September 23rd, 7:45 a.m. In Mut Strasse a person crossed my path and asked me the way to Mut Strasse. In order not to put him to shame, I made no answer. He was not to be put off and asked again, several times; his bearing was courteous. Suddenly his eye fell upon the street sign. He became aware of his stupidity. Instead of withdrawing as fast as he could—as I should have done in his place—he gave way to

the most unmeasured rage and abused me in the vulgarest fashion. Had I not spared him in the first place, I would have spared
myself this painful scene. Which of us was the stupider?"

With that last sentence he proved that he did not draw the
line even at his *own* failings. He was pitiless toward everyone.
Gratified, he put away his notebook and forgot the man in the
Mut Strasse. While he was writing, his books had slipped into
an uncomfortable position. He shifted them into their right
place. At the next street corner he was startled by an Alsatian.
Swift and sure-footed the dog cleared itself a path through the
crowd. At the extremity of a tautened lead it tugged a blind
man. His infirmity—for anyone who failed to notice the dog—
was further emphasized by the white stick which he carried in
his right hand. Even those passersby who were in too much of
a hurry to stare at the blind man, cast an admiring glance at the
dog. He pushed them gently to one side with his patient muzzle. As he was a fine, handsome dog they bore with him gladly.
Suddenly the blind man pulled his cap off his head and, clutching it in the same hand as his white stick, held it out toward
the crowd. "To buy my dog bones!" he begged. Coins show-
ered into it. In the middle of the street a crowd gathered round
the two of them. The traffic was held up: luckily there was no
policeman at this corner to direct it. Kien observed the beggar
from close at hand. He was dressed with studied poverty and
his face seemed educated. The muscles round his eyes twitched
continually—he winked, raised his eyebrows, and wrinkled his
forehead—so that Kien mistrusted him and decided to regard
him as a fraud. At that moment a boy of about twelve came
up, hurriedly pushed the dog to one side, and threw into the
cap a large heavy button. The blind man stared in front of him
and thanked him, perhaps in the slightest degree more warmly
than before. The clink of the button as it fell into the cap had

sounded like the ring of gold. Kien felt a pang in his heart. He caught the boy by the scruff of the neck and cuffed him over the head with his briefcase. "For shame," he said, "deceiving a blind man!" Only after he had done it did he recollect what was in the briefcase: books. He was horrified. Never before had he taken so great a risk. The boy ran off howling. To restore his normal and far less exalted level of compassion, Kien emptied his entire stock of small change into the blind man's cap. The bystanders approved aloud; to himself the action seemed more petty and cautious than the preceding one. The dog set off again. Immediately after, just as a policeman appeared on the scene, both leader and led had resumed their brisk progress.

Kien took a private vow that if he should ever be threatened by blindness, he would die of his own free will. Whenever he met a blind man this same cruel fear clutched at him. Mutes he loved: the deaf, the lame, and other kinds of cripples meant nothing to him; the blind disturbed him. He could not understand why they did not make an end of themselves. Even if they could read braille, their opportunities for reading were limited. Eratosthenes, the great librarian of Alexandria, a scholar of universal significance who flourished in the third century of the pre-Christian era and held sway over more than half a million manuscript scrolls, made in his eightieth year a terrible discovery. His eyes began to refuse their office. He could still see but he could not read. Another man might have waited until he was completely blind. He felt that to take leave of his books was blindness enough. Friends and pupils implored him to stay with them. He smiled wisely, thanked them, and in a few days starved himself to death.

Should the time come this great example could easily be followed even by the lesser Kien, whose library comprised a mere twenty-five thousand volumes.

The remaining distance to his own house he completed at a
quickened pace. It must be past eight o'clock. At eight o'clock
his work began; unpunctuality caused him acute irritation. Now
and again, surreptitiously he felt his eyes. They focused correctly; they felt comfortable and unthreatened.

His library was situated on the fourth and topmost floor of
No. 24 Ehrlich Strasse. The door of the flat was secured by three
highly complicated locks. He unlocked them, strode across the
hall, which contained nothing except an umbrella and coat-
stand, and entered his study. Carefully he set down the briefcase
on an armchair. Then once and again he paced the entire length
of the four lofty, spacious communicating rooms which formed
his library. The entire wall space up to the ceiling was clothed
with books. Slowly he lifted his eyes toward them. Skylights
had been let into the ceiling. He was proud of his roof lighting.
The windows had been walled up several years before after a determined struggle with his landlord. In this way he had gained
in every room a fourth wall space: accommodation for more
books. Moreover illumination from above, which lit up all the
shelves equally, seemed to him more just and more suited to his
relations with his books. The temptation to watch what went on
in the street—an immoral and time-wasting habit—disappeared
with the side windows. Daily, before he sat down to his writing desk, he blessed both the idea and its results, since he owed
to them the fulfilment of his dearest wish: the possession of a
well-stocked library, in perfect order and enclosed on all sides,
in which no single superfluous article of furniture, no single superfluous person could lure him from his serious thoughts.

The first of the four rooms served for his study. A huge old
writing desk, an armchair in front of it, a second armchair in
the opposite corner were its only furniture. There crouched besides an unobtrusive divan, willingly overlooked by its master:

he only slept on it. A movable pair of steps was propped against the wall. It was more important than the divan, and traveled in the course of a day from room to room. The emptiness of the three remaining rooms was not disturbed by so much as a chair. Nowhere did a table, a cupboard, a fireplace interrupt the multicolored monotony of the bookshelves. Handsome deep-pile carpets, the uniform covering of the floor, softened the harsh twilight which, mingling through wide-open communicating doors, made of the four separate rooms one single lofty hall.

Kien walked with a stiff and deliberate step. He set his feet down with particular firmness on the carpets; it pleased him that even a footfall such as his waked not the faintest echo. In his library it would have been beyond the power even of an elephant to pound the slightest noise out of that floor. For this reason he set great store by his carpets. He satisfied himself that the books were still in the order in which he had been forced to leave them an hour before. Then he began to relieve his briefcase of its contents. When he came in, it was his habit to lay it down on the chair in front of the writing desk. Otherwise he might perhaps have forgotten it and have sat down to his work before he had tidied away its contents; for at eight o'clock he felt a very strong compulsion to begin his work. With the help of the ladder he distributed the volumes to their appointed places. In spite of all his care—since it was already late, he was hurrying rather more than usual—the last of the books fell from the third bookshelf, a shelf for which he did not even have to use the ladder. It was no other than Mencius beloved above all the rest. "Idiot!" he shrieked at himself. "Barbarian! Illiterate!" He tenderly lifted the book and went quickly to the door. Before he had reached it an important thought struck him. He turned back and pushed the ladder as softly as he could to the site of the accident. Mencius he laid gently down with both hands on the carpet at the

foot of the ladder. Now he could go to the door. He opened it
and called into the hall:

"Your best duster, please!"

Almost at once the housekeeper knocked at the door which
he had lightly pushed to. He made no answer. She inserted her
head modestly through the crack and asked:

"Has something happened?"

"No, give it to me."

She thought she could detect a complaint in this answer. He
had not intended her to. She was too curious to leave the matter
where it was. "Excuse me, Professor!" she said reproachfully,
stepped into the room, and saw at once what had happened. She
glided over to the book. Below her blue starched skirt, which
reached to the floor, her feet were invisible. Her head was askew.
Her ears were large, flabby, and prominent. Since her right ear
touched her shoulder and was partly concealed by it, the left
looked all the bigger. When she talked or walked her head waggled to and fro. Her shoulders waggled too, in accompaniment.
She stooped, lifted up the book, and passed the duster over it
carefully at least a dozen times. Kien did not attempt to forestall
her. Courtesy was abhorrent to him. He stood by and observed
whether she performed her work seriously.

"Excuse me, a thing like that can happen, standing up on a
ladder."

Then she handed the book to him, like a plate newly polished. She would very gladly have begun a conversation with
him. But she did not succeed. He said briefly, "Thank you,"
and turned his back on her. She understood and went. She had
already placed her hand on the doorknob when he turned round
suddenly and asked with simulated friendliness:

"Then this has often happened to you?"

She saw through him and was genuinely indignant: "Excuse me, Professor." Her "Excuse me" struck through her unctuous tones, sharp as a thorn. She will give notice, he thought; and to appease her explained himself:

"I only meant to impress on you what these books represent in terms of money."

She had not been prepared for so affable a speech. She did not know how to reply and left the room pacified. As soon as she had gone, he reproached himself. He had spoken about books like the vilest tradesman. Yet in what other way could he enforce the respectful handling of books on a person of her kind? Their real value would have no meaning for her. She must believe that the library was a speculation of his. What people! What people!

He bowed involuntarily in the direction of the Japanese manuscripts, and, at last, sat down at his writing desk.

Chapter II: The Secret

Eight years earlier Kien had put the following advertisement in the paper:

A man of learning who owns an exceptionally large library wants a responsibly minded housekeeper. Only applicants of the highest character need apply. Unsuitable persons will be shown the door. Money no object.

Therese Krumbholz was at that time in a good position in which she had hitherto been satisfied. She read exhaustively every morning, before getting breakfast for her employers, the advertisement columns of the daily paper, to know what went on in the world. She had no intention of ending her life in the service of a vulgar family. She was still a young person, the right side of fifty, and hoped for a place with a single gentleman. Then she could have things just so; with women in the house it's not the same. But you couldn't expect her to give up her good place for nothing. She'd know who she had to do with before she gave in her notice. You didn't catch her with putting things in the papers, promising the earth to respectable women. You hardly get inside the door and they start taking liberties. Alone in the world now for thirty-three years and such a thing had never happened to her yet. She'd take care it never did, what's more.

This time the advertisement hit her right in the eye. The phrase "Money no object" made her pause; then she read the sentences, all of which stood out in heavy type, several times backward and forward. The tone impressed her: here was a man. It flattered her to think of herself as an applicant of the highest character. She saw the unsuitable persons being shown the door and took a righteous pleasure in their fate. Not for one second did it occur to her that she herself might be treated as an unsuitable person.

On the following morning she presented herself before Kien at the earliest possible moment, seven o'clock. He let her into the hall and immediately declared: "I must emphatically forbid any stranger whatsoever to enter my house. Are you in a position to take over the custody of the books?"

He observed her narrowly and with suspicion. Before she gave her answer to his question, he would not make up his mind about her. "Excuse me please," she said, "what do you take me for?"

Her stupefaction at his rudeness made her give an answer in which he could find no fault.

"You have a right to know," he said, "the reason why I gave notice to my last housekeeper. A book out of my library was missing. I had the whole house searched. It did not come to light. I was thus compelled to give her notice on the spot." Choked with indignation, he was silent. "You will understand the necessity," he added as an afterthought, as though he had made too heavy a demand on her intelligence.

"Everything in its right place," she answered promptly. He was disarmed. With an ample gesture he invited her into the library. She stepped delicately into the first of the rooms and stood waiting.

"This is the sphere of your duties," he said in a dry, serious tone of voice. "Every day one of these rooms must be dusted from floor to ceiling. On the fourth day your work is completed. On the fifth you start again with the first room. Can you undertake this?"

"I make so bold."

He went out again, opened the door of the flat, and said: "Good morning. You will take up your duties today."

She was already on the stairs and still hesitating. Of her wages, he had said nothing. Before she gave up her present place she must ask him. No, better not. One false step. If she said nothing, perhaps he would give more of his own accord. Over the two conflicting forces, caution and greed, a third prevailed: curiosity.

"Yes, and about my wages?" Embarrassed by the mistake which she was perhaps making, she forgot to add her "excuse me."

"Whatever you like," he said indifferently and closed the door.

She informed her horrified employers—they relied entirely on her, an old piece of furniture in the house for twelve years—

that she wouldn't put up with such goings on any more, she'd rather beg her bread in the street. No arguments could move her from her purpose. She was going at once; when you have been in the same position for twelve years, you can make an exception of the usual month's notice. The worthy family seized the opportunity of saving her wages up to the twentieth. They refused to pay them since the creature would not stay her month out. Therese thought to herself: I shall get it out of him, and went.

She fulfilled her duty toward the books to Kien's satisfaction. He expressed his recognition of the fact by silence. To praise her openly in her presence seemed to him unnecessary. His meals were always punctual. Whether she cooked well or badly he did not know; it was a matter of total indifference to him. During his meals, which he ate at his writing desk, he was busy with important considerations. As a rule he would not have been able to say what precisely he had in his mouth. He reserved consciousness for real thoughts; they depend upon it; without consciousness, thoughts are unthinkable. Chewing and digesting happen of themselves.

Therese had a certain respect for his work, for he paid her a high salary regularly and was friendly to no one; he never even spoke to her. Sociable people, from a child up, she had always despised; her mother had been one of that kind. She performed her own tasks meticulously. She earned her money. Besides, from the very beginning she had a riddle to solve. She enjoyed that.

Punctually at six the Professor got out of his divan bed. Washing and dressing were soon done. In the evening, before going to bed, she turned down his divan and pushed the washstand, which was on wheels, into the middle of the study. It was allowed to stand there for the night. A screen of four sections in Spanish leather painted with letters in a foreign language was so arranged as to spare him the disturbing sight. He could not abide articles of furniture. The wash-trolley, as he called it, was an invention of his own, so constructed that the loathsome object could be disposed of as soon as it had performed its office. At a quarter past six he would open his door and violently expel it; it would trundle all the way down the long passage. Close to the kitchen door it would crash into the wall. Therese would wait in the kitchen; her own little room was immediately adjoining. She would open the door and call: "Up already?" He made no answer and bolted himself in again. Then he stayed at home until seven o'clock. Not a soul knew what he did in the long interval until seven o'clock. At other times he always sat at his writing desk and wrote.

The somber, weighty colossus of a desk was filled to bursting with manuscripts and heavy-laden with books. The most cautious stirring of any drawer elicited a shrill squeak. Although the noise was repulsive to him, Kien left the heirloom desk in this state so that the housekeeper, in the event of his absence from home, would know at once if a burglar had got in. Strange species, they usually look for money before they start on the books. He had explained the mechanism of his invaluable desk to Therese, briefly yet exhaustively, in three sentences. He had added, in a meaningful tone, that there was no possibility of silencing the squeak; even he was unable to do so. During the day she could hear every time Kien took out a manuscript. She wondered how he could put up with the noise. At night he shut all his papers away. Until eight in the morning the writing desk remained mute. When she was tidying up she never found anything on it but books and a few yellow papers. She looked in vain for clean paper covered with his own handwriting. It was clear that from a quarter past six until seven in the morning, three whole quarters of an hour, he did no work whatsoever.

Was he saying his prayers? No, she couldn't believe that. Nobody says their prayers. She had no use for praying. You didn't catch her going to church. Look at the sort of people who go to church. A fine crowd they are, cluttered up together. She didn't hold with all that begging either. You have to give them something because everyone is watching you. What they do with it, heaven knows. Say one's prayers at home—why? A waste of beautiful time. A respectable person doesn't need that sort of thing. She'd always kept herself respectable. Other people could pray for all she cared. But she'd like to know what went on in that room between a quarter past six and seven o'clock. She was not curious, no one could call her that. She didn't poke her nose into other people's business. Women were all alike nowadays. Poking their noses into everything. She got on with her own work. Prices going up something shocking. Potatoes cost double already. How to make the money go round. He locked all four doors. Or else you could have seen something from the next room. So particular as he was too, never wasting a minute!

During his morning walk Therese examined the rooms entrusted to her care. She suspected a secret vice; its nature remained vague. First of all she decided for a woman's body in a trunk. But there wasn't room for that under the carpets and she renounced a horribly mutilated corpse. There was no cupboard to help her speculations; how gladly she would have welcomed one; one against each wall preferably. Then the hideous crime must be concealed somehow behind one of the books. Where else? She might have satisfied her sense of duty by dusting over their spines only; the immoral secret she was tracking down compelled her to look behind each one. She took each out separately, knocked at it—it might be hollow—inserted her coarse, calloused fingers as far back as the wooden paneling, probed about, and at length withdrew them, dissatisfied, shaking her head. Her interest never misled her into overstepping the exact time laid down for her work. Five minutes before Kien unlocked the door, she was already in the kitchen. Calmly and without haste she searched one section of the shelves after another, never missing anything and never quite giving up hope.

During these months of indefatigable research, she couldn't think of taking her money to the post office. She wouldn't lay a finger on it; who knew what sort of money it might be? She placed the notes, in the order in which he gave them to her, in a large clean envelope, which contained, still in its entirety, the stock of notepaper she had bought twenty years before. Overcoming serious scruples she put the whole into her trunk, with the trousseau, specially selected and beautifully worked, which had taken her many years and hard-earned money to accumulate.

Little by little she realized that she would not get to the bottom of the mystery as easily as all that. She knew how to wait. She was very well as she was. If something were to come to light one day—no one could blame her. She had been over every corner of that library with a fine-tooth comb. Of course if you had a friend in the police, solid and respectable, who wouldn't forget you were in a good job, you might say something to him. Excuse me, she could put up with a lot, but she'd no one to rely on. The things people do these days. Dancing, bathing, fooling around, nothing sensible, not a stroke of work. Her own gentleman, though he was sensible enough, had his goings on like anyone else. Never went to bed before midnight. The best sleep is the sleep before midnight. Respectable people go to bed at nine. Very likely it wasn't anything to write home about.

Gradually the horrible crime dwindled into a mere secret. Thick, tough layers of contempt covered it up. But her curiosity remained; between a quarter past six and seven o'clock she was always on the alert. She counted on rare, but not impossible contingencies. A sudden pain in the stomach might bring him out of his room. Then she would hurry in and ask if he wanted anything. Pains do not go away all in a minute. A few seconds, and she would know all she wanted to know. But the temperate and reasonable life which Kien led suited him too well. For the whole eight long years during which he had employed Therese he had never yet had a pain in the stomach.

The very morning on which he had met the blind man and his dog, it happened that Kien urgently wanted to consult certain old treatises. He pulled out all the drawers of the writing desk violently one after the other. A vast accumulation of papers had piled up in them over the years. Rough drafts, corrected scripts, fair copies, anything and everything which had to do with his work, he carefully preserved them all. He found wretched scraps whose contents he had himself long since surpassed and contradicted. The archives went right back to his student days. Merely in order to find a minute detail, which he knew by heart anyway, merely to check a reference, he wasted hours of time. He read over thirty pages and more; one line was all he wanted. Worthless stuff, which had long since served its purpose, came into his hands. He cursed it, why was it there? But once his eye fell upon anything written or printed he could not pass it over. Any other man would have refused to be held up by these digressions. He read every word, from first to last. The ink had faded. He had difficulty in making out the pale outlines. The blind man in the street came into his mind. There was he, playing tricks with his eyes, as if they would last for all eternity. Instead of restricting their hours of service, he increased them wantonly from month to month. Each single paper which he replaced in the drawer cost his eyes a part of their strength. Dogs have short lives and dogs do not read; thus they are able to help out blind men with their eyes. The man who has frittered away the strength of his eyes is a worthy companion of the beast that leads him.

Kien decided to empty his writing desk of rubbish on the following day immediately after he got up; at present he was working.

On the following day, at six o'clock precisely, in the very middle of a dream, he started up from his divan bed, flung himself on the crammed giant, and pulled out every one of its drawers. Screeching filled the air; it shrilled through the entire library, swelling to a heartrending climax. It was as if each drawer had its own voice and each was vying with its neighbor in a piercing scream for help. They were being robbed, tortured, murdered. They could not know who it was who dared to touch them. They had no eyes; their only organ was a shrill voice. Kien sorted the papers. It took him a long time. He disregarded the noise; what he had begun, he would finish. With a pyramid of waste paper in his lean arms, he stalked across into the fourth room. Here, some distance from the screeching, he tore them, cursing, into small pieces. Someone knocked; he ground his teeth. Again that knock; he stamped his feet. The knocking changed to hammering. "Quiet!" he ordered and swore. He would willingly have dispensed with the unseemly row. But he was sorry on account of the manuscripts. Rage alone had given him strength to destroy them. At last he stood, a huge lonely stork on guard over a mountain of scraps of paper. Embarrassed and timid, he stroked them with his fingers, softly mourning over them. So as not to injure them unnecessarily, he lifted a cautious leg and cleared them. The graveyard behind him, he breathed again. Outside the door he found the housekeeper. With a weary gesture, he indicated the pyre and said: "Clear it away!" The screeching had died down; he went back to the writing desk and closed the drawers. They were silent. He had wrenched them open too violently. The mechanism had been broken.

Therese was in the very act of finding her way into the starched skirt which completed her attire, when the screeching had broken loose. Terrified out of her wits, she fastened her skirt provisionally and glided fast to the door of the study. "For Heaven's sake," she wailed, flute-like, "What has happened?" She knocked, discreetly at first, then louder. Receiving no answer, she tried the door, in vain. She glided from door to door. In the last room she heard him, shouting angrily. Here she hammered on the door with all her strength. "Quiet!" he shouted in a rage, in such a rage as she had never heard him. Half indignant, half resigned, she let her hard hands drop against her hard skirt, and stood stiff as a wooden doll. "What a calamity!" she murmured. "What a calamity!" and was still standing there, out of mere habit, when he opened the door.

Slow by nature, this time she grasped in a flash the opportunity which was being offered to her. With difficulty she said "At once," and glided away to the kitchen. On the threshold she had an idea: "Gracious Heaven, he's bolting himself in, just out of habit! Something will happen, at the last minute, that's life! I've no luck, I've no luck!" It was the first time she had said this, for as a rule she regarded herself as a meritorious and therefore as a lucky person. Anxiety made her head jerk to and fro. She sneaked out into the corridor again. She was stooping far forward. Her legs hesitated before she took a step. Her stiff skirt billowed. She would have reached her goal far more quietly by gliding as usual, but that was too ordinary a process. The solemnity of the occasion demanded its own solemnities. The room was open to her: In the middle of the floor the paper was still lying. She pushed a great fold of the carpet between the door and its frame so that it should not be blown to. Then she went back to the kitchen and waited, dustpan and brush in hand, for the familiar rattle of the wash-trolley. She would have preferred to come and fetch it herself, for she had a long time to wait. When at last she heard it crash against the wall, she forgot herself and called, out of habit, "Up already?" She pushed it into the kitchen and, stooping even lower than before, crept into the library. She set down dustpan and brush on the floor. Slowly she picked her way across the intervening rooms to the threshold of his bedroom. After every step she stood still, and turned her head the other way about so as to listen with her right ear, the ear which was the less worn-out of the two. The thirty yards which she traversed took her ten minutes; she thought herself foolhardy. Her terror and her curiosity grew at the same rate. A thousand times she had thought out how to behave when she reached her goal. She squeezed herself tightly against the doorframe. She remembered the crackling of her newly starched skirt too late. With one eye she tried to survey the situation. As long as the other one was in reserve she felt safe. She must not be seen, and she must see everything. Her right arm, which she liked to hold akimbo and which was constantly doubling itself up, she forced into stillness.

Kien was pacing calmly up and down in front of his books, making incomprehensible noises. Under his arm he carried the empty briefcase. He came to a halt, thought for a moment, then fetched the ladder and climbed up it. From the topmost shelf he extracted a book, turned over the pages, and placed it in the briefcase. On the ground again, he continued his pacing up and down, stopped, pulled at a book, which was recalcitrant, wrinkled his forehead, and when he had it at last in his hands, gave it a sharp slap. Then it too disappeared into the briefcase. He selected five volumes. Four small ones and one large one. Suddenly he was in a hurry. Carrying the heavy briefcase he clambered up

to the highest rung of the ladder and pushed the first volume
back into its place. His long legs encumbered him; he had all
but fallen down.

If he fell and hurt himself, there'd be an end of this wicked-
ness. Therese's arm could be controlled no longer; it reached for
her ear and tugged vigorously at it. Both eyes were fixed, gloat-
ing, on her imperiled employer. When his feet at length reached
the thick carpet, she could breathe again. So the books were a
fraud. Now for the truth. She knew every inch of the library, but
secret vices are crafty. There's opium, there's morphia, there's
cocaine—who could remember them all? You couldn't fool her.
Behind the books, that's it. Why for instance did he never walk
straight across the room? He stood by the ladder and what he
wanted was on the shelf exactly opposite. He could fetch it as
easy as anything, but no, he must always go creeping round by
the wall. Carrying that great heavy thing under his arm, he goes
all the way round by the wall. Behind the books, that's it. Murderers are drawn to the scene of the crime. Now the briefcase is
full. He can't get anything more into it; she knows the briefcase,
she dusts it out every day. Now something must happen. It can't
be seven yet. If it's seven he'll go out. Where is it seven? It shan't
be seven.

Shameless and sure of herself, she stooped forward, pressed
her arm to her side, pricked her two large ears, and opened her
little eyes greedily. He took the briefcase by both ends and laid it
firmly on the carpet. His face looked proud. He stooped down
and remained stooping. She was running with sweat and trembling in every limb. Tears came into her eyes, under the carpet
then, that's it. She'd always said, under the carpet. What a fool!
He straightened himself, cracked his joints, and spat. Or did he
only say "There!" He took up the briefcase, extracted a volume,

and slowly replaced it on the shelves. He did the same with all
the others.

Therese came over faint. No thank you, indeed! There's
nothing more worth looking at. So that's your sensible man,
with never a smile or a word! She's sensible herself, and hardworking, but would she demean herself? You could cut her
hand off, you don't find her mixed up in such things. He acts
stupid in front of his own housekeeper. A creature like that to
have money! And so much money, heaps and heaps of money!
Ought to be put away. The way he wastes his money! Anyone
else in her position now, any of that ragtag and bobtail there
is these days, they'd have had the last stitch of clothing off his
back long ago. Doesn't even sleep in a decent bed. What does
he want with all these books and books? He can't be reading all
of them at once. If you ask her, he's nothing but a loony, ought
to have his money taken away before he wastes it all, and then
let him go his own way. She'll teach him! Enticing a respectable woman into his house, indeed. Thinks he can make a fool
of anyone, does he? Nobody can make a fool of her. For eight
years perhaps, but not a moment longer!

By the time Kien had made his second selection of books for
his morning walk, Therese's first anger had evaporated. She saw
that he was ready to go out, glided in her normal, self-possessed
manner back to the heap of paper, and inserted the dustpan underneath it with dignity. She seemed to herself a more interesting and distinguished person than before.

No, she decided, she would not give up her post. But she's
found him out now. Well, that's something to know. If she sees
anything, she knows how to make use of it. She doesn't see
many things. She hasn't ever been outside the town. She's not
one for excursions, a waste of good money. You don't catch her

going bathing, it's not respectable. She doesn't care for traveling, you never know where you are. If she didn't have to go shopping, she'd prefer to stay in all day. They all try to do you down. Prices going up all the time, things aren't the same anymore.

Chapter III: Confucius the Matchmaker

On the following Sunday Kien came back elated from his morning walk. The streets were empty on Sundays at this early hour. Humankind began each holiday by lying late. Then they fell upon their best clothes. They spent their first wakeful hours in devotions before the looking glass. During the remainder they recovered from their own grimaces by looking at other people's. Each thought himself the finest. To prove it he must go among his fellows. On weekdays: sweat and babble to earn a living. On Sundays: sweat and babble for nothing. The day of rest had been first intended as a day of silence. Kien noted with scorn that this institution, like all others, had degenerated into its exact opposite. He himself had no use for a day of rest. Always he worked and always in silence.

Outside the door of his flat he found the housekeeper. She had evidently been waiting for him some time.

"The Metzger child from the second floor was here. You promised him he could come. He would have it, you were in. The maid saw someone tall coming upstairs. He'll be back in half an hour. He won't disturb you, he's coming for the book."

Kien had not been listening. Only at the word "book" did he become attentive and understood in retrospect what the matter was. "He is lying. I promised nothing. I told him I would show him some pictures from India and China if I ever had time. I have no time. Send him away."

"Some people have a cheek. Excuse me, such ragtag and bobtail. The father was a common workingman. Where they get the money from, I'd like to know. But there you are. Everything for the children, these days. Nobody is strict anymore. Cheeky they are; you wouldn't credit it. Playing at their lessons and going for walks with teacher. Excuse me, in my time it was very different. If a child didn't want to learn its parents took it away from school and put it to a trade. With a hard master, so it had to learn. Nothing like that these days. You don't catch people wanting to work now. Don't know their places anymore, that's what it is. Look at young people these days, when they go out on Sundays. Every factory girl has to have a new blouse. I ask you, and what do they do with all their fancy stuff? Go off bathing and take it all off again. With boys, too. Whoever heard of such a thing in my time! Let 'em do a job of work, that'd be more like it. I always say, where does the money come from? Prices going up all the time. Potatoes cost double already. It's not surprising; children have a cheek. Parents don't check them at all. In my days, it was a couple of good smacks, left and right, and the child had to do as it was told. There's nothing good left in the world. When they're little they don't learn, when they grow up they don't do a hand's turn."

Kien had been irritated at first because she was holding him up with a long discourse, but soon he found himself yielding to a kind of astonished interest in her words. So this uneducated creature set great value on learning. She must have a sound core. Perhaps the result of her daily contact with his books. Other women in her position might not have taken color from their surroundings. She was more receptive, perhaps she yearned for education.

"You are quite right," he said, "I am happy to find you so sensible. Learning is everything."

They had entered the flat while they were talking. "Wait a minute!" he commanded and disappeared into the library. He came back with a small book in his left hand. As he turned over the pages, he thrust his thin, hard lips outward. "Listen!" he said and signaled her to stand a little further from him. What he was about to utter called for space. With an abundance of feeling, grotesquely unsuited to the simplicity of the text, he read:

"My master commanded me to learn three thousand characters every day and to write down another thousand each evening. In the short winter days the sun went down early and I had not finished my task. I carried my little tablet onto the veranda which faced the west and finished my writing there. Late in the evening, when I was going through what I had written, I could no longer overcome my weariness. So I placed two buckets of water behind me. When I grew too sleepy, I took off my gown and emptied the first bucket over myself. Naked, I sat down to my work again. Gradually I would grow warmer and sleepy again. Then I would use the second bucket. With the help of two shower baths I was nearly always able to complete my task. In that winter I entered my ninth year."

Moved and ablaze with admiration, he clapped the book to. "That was the way they used to learn! A fragment from the childhood recollections of the Japanese scholar Arai Hakuseki."

During the reading, Therese had drawn closer. Her head waggled in time to his sentences. Her large left ear seemed to reach out of itself toward the words, as he translated freely from the Japanese original. Unintentionally, he was holding the book a little crooked; doubtless she could see the foreign characters and was astonished at the fluency of his rendering. He was reading as if he had a German book in his hands. "Well I never!" she said. He had finished; she took a deep breath. Her amazement amused him. Was it too late, he thought, how old can she be?

It is never too late to learn. But she would have to begin with simple novels.

The bell rang violently. Therese opened the door. The little Metzger boy pushed his head through the crack. "I may come in!" he shouted. "The Professor said I could!" "No books for you!" screamed Therese, and slammed the door. Outside the little boy raged up and down. He yelled threats at the door; he was so angry that they could not understand a word he said. "Excuse me, he takes a whole fistful in one. They'd be dirty in no time. I've seen him eat his piece of bread and butter on the stairs."

Kien was on the threshold of the library: the boy had not seen him. He nodded approvingly to his housekeeper. He was happy to find the interests of his books so well defended. She deserved thanks: "Should you ever wish to read anything, you may always apply to me."

"I make so bold, I often thought of asking."

How she jumped on her opportunity, when books were in question! She was not usually like this. Until this moment she had behaved herself very modestly. He had no intention of starting a lending library. To gain time he answered: "Good. I shall look something out for you tomorrow."

Then he sat down to his work. His promise made him feel uneasy. It was true that she dusted the books every day and had not yet injured one of them. But dusting and reading are different. Her fingers were coarse and rough. Delicate paper must be delicately handled. A hard binding can naturally stand rougher handling than sensitive pages. And how did he know that she *could* read? She must be more than fifty, she had not made much use of her time. "An old man who learned late," Plato called his opponent, the cynic philosopher Antisthenes. Today we have old women who learn late. She wanted to quench her thirst at the fountainhead. Or was she only ashamed of admitting in my presence that she knew nothing? Charity is all very well, but not at other people's expense. Why should the books have to foot the bill? I pay her high wages. I have a right to, it is my own money. But to hand over books to her would be cowardly. They are defenseless against the uneducated. I cannot sit by her all the time she is reading.

That night he saw a man standing, bound fast, on the terrace of a temple, defending himself with wooden clubs from the savage attacks of two upright jaguars on his left and right. Both animals were decked with strange streamers in all colors. They gnashed their teeth, roared, and rolled their eyes so wildly that it made the blood run cold. The sky was black and narrow, and had hidden his stars in his pocket. Tears of glass trickled out of the eyes of the prisoner and splintered into a thousand pieces as they reached the pavement. But as nothing further happened, the savage combat grew boring and made the spectator yawn. Then by chance his eye fell on the feet of the jaguars. They had human feet. Aha, thought the spectator—a lanky, learned man—these are sacrificial priests of ancient Mexico. They are performing a sacred comedy. The victim knows well that he must die in the end. The priests are disguised as jaguars but I see through them at once.

The jaguar on the right seized a heavy stone wedge and drove it into the victim's heart. One edge of it clove sharp through the breastbone. Kien closed his eyes, dazzled. He thought, the blood must spurt up to the very sky; he sternly disapproved of this medieval barbarism. He waited until he thought the blood must have ceased to flow, then opened his eyes. Oh horrible: from the cleft in the victim's wounded breast a book appeared, another, a third, many. There was no end to it, they fell to the ground, they were clutched at by viscous flames. The blood had set fire to the wood, the books were burning. "Shut your breast!" shouted Kien to the prisoner. "Shut your breast!" He gesticulated with his hands; "you must do it like this, quickly, quickly!" The prisoner understood; with a terrific jerk he freed himself of his bonds and clutched both his hands over his heart; Kien breathed again.

Then suddenly the victim tore his bosom wide open. Books poured forth in torrents. Scores, hundreds, they were beyond counting; the flames licked up toward the paper; each one wailed for help; a fearful shrieking rose on all sides. Kien stretched out his arms to the books, now blazing to heaven. The altar was much further off than he had thought. He took a couple of strides and was no nearer. He must run if he was to save them alive. He ran and fell; this cursed shortness of breath; it came of neglecting his physical health; he could tear himself into pieces with rage. A useless creature, when there was need of him he was no use. Those miserable wretches! Human sacrifices he had heard of—but books, books! Now at last he was at the altar. The fire singed his hair and eyebrows. The wood pyre was enormous; from the distance he had thought it quite small. They must be in the very center of the fire. Into it then, you coward, you swaggerer, you miserable sinner!

But why blame himself? He was in the middle of it. *Where are you? Where are you?* The flames dazzled him. And what the devil was this, wherever he reached out, he could get hold of nothing but shrieking human beings. They clutched hold of him with all their strength. He hurled them from him, they came back to him. They crept to him from below and entwined his knees; from above his head burning torches rained down on him. He was not looking up yet he saw them clearly. They seized on his ears, his hair, his shoulders. They enchained him with their bodies. Bedlam broke loose. "Let me go," he shouted,

"I don't know you. What do you want with me! How can I rescue the books!"

But one of them had thrown himself against his mouth, and clung fast to his tightly closed lips. He wanted to speak again, but he could not open his mouth. He implored them in his mind: *I can't save them! I can't save them!* He wanted to cry, but where were his tears? His eyes too were closed fast; human beings were pressing against them too. He tried to step free of them, he lifted his right leg high in the air; in vain, it was dragged back again, dragged down by a burden of burning humankind, dragged down by a leaden weight. He abhorred them, these greedy creatures; could they not be satisfied with the life they had had? He loathed them. He would have liked to hurt them, torment them, reproach them; he could do nothing, nothing! Not for one moment did he forget why he was there. They might hold his eyes forcibly shut, but in his spirit he could see mightily. He saw a book growing in every direction at once until it filled the sky and the earth and the whole of space to the very horizon. At its edges a reddish glow, slowly, quietly, devoured it. Proud, silent, uncomplaining, it endured a martyr's death. Men screamed and shrieked, the book burned without a word. Martyrs do not cry out, saints do not cry out.

Then a voice spoke; in it was all knowledge, for it was the voice of God: "There are no books here. All is vanity." And at once Kien knew that the voice spoke truth. Lightly, he threw off the burning mob and jumped out of the fire. He was saved. Did it hurt then? Terribly, he answered himself, but not so much as people usually think. He was extraordinarily happy about the voice. He could see himself, dancing away from the altar. At a little distance, he turned round. He was tempted to laugh at the empty fire.

Then he stood still, lost in contemplation of Rome. He saw

the mass of struggling limbs; the air was thick with the smell of burning flesh. How stupid men are! He forgot his anger. A single step, and they could save themselves.

Suddenly, he did not know how it could have happened, the men were changed into books. He gave a great cry and rushed, beside himself, in the direction of the fire. He ran, panted, scolded himself, leaped into the flames, and was again surrounded by those imploring human bodies. Again the terror seized him, again God's voice set him free, again he escaped and watched again from the same place the same scene. Four times he let himself be fooled. The speed with which events succeeded each other increased each time. He knew that he was bathed in sweat. Secretly he began to long for the breathing space allowed him between one excitement and the next. In the fourth pause, he was overtaken by the Last Judgment. Gigantic wagons, high as houses, as mountains, high as the heavens, closed in from two, ten, twenty, from all sides upon the devouring altar. The voice, harsh and destructive, mocked him: "Now come the books!" Kien cried out and woke.

This dream, the worst dream he could remember, weighed upon his spirit for half an hour afterward. An ill-extinguished match dropped while he was enjoying himself in the street—and his library would be lost! He had insured it more than once. But he doubted if he would have the strength to go on living after the destruction of twenty-five thousand books, let alone see about the payment of the insurance. He had taken out the policies in a contemptible frame of mind; later he was ashamed of them. He would have liked to cancel them. Indeed he only paid the necessary fees so as not to have to reenter the office in which books and cattle were subject to the same laws, and to be spared the visits of the companies' representatives who would doubtless be sent to call on him at home.

Divided into its elements a dream loses its terrors. He had been looking at Mexican pictorial writings only yesterday. One of them represented the sacrifice of a prisoner by two priests disguised as jaguars. His chance meeting with a blind man a few days before had made him think of Eratosthenes the aged librarian of Alexandria. The name of Alexandria would naturally provoke the recollection of the burning of the famous library. A certain medieval woodcut, whose ingenuousness always made him smile, depicted about thirty Jews on a burning pyre flaming to heaven yet obstinately screeching their prayers. He was a great admirer of Michelangelo; above all he admired his *Last Judgment*. In that picture sinners are being dragged to Hell by pitiless devils. One of the damned, the picture of terror and anguish, covers his cowardly flaccid face with his hands; devils are clutching at his legs but he has never seen the woes of other people and dare not look at his own now. On the height stands Christ, very un-Christlike, condemning the damned with muscular and mighty arm. From all these recollections sleep had concocted a dream.

When Kien pushed the wash-trolley out of his bedroom he heard on an unexpectedly high note the exclamation: "Up already!" Why did the creature speak so loud early in the morning when he was still almost asleep? Very true he had promised to lend her a book. A novel was the only thing worth considering for her. But no mind ever grew fat on a diet of novels. The pleasure which they occasionally offer is far too heavily paid for: they undermine the finest characters. They teach us to think ourselves into other men's places. Thus we acquire a taste for change. The personality becomes dissolved in pleasing figments of imagination. The reader learns to understand every point of view. Willingly he yields himself to the pursuit of other people's goals and loses sight of his own. Novels are so many wedges which the novelist, an actor with his pen, inserts into the closed personality of the reader. The better he calculates the size of the wedge and the strength of the resistance, so much the more completely does he crack open the personality of his victim. Novels should be prohibited by the State.

At seven o'clock Kien once again opened his door. Therese was standing in front of it, as trusting and modest as always, her prominent left ear perhaps a trifle more crooked.

"I make so bold," she reminded him impertinently.

What little blood Kien had rushed to his head. So she would stick to it, this cursed creature in her starched skirt, and exact what had once been thoughtlessly promised. "You want that book," he cried and his voice cracked. "You shall have it."

He slammed the door in her face, strode with quivering steps into the third room, inserted one finger into the shelves, and extracted *The Trousers of Herr von Bredow*. He had possessed this book from his earliest schooldays, had then lent it to all his classmates, and on account of the deplorable condition in which it had been ever since could not bear the sight of it. He looked with malice at its grease-spotted binding and sticky pages. Calm now, he went back to Therese and held the book close to her eyes.

"That was unnecessary," she said and pulled out from under her arm a thick bundle of paper, packing paper, as he now noticed for the first time. With some ceremony she selected a suitable piece and wrapped it round the book like a shawl round a baby. Then she selected a second piece of paper and said, "A stitch in time saves nine." When the second piece of paper did not lie smoothly enough, she tore it off and tried a third one.

Kien followed her movements as though he were seeing her for the first time. He had underestimated her. She knew how to handle a book better than he did. This old thing was loathsome

to him, but she wrapped it carefully up in two layers of paper.
She kept the palms of her hands clear of the binding. She worked
with her fingertips alone. Her fingers were not so coarse after
all. He felt ashamed of himself and pleased with her. Should he
fetch her something else? She deserved something less shabby.
Still, for a beginning she could make do with this one. Even
without encouragement she would soon be asking for another.
For eight long years his library had been safe in her care; he had
not known it.

"I have to leave tomorrow," he said suddenly, as she was
smoothing down the paper cover with her knuckles. "For some
months."

"Then I shall be able to dust properly for once. Is an hour
long enough?"

"What would you do if a fire broke out?"

She was horrified. She dropped the paper to the ground.
The book remained in her hand. "Gracious Heavens, save the
books!"

"But I am not really going away: I was only joking." Kien
smiled. Carried away by this picture of extreme devotion—
himself absent and the books alone—he came closer to her and
patted her on the shoulder with his bony fingers, saying in a
tone almost friendly, "You're a good creature."

"I must have a look at what you've chosen for me," she said,
and the corners of her mouth seemed to reach out almost to her
ears. She opened the book and read aloud, *The Trousers*—she
interrupted herself but did not blush. Her face was bedewed
with a light sweat.

"Excuse me, Professor," she exclaimed, and glided away,
swiftly triumphant, toward her kitchen.

During the ensuing days Kien exerted himself to recover his
old power of concentration. He too knew moments when he

was tired of his services to the written word and felt a secret desire for more of the company of humankind than his strength of character normally permitted. When he entered into open conflict with such temptations he wasted much time; they tended to grow stronger if he fought them. He had contrived a more ingenious method: he out-maneuvered them. He did not pillow his head on the writing desk and lose himself in idle desires. He did not walk up and down the streets and enter into trivial conversations with fools. On the contrary he filled the library with the distinguished friends he had read. Mostly he inclined to the ancient Chinese. He commanded them to step out of the volume and the shelf to which they belonged, beckoned to them, offered them chairs, greeted them, threatened them, and according to his taste put their own words into their mouths and defended his own opinions against them until at length he had silenced them. When he entered into written controversy he found his words acquired from this practice an unexpected force. In this way he practiced speaking Chinese and took pride in the clever phrases which flowed from his lips so easily and so emphatically. If I go to the theater (he thought) I hear a conversation in double Dutch which is entertaining but not instructive, and in the end not even entertaining, only boring. Two or even three whole valuable hours must I sacrifice only to go to bed feeling irritated. My own dialogues do not go on so long and have meaning and balance. In this way he justified to himself the harmless game which might have seemed odd to a spectator.

Sometimes Kien would meet, either in the street or in a bookshop, a barbarous fellow who amazed him by uttering a reasonable sentiment. In order to obliterate any impression which contradicted his contempt for the mass of mankind he would in such cases perform a small arithmetical calculation. How many words does this fellow speak in a single day? At a conservative reckoning ten thousand. Three of them are not without sense. By chance I overheard those three. The other words which whirl through his head at a rate of several hundred thousand per day, which he thinks but does not even speak—one imbecility after another—are to be guessed merely by looking at his features; fortunately one does not have to listen to them.

His housekeeper, however, spoke little, since she was always alone. At a flash, they seemed to have something in common; his thoughts recurred to it hourly. Whenever he saw her, he remembered at once how carefully she had wrapped up *The Trousers of Herr von Bredow*. The book had been in his library for years. Every time he passed it the sight of its back alone smote his heart. Yet he had left it, just as it was. Why had it not occurred to him to care for its improvement by providing it with a handsome wrapper? He had lamentably failed in his duty. And now came a simple housekeeper and taught him what was tight and seemly.

Or was she playacting for his benefit? Perhaps she was merely flattering him into a sense of false security. His library was famous. Dealers had often besieged him for unique editions. Perhaps she was planning some vast robbery. He must find out how she acted when she was alone with the book.

One day he surprised her in the kitchen. His doubts tormented him; he longed for certainty. Once unmasked, he would throw her out. He wanted a glass of water; she had evidently not heard him calling. While she made haste to satisfy his wishes, he examined the table at which she had been sitting. On a small embroidered velvet cushion lay his book. Open at page twenty. She had not yet read very far. She offered him the glass on a plate. It was then he saw that she had white kid gloves on her hands. He forgot to close his fingers round the glass; it fell to the floor, the plate after it. Noise and diversion were welcome to him. He could not have brought a word to his lips. Ever since he was five years old, for thirty-five years, he had been reading. And the thought had never once crossed his mind, to put on gloves for the purpose. His embarrassment seemed ridiculous, even to himself. He pulled himself together and asked casually: "You have not got very far yet?"

"I read every page a dozen times, otherwise you can't get the best out of it."

"Do you like it?" He had to force himself to go on speaking, or he would have fallen to the ground as easily as the glass of water.

"A book is always beautiful. You need to understand it. There were grease spots on it, I've tried everything but I can't get them out. What shall I do now?"

"They were there before."

"All the same, it's a pity. Excuse me, a book like this is a treasure."

She did not say "must cost a lot," she said "is a treasure." She meant its intrinsic value, not its price. And he had babbled to her of the capital which was locked up in his library! This woman must despise him. Hers was a generous spirit. She sat up night after night trying to remove old grease spots from a book, instead of sleeping. He gave her his shabbiest, most dog-eared and worn-out book out of sheer distaste, and she took it into loving care. She had compassion, not for men (there was nothing in that) but for books. The weary and heavy-laden could come to her. The meanest, the most forsaken and forgotten creature on the face of God's earth, she would take to her heart.

Kien left the kitchen in the deepest perturbation. Not one word more did he say to the saint.

In the lofty halls of his library he paced up and down and called on Confucius. He came toward him from the opposite wall, calm and self-possessed—it is easy to be self-possessed when you have been dead for centuries. With long strides Kien went to meet him. He forgot to make any obeisance. His excitement contrasted strangely with the bearing of the Chinese sage.

"I think that I am not wholly without education!" he shouted from a distance of five paces. "I think I am not wholly without tact. People have tried to persuade me that education and tact are the same thing, that one is impossible without the other. Who tried to persuade me of this? You!" He was not shy of Confucius; he called him "you" straight out. "Here comes a person without a spark of education and she has more sensibility, more heart, more dignity, more humanity than I or you and all your learned disciples put together!"

Confucius was not to be put out of countenance. He did not even forget to make his bow before he was spoken to. In spite of these incredible accusations, he did not even raise his eyebrows. Beneath them, his eyes, very ancient and black, were wise as those of an ape. Deliberately he opened his mouth and uttered the following saying:

"At fifteen my inclination was to learning, at thirty I was fixed in that path, at forty I had no more doubts—but only when I was sixty were my ears opened."

Kien had this sentence firmly fixed in his head. But as an answer to his violent attack, it disturbed him greatly. Quickly he compared the dates to see if they fitted. When he was fifteen he had been secretly devouring book after book, much against his mother's will, by day at school, and by night under the bedclothes, with a tiny pocket flashlight for sole wretched illumination. When his younger brother George, set to watch by his mother, woke up by chance during the night, he never failed to pull the bedclothes off him, experimentally. The fate of his read-

ing program for the ensuing nights depended on the speed with
which he could conceal flashlight and book underneath his body.
At thirty he was fixed in the path of knowledge. Professorial
chairs he rejected with contempt. He might have lived comfort-
ably on the income from his paternal inheritance. He preferred
to spend the capital on books. In a few more years, three perhaps, it would all be spent. He never even dreamed of the threatening future, he did not fear it. He was forty. Until this day he
had never known a doubt. But he could not get over *The Trousers of Herr von Bredow*. He was not yet sixty, otherwise his ears
would have been opened. But to whom should he open them?

Confucius came a step closer to him, as if he had guessed the
question, bowed, although Kien was at least two heads taller,
and gave him the following confidential advice:

"Observe the manner of men's behavior, observe the motives of their actions, examine those things in which they find
pleasure. How can anyone conceal himself! How can anyone
conceal himself!"

Then Kien grew very sad. What had it availed him to know
these words by heart? They should be applied, proved, confirmed. For eight long years he had had a human being in the
closest proximity, and all for nothing. I knew how she behaved,
he thought, I never thought of her motives. I knew what she did
for my books. I had the evidence of it daily before my eyes. I
thought, she did it for money. Now that I know what she takes
pleasure in, I know her motives better. She takes the grease spots
off wretched and rejected books for which no one else has a
good word to say. That is her recreation, that is her rest. Had I
not surprised her in the kitchen, out of shameful mistrust, her
deeds would never have come to light. In her solitude she had
embroidered a pillow for her foster-child and laid it softly to
rest. For eight long years she never wore gloves. Before she

could bring herself to open a book, and *this* book, she went out
and bought with her hard-earned money a pair of gloves. She is
not a fool, in other things she is a practical woman, she knows
that for the price of the gloves she could have bought the book,
new, three times over. I have committed a great sin, I was blind
for eight years.

Confucius gave him no time to think again. "To err without
making amendment is to err indeed. If you have erred, be not
ashamed to make the fault good."

It shall be made good, cried Kien. I will give her back her
eight lost years! I will marry her! She is the heaven-sent instrument for preserving my library. If there is a fire I can trust in
her. Had I constructed a human being according to my own de-
signs, the result could not have been more apt for the purpose.
She has all the elements necessary. She is a born foster-mother.
Her heart is in the right place. There is room for no illiterate
fools in her heart. She could have had a lover, a baker, a butcher,
a tailor, some kind of barbarian, some kind of an ape. But she
cannot bring herself to it. Her heart belongs to the books. What
is simpler than to marry her?

He took no more notice of Confucius. When he chanced to
look in his direction, he had dissolved into air. Only his voice
could still be heard, saying faintly but clearly: "To see the right
and not to do it is to lack courage."

Kien had no time to thank him for this last encouragement.
He flung himself toward the kitchen, and seized violently upon
the door. The handle came off in his hand. Therese was seated
in front of the cushion and made as if she were reading. When
she sensed that he was already behind her, she got up, so that
he could see what she had been reading. The impression of his
last conversation had not been lost on her. She had gone back to
page three. He hesitated a moment, did not know what to say,

and looked down at his hands. Then he saw the broken door handle; in a rage he threw it to the ground. He took his place stiffly in front of her and said: "Give me your hand!" "Excuse me," breathed Therese and stretched it out to him. Now for the seduction, she thought and began to sweat all over. "No," said Kien; he had not meant her hand in that sense. "I want to marry you!" So sudden a decision had been beyond Therese's expectations. She twisted her astonished head round in the opposite direction and replied proudly, though with an effort not to stammer: "I make so bold!"

Chapter IV: The Mussel Shell

The wedding took place quietly. The witnesses were an odd-man who could still strike a few last sparks from his tottering frame, and a worthy cobbler who, having cunningly evaded marriage himself, for the drink-sodden life of him, enjoyed watching other people's. Superior clients he would urgently press to have sons and daughters who would marry soon. He had convincing arguments in favor of early marriage. "Settle your children properly, you'll have grandchildren in no time. Look sharp and get your grandchildren settled, and you'll have great-grandchildren!" In conclusion he would point to his good suit which could mix with anybody. Before grand weddings he had it pressed at the cleaners, for ordinary ones he ironed it himself at home. Only one thing he begged leave to ask, and that was reasonable notice. When his services had not been in request for some time, he would offer—slow worker though he was by temperament—repairs while-you-wait for nothing. Usually unreliable, in this sphere he was a man of his word, did the shoes on the spot and charged really very little. Children—mostly

young girls—so lost to their duty as to marry without their
parents' knowledge, but not so lost as to dispense with marriage
altogether, sometimes made use of him. Indiscretion incarnate,
he was in these matters silent as the grave. Not by a flicker did
he betray his clients, even though he recounted in pompous detail the tale of her daughter's wedding to her own unsuspecting
mother. Before setting off for his "little bit of heaven"—as he
called it—he would fix to the door of his workshop an enormous notice. On it could be read in writhing, soot-black letters
the message: "Out on my business. Back sooner or later. The
undersigned: Hubert Beredinger."

He was the first to learn Therese's luck and doubted the truth
of her story until, offended, she invited him to the registry office.
When all was over, the witnesses followed the happy pair into the
street. The oddman received his tip bowed down with gratitude.
Muttering his congratulations he made his way off. ". . . at your
service any other time . . ." echoed in the ears of Mr. and Mrs.
Kien. Ten paces off, his empty mouth was still mumbling with
zeal. But Hubert Beredinger was bitterly disappointed. He did
not hold with this sort of wedding. *He* had sent his suit out to
be pressed; the bridegroom was in his working clothes, his shoes
trodden over, his suit threadbare; without love or joy, instead of
looking at the bride, he had been reading the words in the book.
He said "I will" no different from "thank you"; then never even
gave his arm to the old stick, and as for the kiss, the kiss on which
the cobbler lived for weeks—a kiss by proxy was worth twenty
of his own—the kiss which he'd have paid good money for, the
kiss which was the "business" hung up on his workshop door;
the public kiss under official eyes; the bridal kiss; the kiss for all
eternity; that kiss, that kiss had never happened at all. When they
parted the cobbler refused his hand. He disguised his resentment
under a hideous grin. "Just a moment please," he giggled, like a

photographer, while the Kiens hesitated. Suddenly he bent down toward a woman, chucked her under the chin, smacked his lips loudly, and with eager gestures outlined her opulent figure. His round face grew rounder and rounder, his cheeks blew out to bursting, his double chin splayed out far and wide, the lines round his eyes twitched, tiny nimble snakes; his tensed hands drew ever broader curves. From second to second the woman grew fatter. Twice he looked at her, the third time, encouragingly, at the bridegroom. Then he gathered her into his arms and felt with his left hand shamelessly for her bosom.

True, the woman with whom the cobbler was fooling was not there, but Kien understood the shameless dumb show and drew the watching Therese quickly away.

"Drunk even before lunch!" said Therese, and clamped herself to her husband's arm; she too was indignant.

At the next stop, they waited for the tram. To make it clear that one day—even a wedding day—was no different from any other Kien took no taxi. The tram came up; he mounted the step before her. One foot on the platform, he recollected that his wife ought to go first. His back to the street, he stepped off again and collided violently with Therese. Exasperated, the conductor rang the bell. The tram went on without them. "What's the matter?" Therese asked reproachfully. He had certainly hurt her a good deal. "I wanted to help you up—that is, to help you, my dear." "Oh," she said, "that would be a nice thing."

When they were at last seated, he paid for both of them. He hoped this would make amends for his clumsiness. The conductor gave the tickets to her. Instead of thanking him, she grinned broadly and nudged her husband with her shoulder. "What?" he asked. "The things people think of!" she giggled and flourished the tickets at the stout back of the conductor. She was making fun of him, thought Kien, and he said nothing.

He began to feel uncomfortable. The tram filled up. A woman sat down opposite him. She had, in all, four children with her, each smaller than the next. Two of them she clutched tightly on her lap, two of them remained standing. A gentleman, sitting on Therese's right, got out. "Over there!" cried the mother, pushing her little brood across the gangway. The children made a rush for it, a little boy and a little girl, well under school age, the two of them. From the opposite direction an elderly gentleman was approaching. Therese put out her hand to protect the free seat. The children crept underneath it. They were in haste to show they could manage by themselves. Close by the seat, their little heads popped up. Therese flicked them away like specks of dust. "My children!" screamed their mother. "What are you thinking of?"

"I ask you," countered Therese and gave a meaningful look at her husband. "Children last." By this time the elderly gentleman had reached the goal, thanked her, and sat down.

Kien understood the look in his wife's eyes. He wished his brother George were here. He had set up as a gynecologist in Paris. Not yet thirty-five years old, he enjoyed a suspiciously high reputation. He knew far more about women than about books. A bare two years after he had completed his studies, society had placed itself in his hands in so far as it was ill, and it was always ill, all those sickly women anyway. This outward sign of success had earned him Peter's well-deserved contempt. He might perhaps have forgiven George his good looks, they were congenital, he was not to blame. He could never have forced himself to undergo a plastic operation in order to escape the injurious results of so much beauty; his was unhappily a weak character. How weak was clear from the fact that he had abandoned the special branch of medicine which he himself had first chosen in order to pass with flying colors into the realms of psychiatry. It was alleged that he had done some good work in this field. In his heart he had remained a gynecologist. Loose living was in his blood. Eight years before, indignant at George's vacillation, Peter had abruptly broken off all correspondence with him and had subsequently torn up a whole series of anxious letters. He was not in the habit of answering letters which he had torn up.

His marriage would make the best possible occasion for resuming relations with him. Peter's suggestions had first awakened in George his taste for a career of learning. It would be no disgrace to ask for his advice on a subject which lay within the domain of his real and natural branch of medicine. What was the right way to treat this timid, reserved creature? She was no longer young and took life very seriously. The woman who sat opposite was certainly a great deal younger, but she already had four children; Therese had none. "Children last." That sounded straightforward enough, but what did she really mean by it? She probably wanted no children; neither did he. He had never thought about children. For what purpose had she said that? Perhaps she took him for a person of no morals. But she knew his life. For eight years she had been aware of all his habits. She knew that he was a man of character. Did he ever go out at night? Had a woman ever called on him, even for a quarter of an hour? When she had first taken up her post with him, he had most emphatically explained to her that he received no visitors on principle, male or female, of whatever age, from infants in arms to octogenarians. She was to send everyone away. "I have no time!" Those had been his very words. What devil had got into her? That shameless cobbler, perhaps? She was an innocent ingenuous creature; how otherwise, uneducated as she was, could she have acquired so great a love for books? But that dirty fellow's pantomime had been all too obvious. His gestures were self-explanatory; a child, without even knowing the reasons for his movements, would have understood that he had a woman in his arms. People of that kind, capable of losing control of themselves in the open street, ought to be segregated in asylums. They induce ugly thoughts in hardworking people. She was a hardworking woman. The cobbler had insinuated ideas into her head. Why else should children have occurred to her? It was not impossible that she might have heard something about such things. Women talk among themselves. She had perhaps been present at a birth, when she was in some other service. What did it signify if she did indeed know all there was to know? Better perhaps than if he had to explain it to her himself. There was a certain bashfulness in her expression; at her age it was faintly comic.

I never thought of asking anything so vulgar of her; it did not cross my mind. I have no time. I need six hours' sleep. I work until twelve, at six o'clock I get up. Dogs and other animals may do such things by day. Perhaps she expects something of the kind from marriage. Hardly. Children last. Fool. All she meant was that she knew what was necessary. She knew the chain of circumstances whose conclusion is the perfected child. She was trying to explain herself gracefully. She took the occasion of this little incident, the children were importunate, the words were apt, but her eyes were fixed on me alone; it did for a confession. Most understandable. Such admissions are naturally painful. I married because of the books; children last. That means nothing at all. I remember her saying that children learned too little. I read out to her a paragraph of Arai Hakuseki. She was quite carried away. That was how she first betrayed herself. Who knows how otherwise I could have guessed her feeling for books. At that moment we were drawn together. Probably she only meant to remind me of that. She is still the same. Her views on children have not altered since then. My friends are her friends. My enemies will be her enemies. The brief speech of an innocent mind. She had no conception of any other relationship. I must be careful. She might be frightened. I shall act very cautiously. How shall I open the subject to her? It is difficult to speak of it. I have no books on it. Buy one? What would the bookseller think? I am not that kind of man. Send someone for it? But who? She herself—for shame—my own wife! How can I be so cowardly. I must try myself. I, myself. But suppose she is unwilling. Suppose she screams. The people in the other flats—the caretaker—the police—the mob. But they can do nothing to me. I am married to her. I have a right. How disgusting! How came I to think of it? I am the one whom that cobbler has infected. Shame on you. After forty years. And now to behave in this way. I shall spare her. Children last. If I only knew what she meant. Sphinx.

The mother of the four children stood up. "Look out!" she urged them, and shepherded them forward on her left. On the right, on Therese's side, she exposed herself only, a valiant commander. Contrary to Kien's expectation, she bobbed her head at her enemy, greeted her affably, and said: "You're the lucky one, still single," and laughed, her gold teeth glittering a parting signal. Only when she had gone did Therese explode, screaming in a voice of fury, "I ask you, my husband, I ask you, my husband! No children for us! I ask you, my husband!" She pointed at him, she pulled at his arm. I must calm her, he thought. The scene was painful to him, she needed his protection, she screamed and screamed. At last he drew himself to his full height and spoke out before their fellow travelers: "Yes," he said. She had been insulted, she had to defend herself. Her counter-attack was as coarse as the attack had been. She was not to blame. Therese relaxed in her seat. No one, not even the gentleman next to her

for whom she had saved the seat, took her part. The world was
corrupt with kindness to children. Two stops further the Kiens
got out. Therese went first. Suddenly he heard someone saying
just behind him: "Her skirt is the best thing about her." "What a
bulwark!" "Poor fellow!" "What can you expect, the old starch
box." They were all laughing. The conductor and Therese, already peacefully on the outer platform, had heard nothing. But
the conductor was laughing. In the street Therese received her
husband joyfully: "A jolly fellow!" she observed. The jolly fellow leaned out of the moving tram, put his hand to his mouth,
and bellowed two incomprehensible syllables. He was shaking
all over, doubtless with laughter. Therese waved and excused
herself, seeing his astonished look, with the words: "He'll be
falling out in a minute."

But Kien was surreptitiously contemplating the skirt. It was
even bluer than usual and had been more stiffly starched. Her
skirt was a part of her, as the mussel shell is a part of the mussel. Let no one try to force open the closed shell of a mussel. A
gigantic mussel as huge as this dress. They have to be trodden
on, to be trampled into slime and splinters, as he had once done
when he was a child at the seaside. The mussel yielded not a
chink. He had never seen one naked. What kind of an animal did
the shell enclose with such impenetrable strength? He wanted
to know, at once: he had the hard, stiff-necked thing between
his hands, he tortured it with fingers and fingernails; the mussel
tortured him back. He vowed not to stir a step from the place
until he had broken it open. The mussel took a different vow.
She would not allow herself to be seen. Why should she be so
modest, he thought, I shall let her go afterward, as far as I'm
concerned I shall shut her up again, I shan't hurt her, I promise
I shan't, if she's deaf then God can surely explain to her what
I'm promising. He argued with her for several hours. But his

words were as impotent as his fingers. He hated roundabout methods, he liked to reach his goal the direct way. Toward evening a great ship passed by, far out at sea. His eyes devoured the huge black letters on its side and read the name *Alexander*. Then he laughed in the midst of his rage, pulled on his shoes in a twinkling, hurled the mussel with all his strength to the ground, and performed a Gordian dance of victory. Now her shell was utterly useless to her. His shoes crushed it to pieces. Soon he had the creature stark naked on the ground, a miserable fleck of fraudulent slime, not an animal at all.

Therese without her shell—without her dress—did not exist. It was always immaculately ironed. It was her binding, blue cloth. She set great store by a good binding. Why did the folds not crumple up after a time? It was evident that she ironed it very often. Perhaps she had two. There was no visible difference. A clever woman. I must not crush her skirt. She would faint with grief. What shall I do if she suddenly faints? I shall ask her to excuse me beforehand. She can iron her skirt again immediately afterward. While she is doing it I shall go into another room. Why does she not simply put on the other one though? She puts too many difficulties in my way. She was my housekeeper, I have married her. She can buy herself a dozen skirts and change more often. Then it will be quite sufficient to starch them less stiffly. Exaggerated hardness is absurd. The people in the tram were right.

It was not easy going up the stairs. Without noticing it, he slackened his pace. On the second floor he thought he was already at his own door at the top, and started back. The little Metzger boy came running down the stairs singing. Hardly had he seen Kien, when he pointed to Therese and complained: "She won't let me in! She always shuts the door in my face. Scold her, Professor!"

"What is the meaning of this?" asked Kien threateningly, grateful for a scapegoat in the hour of need.

"You said I could come. I told her you said so."

"'Her.' Who is that?"

"Her."

"Her?"

"Yes, my mother said, she's no right to be rude, she's only a servant."

"Miserable brat!" shouted Kien and reached out to box his ears. The child ducked, tripped, fell forward, and to save himself from shooting down the stairs clutched at Therese's skirt. There was the sound of starched linen cracking.

"What!" cried Kien. "More impertinence!" The brat was making fun of him. Beside himself with rage, he gave him a couple of kicks, dragged him panting to his feet by the hair, boxed his ears once or twice with his bony hands, and pushed him out of the way. The child ran up the stairs whimpering. "I'll tell Mother! I'll tell Mother!" A door on the floor above was opened and closed again. A woman's voice was heard raised in protest.

"It's a shame for the beautiful skirt," Therese excused the violence of the blows, stood still, and looked in a special way at her protector. It was high time to prepare her for what was to come. Something must be said. He too stood still.

"Yes, indeed, the beautiful skirt. 'Youth's a stuff will not endure,'" he quoted, happy for the chance of indicating in the words of a beautiful ancient poem what must later come to pass. A poem was always the best way of saying something. Poems can be found for every occasion. They call things by the most formal of names and yet they are perfectly comprehensible. As he walked on up the stairs, he turned back toward her and said:

"A beautiful poem, don't you think?"

"Oh yes, poems are always beautiful. You've got to understand them, though."

"Many things need understanding," he said slowly, and blushed.

Therese jogged him in the ribs with her elbow, shrugged up her right shoulder, twisted her head round the opposite way, and said pointedly and with a challenge in her voice: "We shall see what we shall see. Still waters run deep."

He had the feeling that she meant him. He took her remarks for a sign of disapproval. He regretted his immodest hints. The mocking tone of her answer robbed him of the rest of his courage.

"I—er, I didn't mean it quite like that," he faltered.

The door of his own flat saved him from further embarrassment. He was relieved to be able to dive into his pocket for the keys. It gave him at least a reasonable excuse for lowering his eyes. He could not find the keys.

"I have forgotten the keys," he said. Now he would have to break open his own flat, as he had once broken open the mussel. One difficulty after another; he could do nothing right. With a sinking heart he dived into the other trouser pocket. No, the keys were nowhere to be found. He was still searching, when he heard a sound from the lock of the door. Burglars! The idea flashed through his mind. At the same moment he saw her hand on the lock.

"That's why I brought mine with me," she said, puffing herself out with satisfaction.

How fortunate he had not shouted for help. The cry had been on the tip of his tongue. He would never have been able to look her in the face again. He was behaving like a small boy. Not to have his keys with him, such a thing had never happened before.

At last they were inside the flat. Therese opened the door to the room in which he slept and signed him to go in. "I shall be back at once," she said, and left him there alone.

He looked round and breathed deeply, a man set free.

Yes, this was his home. Here no harm could come to him. He smiled at the mere idea that any harm could come to him here. He avoided looking at the divan on which he slept. Every human creature needed a home, not a home of the kind understood by crude knock-you-down patriots, not a religion either, a mere insipid foretaste of a heavenly home: no, a real home, in which space, work, friends, recreation, and the scope of a man's ideas came together into an orderly whole, into—so to speak—a personal cosmos. The best definition of a home was a library. It was wisest to keep women out of the home. Should the decision however be made to take in a woman, it was essential to assimilate her first fully into the home, as he had done. For eight long, quiet, patient years the books had seen to the subjugation of this woman for him. He himself had not so much as lifted a finger. His friends had conquered the woman in his name. Certainly there is much to be said against women, only a fool would marry without a certain testing time. *He* had been clever enough to put off the event until his fortieth year. Let others seek to emulate his eight years of testing! Gradually the inevitable had borne fruit. Man alone was master of his fate. When he came to think it over carefully, he saw that a wife was the only thing he had lacked. He was not a man of the world—at the words "man of the world" he saw his brother George the gynecologist before his eyes—he was everything else, but not a man of the world. Yet the bad dreams of these last days were doubtless connected with the exaggerated austerity of his life. Everything would be different now.

It was ridiculous to feel any more depression at the task

before him. He was a man, what was to happen next? Happen? No, that was going too far. First he must decide when it was to happen. Now. She would put up a desperate defense. No matter. It was understandable, when a woman was fighting to save her last secret. As soon as it was over, she would fall in admiration before him, because he was a man. All women are said to be like that. The hour had struck. Resolved. He gave himself his word upon it.

Next: where was it to happen? An ugly question. True, all this time he had been staring straight at a divan bed. His eyes had been gliding over the bookshelves, and the divan bed with them. The mussel from the seashore lay on it, gigantic and blue. Wherever his eyes rested, the divan bed rested too, oppressed and clumsy. It looked as if it had to bear the whole burden of the bookshelves. When Kien found himself in the neighborhood of the real divan bed, he would twist his head round and the bed would come gliding all the way back to its right place. Now that he had made a resolution on his word of honor, he examined it more accurately and at greater length. His eyes indeed, out of habit no doubt, still wandered from time to time. But in the end they came to rest. The divan bed, the real live divan bed was empty and had neither mussels nor burdens upon it. But suppose it were made to carry a burden? Suppose it were covered with a layer of beautiful books? Suppose it were covered all over with books, so that it could not be seen at all?

Kien obeyed his inspired impulse. He collected a mass of books together and carefully piled them up on the divan. He would have preferred to select some from the top shelves but time was short; she had said she would be back directly. He renounced the idea, left the stepladder as it was and made do with selected works from the lower shelves. He laid four or five heavy volumes one on top of another, fondled them briefly, and hurried off in search of others. Inferior works he rejected, so as not to hurt the woman's feelings. True she knew nothing about them, but he selected carefully on her behalf all the same, for she had insight and sensibility where books were concerned. She would be coming directly. As soon as she saw the divan bed covered with books, orderly woman that she was, she would go up to it and ask where the volumes belonged. In this way he would lure the unsuspecting creature into the trap. A conversation would easily arise on the titles of the books. Step-by-step he would go on ahead, guiding her gradually on the way. The shock which lay before her was the crowning event in a woman's life. He would not frighten her, he would help her. There was only one way of acting, boldly and with determination. Precipitancy was hateful to him. He blessed the books in silence. If only she didn't scream.

A little while before he had heard a faint sound as though the door in the fourth room had been opened. He took no notice, he had more important things to do. He contemplated the armored divan from his writing desk, to see the effect, and his heart overflowed with love and gratitude toward the books. Then he heard her voice:

"Here I am."

He turned round. She was standing on the threshold of the neighboring room, in a dazzling white petticoat with wide lace insertions. He had looked first for the blue, the danger. Horrified, his eyes traveled up her figure; she had kept on her blouse.

Thank God. No skirt. Now there would be no need to crush anything. Was this respectable? But how fortunate. I would have been ashamed. How could she bring herself to do it? I should have said: Take it off. I couldn't have done it. So naturally she stood there. As though we had known each other for a long time. Naturally, my wife. In every marriage. How did she know? She was in service. With a married couple. She must have seen things. Like animals. They know what to do by nature. She had no books in her head.

Therese approached swinging her hips. She did not glide, she waddled. The gliding was simply the effect of the starched skirt. She said gaily: "So thoughtful? Ah, men!" She held up her little finger, crooked it menacingly, and pointed down at the divan. I must go to her, he thought, and did not know how but found himself standing at her side. What was he to do now—lie down on the books? He was shaking with fear, he prayed to the books, the last stockade. Therese caught his eye, she bent down and, with one all-embracing stroke of her left arm, swept the books onto the floor. He made a helpless gesture toward them, he longed to cry out, but horror choked him, he swallowed and could not utter a sound. A terrible hatred swelled up slowly within him. This she had dared. The books!

Therese took off her petticoat, folded it up carefully, and laid it on the floor on top of the books. Then she made herself comfortable on the divan, crooked her little finger, grinned, and said, "There!"

Kien plunged out of the room in long strides, bolted himself into the lavatory, the only room in the whole house where there were no books, automatically let his trousers down, took his place on the seat, and cried like a child.

6.

From *Notes from Hampstead*

The infusion of Platonism in Cervantes is interesting only in the places where it becomes negative. When ideas are delusion, they lose the hollow, worn-out falseness they have accreted in the course of an overlong literary tradition. Of course, this is the great thing about Don Quixote: the idea and the ideal as madness, in all its consequences, uncovered and skewered. Whether this is ridiculous or not is not the issue: to me it seems terribly serious.

The moral quality of Cervantes is his desperate attempt to cope with the wretched circumstances of his daily life, his conforming to the official conventions of the powers of his time. This is why he is careful that virtue wins out and why he behaves like a Christian. Fortunately his substance, the misery of his real life, is so immeasurably great that conformism could never quite smother it.

Tremendous affection for Cervantes because he knew better than the conventional wisdom of his age and because his hypocrisy, which perhaps he himself didn't see through, is nonetheless transparent. I admire his *spatial* breadth; his fate, which so drove him hither and yon, gave him breadth instead of lessening him. Also I love the fact that he became known so late and that despite, or even because of, this he never gave up hope. Despite the many falsifications of life that he allowed into his "ideal" tales, he loved life as it is.

For me, this is the sole criterion of the epic talent: a knowledge of life even at its most horrific, a passionate love for it nonetheless, a love that never despairs, for it is inviolable even in its desperation. Nor is it really tied to a belief, for it originates in the variety of life, its unknown, astonishing, wondrous variety, its unpredictable twists and turns. For those who cannot stop pursuing life, it changes in the pursuit into a hundred new, overwhelmingly remarkable creatures; and for those who just as tirelessly chase after all hundred of them, they will change into a thousand others, all just as new.

The superior "higher" people in Cervantes's novellas are no less "high" than in Shakespeare. But it is welcome when, in Cervantes, the children of these higher characters run off for at least a few years of "low" living. The young nobleman who for love becomes a Gypsy (though his lover turns out not to be a Gypsy after all) or the young man in "The Highborn Barn Maid" who bolts for freedom, returning three years later without his upper-class parents' suspecting where he really was. If we could only know what lies he tells them before running off again! With Cervantes, love is really a "lowlife" concern, but to become famous for knowing it so well, he sets the "high" impossibly high, to flatter those who could be his patrons. But there is more here than mere flattery: he would rather *be* in their shoes. Should we think it lucky that his wretched lot never did improve?

We really cannot say. The effect of privation on invention is different with everyone, and without knowing the person at hand well, we will never know whether there was too much

or too little of it, whether it helped or hindered the power of
invention.

Stendhal has become so important to me that I have to turn back
to him every five or six months. It does not matter at all which
work it is, so long as the sentences contain the breath of his
spirit. Sometimes I'll read twenty or thirty pages of Stendhal
and think I will live forever. I have countless projects of my own
before me, and then with incredulous horror I tell myself that
he died at fifty-nine.

Stendhal's head was filled with things of "culture"—pictures,
books, music—many of which are as important to me today as
they were to him then. Many more are indifferent or repellently
"sentimental"; the important point is *how* he was taken up by
these things. He extracts from everything only that which is like
himself. Thus I can perhaps console myself for being so preoccupied with barbarians and religions, since it is possible that
they have become very much like me. Whether it's Canova or
Wotruba, the accident of birth plays only an external role here.
The passion with which one possesses every object and the passion with which one distances oneself in contemplation of it—
that is everything.

I so often agree with Tolstoy's way of thinking: how is it possible that his manner of expression disappoints and repels me?
It irritates me that he forgoes *surprise*. For clarity and simplicity
he states at the very outset how he will end things. The moral is
there from the beginning; he never forgets it, nor does he change
it. But he really ought to tell the story as if he had forgotten it
and lost it; he should have forgotten it in the course of telling the
story. Its sudden rediscovery would then be a revelation for the
reader instead of being a storybook moral.

But one should not forget that he knew that most Russian people of his time were illiterate. So he may have viewed his task too broadly, deciding that he had to create books that would enable people to comprehend morality without outside help, each person for himself.

But he was also led astray by overplaying the significance of simple relationships. He liked to see people as *simple*, which they are not. Like all people, he was basically opposed to lies, to transformations. But this way of thinking ignores a major characteristic of humanity, and any further ideas that may be expressed are boring, as if meant for creatures who don't exist: the great advantage of the Greeks, whose learning starts with the *Odyssey*, a "lie" that here seems fortunate: namely, transformation.

Tolstoy cannot dictate laws to men since his whole critique of humanity is simply the residuum of his own past life, once rich and colorful. And it is just this, life's richness and color, that people will not be cheated of.

Brecht's preachiness as ersatz Bible proverbs: you need only to hold his sayings up against the power of the biblical ones he cites to see how dubious and poor his own are. Theater is not school, for it employs transformation as its most important method. Learning takes place only through the right kind of transformation—but this has not yet been found. Brecht objects to transformation because he knows and fears what it can do; thus his prohibition of it, his "alienation effect."

Dante's project appears to me to be ever more monstrous. Who could emulate him and call together the names of *our* time before such a bar of justice as his poem is? Today the hardest thing to manage is merely to judge *oneself*, and how proud one is just to succeed honestly in that!

No one has the integrity and trustworthiness of a judge anymore.

The judge is suspect even to himself. We don't believe that he is a judge; we don't believe he isn't ashamed of it. This shame is the creation of Kafka.

Chuang-tze contains both the very *small* and the very *large*. One half is like Kafka, but there's another half as well—thus, he's all the more complete.

Nowhere but in Confucius does there exist such a conscious and systematic depiction of models. Through him, the rulers of the ancient world (and there are any number of them) all partake of a certain similarity—basically they are *like him*.

7.

From *Auto-da-Fé*

Part II: "Headless World"

Chapter I: The Stars of Heaven

Since Kien had been thrown out of his flat, he had been overwhelmed with work. From morning to night with a measured and persistent tread he walked through the town. Already at dawn his long legs were in motion. At midday he didn't permit himself either rest or food. So as to husband his strength, he divided the scene of his activities into sections to which he kept rigorously. In his briefcase he carried a vast plan of the town, scale 1:5,000, on which the bookstores were designated by cheerful red circles.

He entered a bookshop and demanded the proprietor himself. If he was away or out at lunch he contented himself with the head assistant. "I urgently require, for a work of scholarship, the following books," he said, and from a nonexistent paper read out a long catalogue. To avoid repeating himself he pronounced the authors' names with perhaps exaggerated distinctness and deliberation. For he was concerned with rare works and the ignorance of such people is hardly to be conceived.

Despite reading he could spare a watchful side-glance for the
listening faces. Between one title and the next he introduced
brief pauses. He delighted in hurling the next title rapidly at the
listener, who had as yet not fully recovered from the preceding one. The bewildered expressions amused him. Some asked
for "One moment, please!" Others clutched at their forehead or
temples, but he continued to read unperturbed. His paper included between two and three dozen volumes. At home he had
them all. But here he acquired each afresh. These duplicates, at
present oppressive to him, he planned to exchange or sell later
on. For the rest, his new activity cost him not a penny. In the
street he prepared his lists. In each new bookshop he read out a
new one. When he had finished he folded up his piece of paper
with a few assured movements, replaced it with the others in his
note case, bowed contemptuously low, and left the shop. He
waited for no answer. What could these numbskulls have answered? If he involved himself in discussions about the required
books it would only be a waste of time. Already he had lost
three whole weeks in the strangest circumstances, stiff and stark
at his writing desk. To make up for the loss he walked all day, so
cleverly, persistently, industriously that, without a suspicion of
self-complacency, he could feel pleased with himself, as he was.

The people with whom his profession brought him into
contact behaved, according to their mood and temperament, in
different ways. A few felt affronted at not being given time to
answer, the majority were glad enough to listen. His gigantic
learning could be both seen and heard. One of his sentences
outweighed the contents of a well-filled shop. His full importance was rarely recognized. Else the poor fools would have left
their work, crowded about him, pricked up their ears, and hark-
ened until their eardrums split. Would they ever again encounter such a prodigy of learning? But mostly a lone assistant took

FROM AUTO-DA-FÉ   161

advantage of the opportunity of hearing him. He was shunned, as all great men are, he was too strange and remote, and their embarrassment, which he had determined not to notice, smote him to his inmost core. As soon as he turned his back on them, for the rest of the day, they would talk of nothing but him and his lists. Strictly speaking, proprietors and staff functioned as his own private servants. He would not grudge them the honor of a collective mention in his biography. After all, they did not behave themselves ill, admired him, and provided him with everything of which he had need. They divined who he was, and at least had the strength to be silent in his presence. For he never entered a bookstore twice. When he did so once in error, they threw him out. He was too much for them, his appearance oppressed them and they freed themselves of it. He sympathized with their humiliation and on that occasion bought the plan of the town with the red circles. In the circles denoting bookshops he had already dealt with, he made a small cross; for him they were dead.

Besides, his activity had a pressing purpose. From the first moment when he found himself in the street his sole interest was for his theses at home. He was determined to complete them: without a library this was impossible. He therefore considered and compiled lists of the specialized books he needed. These lists came into being by necessity; caprice and desire were excluded, he only permitted himself to buy books indispensable to his work. Circumstances forced him to shut up his library at home for the time being. He apparently submitted to his fate, but in fact he outwitted it. He would not yield an inch of ground in this matter of learning. He bought what he needed and in a few weeks would resume his work; his plan of campaign was largely conceived and well-adapted to the peculiar circumstances, he was not to be subdued; in freedom he

spread his wise wings; with each glorious day of independence
he grew in stature, and this interim collection of a small new
library comprising a few thousand volumes was reward enough
for his pains. He was even afraid that the collection might grow
too big. Every night he slept in a different hotel. How was he to
carry away the increasing burden? But he had an indestructible
memory and could carry the entire new library in his head. The
briefcase remained empty.

In the evenings after closing time he became aware of his fatigue, and sought, the moment he had left the last bookshop, the
nearest hotel. Without luggage as he was, and in his shabby suit,
he aroused the porters' suspicions. Pleased in advance at the
way in which they would send him packing, they allowed him
to speak his three or four sentences. He required a large, quiet
room for the night. If none was to be had except in the vicinity of women, children, or common people, he requested them
to tell him so at once, since in that case he would be compelled
to refuse it. At the phrase "common people" every porter was
disarmed. Before his room was allotted to him, he pulled out
his wallet and declared his intention of paying in advance. He
had drawn his remaining capital out of the bank; the wallet was
crammed with highly respectable banknotes. For love of these
the porters laid bare regions of their eyeballs which no one, not
even titled travelers or Americans, had ever seen before. In his
precise, tall, angular writing Kien filled in the usual form. His
profession he declared to be: "Owner of a library." He would
not state whether married or single; he was neither married
nor single nor divorced and he indicated this by a crooked pen
stroke. He gave the porters fantastic tips, about 50 percent on
the price of the room. Every time he paid he rejoiced that his
bankbook had escaped Therese. Their enthusiastic bows placed
a coronet on his head; he remained unmoved, an English lord.

Contrary to his custom—technical simplifications were odious to him—he made use of the lift, for in the evening, tired as he was, the library in his head weighed heavy. He had his dinner brought up to his room: it was the only meal in the day. Relaxing for a short while he set down his library, and then looking round decided whether there was enough room for it.

At first, when his liberty was yet young, he was not concerned with the kind of room he had taken; it was after all only a matter of sleeping and the sofa could hold his books. Later he used the wardrobe as well. Soon the library had outgrown both. The dirty carpet had to be used so he rang for the maid and asked for ten clean sheets of brown paper. He spread them out on the carpet and over the whole floor; if any were left over he covered the sofa with them and lined the wardrobe. Thus for a time it became his habit to order paper every evening as well as food; he left it behind every morning. The books built themselves up higher and higher, but even if they fell they would not be soiled for everything was covered with paper. Sometimes at night when he awoke, filled with anxiety, it was because he had most certainly heard a noise as of falling books.

One evening the piles of books were too high even for him; he had already acquired an amazing number of new ones. He asked for a pair of steps. Questioned why he wanted it, he replied, cuttingly, "That is not your business!" The maid was of a rather timid nature. A burglary, which had recently occurred, had all but cost her her place. She ran to the porter and told him, excitedly, what the gentleman in No. 39 wanted. The porter, a character and man of the world, knew what he owed to his tip, although it was safe in his pocket.

"Go and get some sleep, sweetie." He grinned at her. "I'll deal with the murderer!"

She didn't move. "Strange, isn't he," she said shyly. "Looks

like a flagpole. First he asked for paper and now he wants a pair
of steps. The floor's covered with paper."

"Paper?" he asked; this information made an excellent impression on him. Only the most remarkable people carry precautions to that length.

"Yes, what do you think?" she said proudly; he had listened
to her.

"Do you know who the gentleman is?" he asked. Even talking to the maid he didn't say "he"; he said "the gentleman." "Proprietor of the Royal Library, that's what he is!" Each syllable of
this glorious profession he launched into the air like an article
of faith. To shut the girl up he added "Royal" on his own account. And he realized how very refined the gentleman upstairs
was since he had omitted "Royal" when filling in the form.

"There aren't any Royals now, anyway."

"But there's a Royal Library! Clever, aren't you? What do
you think they did with the books, swallowed them?"

The girl was silent. She loved to make him angry because he
was so strong. He only noticed her when he was furious. She
came running to him with every little thing. For a couple of
minutes he bore with her. Once he was enraged, you had to look
out for yourself. His fury gave her strength. She gladly carried
the steps to Kien. She could have asked the boots to do it, but
she did it herself; she wanted to obey the porter. She asked the
gentleman proprietor of the Royal library if she could help him.

He said: "Yes, by leaving this room at once!" Then he locked
the door—for he mistrusted the officious creature—stopped up
the keyhole with paper, placed the steps cautiously between the
piles of books, and climbed up. One parcel after another, arranged according to the lists, he lifted out of his head, filling
the entire room with them up to the ceiling. Despite the heavy
weight he managed to keep his balance on the steps; he felt like

an acrobat. Now, his own master again, he overcame difficulties easily. He had just finished when there was an obsequious knock at the door. He was annoyed at being disturbed. Since his experiences with Therese he was in mortal terror of any uninitiate looking at his books. It was the maid (who out of devotion to the porter) timidly asked him for the steps back again.

"Please, sir, excuse me, sir, you won't want to be sleeping with the steps in the room!" Her zeal was genuine; she stared at the strange flagpole with curiosity, love, and envy and wished that the porter would take as much interest in her.

Her language reminded Kien of Therese. Had she been Therese he would have been afraid. But as she only reminded him of her he shouted: "The steps remain here! I shall sleep with the steps!"

Gracious heavens, this is a fine gentleman, thought the young thing and disappeared, frightened. She had not realized that he was so very refined that you couldn't address a single word to him.

He drew his own conclusions from this experience. Women, whether housekeepers, wives, or maids had to be avoided at all costs. From then onward he asked for bedrooms so large that a pair of steps would have been senseless and superfluous, and he carried his own paper in his briefcase. The waiter, for whom he rang to order his meal, was, happily, a man.

As soon as his head felt relieved of the weight, he lay down on the bed. Before going to sleep he compared his previous circumstances with his present situation. In any case, toward the evening his thoughts reverted to Therese with pleasure, because he paid his expenses with the money he had rescued from her by his personal valor. Money matters promptly conjured up her picture. All day he had nothing to do with money, not only did he refuse himself lunch but also trams, and with good reason.

The serious and glorious undertaking on which he was now engaged was not to be smirched with any Therese. Therese was
the penny soiled by a thousand hands. Therese was the word in
the mouth of an illiterate. Therese was the weight on the spirit
of man. Therese was madness incarnate.

Imprisoned for months with a lunatic, he had in the end been
unable longer to resist the evil influence of her disease and had
himself been infected. Grasping to excess, she had imparted a
portion of her greed to him. A devouring lust for other books
had estranged him from his own. He had almost robbed her of
the million which he believed her to possess. His character, per-
petually in close and violent contact with hers, had been all but
dashed to pieces on this rock of money. But it had sustained the
shock. His body invented a defense. Had he continued to move
about the flat freely for much longer he would have succumbed
irremediably to her disease. For that reason he had played that
trick of the statue. Naturally he could not transform himself
into concrete stone. It was enough that *she* had taken him for
that. She was frightened by the statue and made a wide circle
round it. His ingenuity in sitting rigidly on a chair for weeks
had perplexed her. She had been perplexed already. But after
this adroit ruse she no longer knew who he was. This gave him
time to free himself from her. Gradually his wounds healed. Her
power over him was broken. As soon as he was strong enough
he resolved on a plan of escape. It was essential to escape from
her, and yet to keep her in custody. So that his escape should be
successful, she had to believe that it was she who had thrown
him out. Thus he hid his bankbook. For many a long week she
searched the flat for it. This indeed was the nature of her disease, she must always look for money. Nowhere did she find
the bankbook. Finally she ventured as far as the writing desk.
But here she collided with him. Her disappointment provoked

her to fury. He irritated her more and more, until, beside herself with rage, she threw him out of his own flat. There he stood outside, redeemed. She thought herself the victor. He locked her into the flat. She could never escape, and now he was completely safe from her attack. True he had sacrificed his flat, but what will not a man do to save his life, if that life belongs to the sacred cause of Learning?

He stretched himself out under the blanket and touched with his body as much as possible of the linen sheet. He begged the books not to fall down, he was tired and at last would like to rest. Half asleep, he mumbled, "Good night."

For three weeks he enjoyed his new freedom. With admirable diligence he made use of every minute; when the three weeks were over he had exhausted every bookshop in the town. One afternoon he did not know where else he was to go. Begin again at the beginning, and visit all over again in the same order? He might be recognized? He would prefer to avoid unpleasantness. His face—was it one of those which anyone would remember from a single glance? He stopped in front of the mirror outside a hairdresser's and surveyed his features. Watery blue eyes, and no cheeks at all. His forehead, ridged as a rock face, from which his nose plunged at right angles toward the abyss, an edge dizzily narrow. At its base, almost hidden, cowered two minute black insects. No one would have guessed them to be nostrils. His mouth as the slot of a machine. Two sharp lines, like artificial scars, ran from his temples to his chin and met at its point. These and his nose divided his long and lean face into five strips of a terrifying narrowness; narrow, but strictly symmetrical; there was no room to linger anywhere and Kien did not linger. For when he saw himself—he was not used to seeing himself—he suddenly felt very lonely. He decided to lose himself among a crowd of people. Perhaps he would then forget how lonely his face was, and perhaps he would think of a way of carrying on his activities.

He turned his eyes to the names above the doors, a feature of the town to which he was otherwise blind, and read The Stars of Heaven. He entered with pleasure. He thrust back the thick curtains over the door. An appalling fog almost took his breath away. Mechanically, as if in self-defense, he walked two steps further. His narrow body cut the air like a knife. His eyes watered: he opened them wide to see. They watered more and he could see nothing. A black figure escorted him to a small table and told him to take a seat. He obeyed. The figure ordered him a large black coffee and disappeared in the fog. Here in this alien quarter of the world, Kien clutched at the voice of his escort and identified it as male, but blurred and therefore distasteful. He was pleased to find yet another creature as despicable as he held all mankind to be. A thick hand pushed a large coffee in front of him. He thanked it politely. Surprised, the hand paused a moment, then pressed itself flat against the marble and stretched out all five fingers. What can it be grinning for? Kien asked himself, his suspicions aroused.

By the time the hand, with the man attached to it, had withdrawn, he was once again in possession of his eyes. The fog was parting. Kien's glance followed the figure, long and thin as he was himself, with distrust. It came to a halt in front of a bar, turned itself round, and indicated with an outstretched arm the newcomer. It said some incomprehensible words and shook with laughter. To whom was it speaking? In the vicinity of the bar, on every side, not a soul was standing. The place was unbelievably neglected and dirty. Behind the bar there was most clearly to be seen a heap of many colored rags. These people were too lazy even to open a wardrobe door; they used the space between the bar and the mirror at the back of it to throw their things down.

They were not even ashamed in front of their customers! Those too now began to interest Kien. At almost every little table sat a hairy object with a face like an ape, staring doggedly in his direction. Somewhere at the back strange girls yelled. The Stars of Heaven were very low and daubed between smeary gray-brown clouds. Here and there the remains of one of them broke through the dreary layers. Once the whole of the sky had been sprinkled with golden stars, but most of them had been extinguished by smoke, the rest were dying for lack of daylight. The world beneath this sky was small. It would easily have been got into a hotel bedroom. Only as long as the fog deceived the eye it had seemed wide and wild. Each little marble table had its own planetary existence. The stink of the world was generated by each and all. Everyone was smoking, silent, or battering his fist upon the hard marble. From tiny alcoves smothered cries for help could be distinguished. Suddenly an old piano made itself heard. Kien looked about for it in vain. Where had they hidden it? Old fellows dressed in rags, with cloth caps on their heads, pushed the heavy door-curtains aside with tired movements and slowly drifted about among the planets, greeting this one, threatening that, and finally settling down where they were least welcome. In a short time the place changed entirely. Movement became impossible. Who would dare to tread on the toes of such neighbors as these! Kien only was still sitting alone. He was afraid to stand up and remained where he was. Between the tables insults were bandied about. Music inspired these people with strength and fight. As soon as the piano stopped they slumped down wretchedly into themselves. Kien clutched at his head. What kind of creatures were these?

Suddenly a vast hump appeared close to him and asked, could he sit there? Kien looked down fixedly. Where was the mouth out of which speech had issued? And already the owner of the hump, a dwarf, hopped up onto a chair. He managed to seat himself and turned a pair of large melancholy eyes toward Kien. The tip of his strongly hooked nose lay in the depth of his chin. His mouth was as small as himself—only it wasn't to be found. No forehead, no ears, no neck, no buttocks—the man consisted of a hump, a majestic nose, and two black, calm, sad eyes. For a long time he said nothing; he was doubtless waiting while his appearance made its own impression. Kien accustomed himself to the new circumstance. Suddenly he heard a hoarse voice underneath the table:

"How's business?"

He looked down at his legs. The voice rasped, indignantly: "I'm not a dog, am I?" Then he knew that the dwarf had spoken. What he was to say about business he did not know. He considered the all-pervading nose of the manikin, it inspired him with mistrust. As he was not a businessman he shrugged his shoulders slightly. His indifference made a great impression.

"Fischerle is my name!" The nose pecked at the table. Kien was distressed for his own good name. He did not therefore respond with it and only inclined himself stiffly, in a manner which might have passed equally well for dismissal or for greeting. The dwarf interpreted it as the latter. He dragged two arms into view—as long as the arms of a gibbon—and reached for Kien's briefcase. Its contents provoked him to laughter. The twitching corners of his mouth, appearing on both sides of the nose, at last proved the existence of the mouth itself.

"You're in the paper racket, or aren't you?" he croaked, and held up the clean folded paper. At the sight of it the whole world beneath the Stars of Heaven broke into neighing laughter. Kien, well aware of the deeper significance of his paper, felt like shouting "Insolence!" and snatching it out of the dwarf's hand. But the very intention, bold as it was, appeared to him as a colossal crime. To atone for it he put on an unhappy and embarrassed expression.

Fischerle did not let go. "Here's a novelty for you. Ladies and gentlemen, here's a novelty! A dumb salesman!" He waved the paper about in his crooked fingers and crushed it in at least twenty places. Kien's heart bled. The cleanliness of his library was at stake. Was there no means by which he could rescue it? Fischerle climbed up onto his chair—now he was just as tall as the sitting Kien—and sang in a cracked voice. "I'm a fisherman— He's a fish!" At "I" he clapped the paper against his hump, at "he" he flicked it at Kien's ears. Kien bore it all patiently. He thought himself lucky that the raving dwarf hadn't murdered him. But his behavior was growing painful. His clean library was already defiled. He grasped that a man without a racket was of no account in this company. During the long drawn-out interval between "I" and "he" he stood up, made a deep bow, and declared resolutely: "Kien, book racket."

Fischerle broke off before the next "he" and sat down. He was satisfied with his success. He shrank back into his hump and asked with utter humility: "Do you play chess?" Kien expressed his regret.

"A person who can't play chess, isn't a person. Chess is a matter of brain, I always say. A person may be twelve foot tall, but if he doesn't play chess, he's a fool. I play chess. I'm not a fool. Now I'm asking you; answer me if you like. If you don't, don't answer me. What's a man got brains for? I'll tell you, or you'll be worrying your head about it, wouldn't that be a shame? He's got brains to play chess with. Do you get me? Say yes, then that's that. Say no, I'll explain it all over again, for you. I've always liked the book racket. May I point out to you that I learned it on my own, not out of a book. What do you think, who's the champion in this place? I bet you don't

know that one. I'll tell you who it is. The champion's called
Fischerle and sitting at the same table as you are. And why do
you think he came to sit here? Because you look such a misery.
Now maybe you'll be thinking I always make for the miseries. Wrong, rubbish, not a bit of it. Have you any idea what a
beauty my wife is! Such a rare creature as you don't often see!
But, say I, who's got the brains? The miseries have got brains,
that's what I say. What's the good of brains to a handsome fellow? Earning? His wife works for him. He wouldn't play chess
because he'd have to stoop, might spoil his figure; now what's
the conclusion? The miseries get all the brains there are. Look at
chess champions—all miseries. Look here, when I see a famous
man in the picture paper and he's anything to look at, Fischerle,
I say to myself, there's something fishy. They've got the wrong
picture. Well, what do you expect, piles and piles of photos, every
one supposed to be someone famous. What's a picture paper to
do? Picture papers are only human. Tell you what, it's queer you
don't play chess. Everyone in the book racket plays chess. No
wonder, considering the racket. They just open the book and
learn the moves by heart. But do you think one of them's ever
got me beaten? No man in the book racket ever beat me. As true
as you're in it yourself, if you are."

To obey and to listen was the same for Kien. Since the manikin had got onto the subject of chess he was the most harmless
little Jew in the world. He never paused, his questions were rhe-
torical but he answered them himself. The word "chess" rang
in his mouth like a command, as though it depended on his
gracious mercy, whether he would not add the mortal "checkmate." Kien's silence, which had irritated him at first, now appeared to him as attentiveness and flattered him.

During games his partners were far too much afraid of him to
interrupt him with objections. For he took a terrible vengeance

and would hold up the foolishness of their moves to the general derision. In the intervals between games—he passed half his life at the chessboard—people treated him as his shape and size warranted. He would have preferred to go on playing forever. He dreamed of a life in which eating and sleeping would be got through while his opponent was making his moves. When he had won uninterrupted for six hours and managed to find yet another victim, his wife interfered and forced him to stop, otherwise he would get above himself. He was as indifferent to her as if she were made of stone. He stuck to her because she provided his meals. But when she snapped off the chain of his triumphs, he would dance raging round about her, hitting her in the few sensitive parts of her coarsened person. She stood it all quietly, strong as she was, and let him do as he liked. Those were the only expressions of conjugal tenderness with which he favored her. For she loved him; he was her child. Business considerations forbade any other. She enjoyed great respect under the Stars of Heaven, because she alone of the poverty-stricken and low-priced girls of the establishment had a regular elderly gentleman, who for eight years had visited her every Monday with undeviating fidelity. On account of this regular income she was known as the Capitalist. During her frequent scenes with Fischerle, the whole place roared, but no one would have dared to start a new game against her orders. Fischerle only hit her because he knew this. For her clients, he felt tenderness, if indeed his love for chess left him any to spare. As soon as she had disappeared with one of them he could race across a chessboard to his heart's content. He had priority claims on any stranger whom chance brought to the place. Each one might be a world champion who might teach him something new. But he took it for granted that he would beat him. Only when his hope for new combinations had been shattered he introduced his wife to

the stranger and got rid of her for a time. Secretly he advised the
man to stay with her as long as he cared to; he, Fischerle, had
always liked the man's particular racket; she was easygoing, she
knew how to value a man with a bit of life in him. But he begged
not to be given away, business was business and he was acting
against his own interests.

Earlier, many years ago, before his wife was a Capitalist, and
when she had too many debts to be able to pack him off to a
café, whenever she brought a client into her narrow little room,
Fischerle, in spite of his hump, had to creep under the bed. There
he listened carefully to everything the man said—he didn't care
what his wife said—and soon he developed an instinct whether
the man was a chess player or not. The moment he was sure of
this, he crawled out as fast as he could—often hurting his hump
very much—and challenged the unsuspecting visitor to a game
of chess. Some men agreed at once, as long as the game was for
money. They hoped they would win back from the shabby Jew
the money they had given his wife under a more insistent pressure. They thought themselves well justified because they would
certainly not now have agreed to their original bargain. But they
always lost as much money again. Most of them refused Fischerle's offer, tired, suspicious, or indignant. Not one of them was
puzzled by his sudden appearance. But Fischerle's passion grew
with the years. Each time it was harder for him to postpone his
challenge long enough. Often he was forcibly overcome by the
conviction that just above his head an international champion
was lying incognito. Much too early he would appear at the bed-
side, and with his finger or his nose tap the unknown celebrity on
the shoulder until he became aware not of the insect he suspected
but of the dwarf and his challenge. This was too much for all of
them, and not one but instantly used the occasion to demand
his money back. After this had happened several times—once an

infuriated cattle dealer even fetched the police—his wife declared categorically that things must change or she would get herself someone else. Whether things were going well or not, Fischerle was sent henceforth to the café and was not allowed to come home before four in the morning. Soon after that the regular old gentleman who came every Monday settled himself in and the worst times were over. He stayed all night. Fischerle would find him still there when he came home, and was regularly greeted by him with "Hallo, World Champion!" This was intended for a good joke—in time it grew to be eight years old—but Fischerle took it for an insult. If the gentleman, whose name nobody knew—he even concealed his Christian name—was particularly satisfied, he took pity on the little man and quickly let himself be beaten by him. The gentleman was one of those people who like to settle the superfluities of life all at once. When he left the little room he had got rid of both love and pity for a week. His voluntary defeat by Fischerle saved him the pennies he would otherwise have had ready for beggars in the shop he presumably kept. On its door was a notice which ran: "Beggars will be given nothing here."

There was, however, one type of man in the world whom Fischerle hated—International Chess Champions. With a kind of rabid fury he pursued every important tournament which came to his notice in papers or magazines. Once he had played them through for himself, he could keep them in his head for years. Owing to his unchallenged championship in the café, it was easy for him to prove to his friends the worthlessness of these great players. Move by move, he would show them—they relied unquestioningly on his memory—what had happened at this or that tournament. When their admiration for such a match reached a pitch which annoyed him, he made up a few false moves and thence carried on the game just as it suited him.

Rapidly he would steer toward the catastrophe; they knew, of
course, who had suffered it, for here too, names were a fetish.
Voices were raised to say that Fischerle himself would have
done no better. Nobody had recognized the mistake made by
the defeated party. Then Fischerle would push his chair so far
back from the table that his outstretched arm could just reach
the pieces. This was his particular way of showing contempt,
since his mouth, the organ which other men use for the purpose,
was almost entirely hidden by his nose. Then he would croak:
"Give me a handkerchief. I'll win the game blind." If his wife
was there she would hand him her dirty scarf; she knew that she
must not interfere with his chess tournament triumphs which
only took place about once every few months. If she were not
there, one of the other girls would put her hands over his eyes.
Swift and sure, he would take the game back move for move.
At the place where the original mistake had occurred he would
stop. It was the very point where he had begun to cheat. Cheating again he carried the opposing party with equal boldness to
victory. Every move was breathlessly followed. Everyone was
amazed. The girls fondled his hump and kissed his nose. The
men, even the good-looking ones who knew little or nothing
about chess, beat their fists on the marble tables and asserted,
in just indignation, that it would be a dirty swindle if Fischerle were not to become the world champion. They shouted so
loudly that they at once recaptured the girls' attention. Fischerle
didn't care. He pretended that their applause meant nothing to
him, and only remarked drily: "What do you expect, I'm only a
poor devil. If someone gave me the deposit, now, I'd be world
champion tomorrow!" "Today!" they all cried. That was an end
of their enthusiasm.

Thanks to the fact that he was an unrecognized genius
at chess, and thanks to the regular customer of his wife's, the

Capitalist, Fischerle enjoyed one important privilege beneath the Stars of Heaven. He was allowed to cut out and keep all the printed chess problems in the papers, although these, which had already passed through half a dozen hands were—after several months—sent on to an even more miserable café. But Fischerle did not keep the scraps of checkered paper; he tore them into tiny fragments and threw them down the lavatory with disgust. He lived in mortal terror lest anyone should want to refer to one of them. He was by no means convinced of his importance. He racked his brains over the actual moves which he concealed. Therefore he loathed world champions like the plague.

"Where would I be, d'you think, if I was given a stipendium?" he said to Kien. "A man without a stipendium is a cripple. Twenty years I've been waiting for a stipendium. You don't think I'd take anything from my wife, do you? I want peace, and I want a stipendium. Move in with me says she. I was a boy then. No, I said, what does Fischerle want with a wife? What *do* you want then, says she, she couldn't leave me alone. What do I want? A stipendium's what I want. Nothing for nothing. You wouldn't start a firm without capital. Chess too's a racket, why shouldn't it be? There's nothing that isn't a racket, come to think of it. Very good, says she, you move in with me and you'll get your stipendium. Now, I ask you, do you understand what I'm talking about? D'you know what a stipendium is? I'll tell you in any case. If you know already, it'll do no harm, if you don't it'll do no harm either. Now listen: 'stipendium' is a refined word. This word comes from the French and means exactly the same as 'capital' does in Jewish!"

Kien swallowed. By their etymology shall ye know them. What a place! He swallowed and was silent. It was the best thing to do in this den of thieves. Fischerle made a minute pause in order to observe the effect of the word "Jewish" on his companion.

You never can tell. The world is crawling with anti-Semites. A
Jew always has to be on guard against deadly enemies. Hump-
backed dwarfs and others, who have nevertheless managed to
rise to the rank of pimp, cannot be too careful. The swallow-
ing did not escape him. He interpreted it as embarrassment, and
from that moment decided that Kien must be a Jew, which he
certainly was not.

Reassured he went on: "You can only make use of it in better-
class professions," he said, meaning the stipendium; "when she
swore by the Holy Saints I moved in with her. Do you know
how long ago that was? I can tell you because you're my friend;
that was twenty years ago. Twenty years she's been scraping
and saving, doesn't allow herself anything, doesn't allow me
anything. Do you know what a monk is? No, you wouldn't
know that because you're a Jew, we don't have monks among
the Jews, monks, never mind, we live like monks, I'll tell you
a better one, perhaps you'll understand it now since you don't
understand much: we live like nuns, nuns are the wives of the
monks, see? Every monk has a wife and she's called a nun. But
you can't imagine how separately they live. That's the sort of
marriage everyone would like, the Jews ought to have that kind
too! And would you believe it, we haven't got that stipendium
together yet? Add it up now, you must be able to add! You'd
give twenty schillings right away. But not everyone would give
that. Nowadays a gentleman's a rarity. Who can afford such stupidity? You're my friend. Like the good chap you are, you say
to yourself Fischerle must have his stipendium. If not, he'll be
ruined. Can I let a man like Fischerle ruin himself? That would
be a shame, no, I can't do a thing like that. What shall I do? I'll
give his wife twenty schillings, she'll take me along with it and
my friend'll have his fun. There's nothing I wouldn't do for a

friend. I'll prove it to you. You bring your wife here, until I got my stipendium that is, and I swear to you I'm not a coward. D'you think I'm afraid of a woman? What harm can a woman do? Have you a wife?"

This was the first question to which Fischerle expected an answer. True he was as sure of the wife, whose existence he was questioning, as he was of his hump. But he longed for a game, he had been watched now for three hours and could bear it no longer. He was determined to bring the discussion to a practical conclusion. Kien was silent. What could he have said? His wife was his sore point; with the best intention in the world nothing true could be said of her. He was, actually, neither married, nor single, nor divorced. "Have you a wife?" asked Fischerle a second time. But already it sounded threatening. Kien was worried about the truth. The same thing which had happened before over the book racket was happening again. Necessity makes liars of us all. "I have not a wife!" he asserted with a smile which lit up his austerity. If he must lie, he would choose the pleasantest alternative. "Then I'll give you mine!" burst out Fischerle. Had the man in the book racket had a wife, Fischerle's offer would have been differently worded: "Then I'll make you a nice change from her." Now he shouted loudly across the café: "Are you coming, or not?"

She came. She was large, fat, and round, and half a century old. She introduced herself by shrugging a shoulder in Fischerle's direction and adding, not without a breath of pride, "My husband." Kien stood up and bowed low. He was terrified of whatever was going to happen now. Aloud he said: "Delighted!" To himself softly, inaudibly: "Strumpet." With this archaic word he reduced her to nothing. Fischerle said: "Well then, sit down." She obeyed. His nose reached up to her bosom. Nose and bosom leaned side by side over the marble table. Suddenly the manikin burst out and rattled rapidly as if he had forgotten the most important thing: "Book racket!"

Kien was again silent. The woman found him repulsive. She compared his boniness to her husband's hump and found the latter beautiful. Her rabbit-face always had something to say for himself. He wasn't born dumb. There was a time when he even talked to her. Now she was getting too old for him. He's quite right. It's not as though he goes with other girls. He's got a heart of gold, that kid. Everybody thinks they're still carrying on with each other. Every one of her girlfriends is after him. You can't trust women. She's different. You can trust her. Men aren't to be trusted either. But you can trust Fischerle. Rather than have anything to do with a woman, he says, he'd have nothing to do with anyone. She agrees to everything. She doesn't want any of that. But he mustn't talk about it, that's all. He's so modest. He's never wanted a thing out of her. A pity he doesn't look after his clothes a bit more. Time and again you'd think he'd scrambled straight out of the dustbin. If that Ferdy hasn't given Mizzi an ultimatum: he'll wait another year for that motorbike she promised him. If she hasn't got it by the end of the year, sh— him if he doesn't find himself another girl. Now she's scraping and saving, but where's she going to get a motorbike from? Her rabbit-face wouldn't do a thing like that. The beautiful eyes he's got! He can't help his hump, can he!

Always when Fischerle found her a client she felt that he wanted to be rid of her and was grateful to him for his love. Later on she would find him too conceited again. But on the whole she was a contented creature, and in spite of her squalid life had little hate in her. That little was all for chess. While the other girls knew the first principles of the game, in all her life she had never understood why the different pieces had differ-

ent moves. It disgusted her that the king should be so powerless. She'd teach that pert thing the queen a thing or two! Why
should she have it all her own way and the king not at all? Often she would watch the game tensely. A stranger would have
judged her by her expression a pronounced connoisseur. In fact
she was simply waiting for the queen to be taken. If that happened she burst into triumphant crooning and left the table at
once. She shared her husband's hate for the stranger queen, and
was jealous of the love with which he guarded his own. Her girlfriends, more independent than she was, placed themselves at
the top of the social hierarchy and called the queen the tart, the
king the pimp. Only the Capitalist still clung to the existing order from whose lowest rank, by virtue of her regular gentleman,
she had already climbed. She, who otherwise set the tone for the
most outspoken jokes, would not join in against the king. As for
the queen, "tart" was too good a name for her. The castles and
the knights pleased her, because they looked like real ones, and
when Fischerle's knight charged full gallop across the board she
would laugh out loud in her calm husky voice. Twenty years
after he had first come to her with his chessboard she would
still ask him in all innocence why the castles could not be left
standing at the corners of the board where they had been at the
beginning of the game; they looked ever so much nicer there.
Fischerle spurned her woman's witlessness and said not a word.
When she bored him with her questions—she only wanted to
hear him speak, she loved his croaking, nobody else had such a
raven-voice—he would shut her up with some drastic assertion:
"Have I a hump or haven't I? And suppose I have? You can take
yourself out sliding! Maybe that'll knock a little sense into your
head." His hump distressed her. She'd rather have overlooked
it. She had a feeling as if she were answerable for the misshapen-
ness of her child. As soon as he had discovered this trait in her,

which seemed to him quite mad, he made use of it as blackmail. His hump was the one dangerous threat on which he could rely.

At this very moment she was gazing lovingly upon him. His hump compared to this skeleton was beautiful. She was happy that he had called her to his table. She gave herself no trouble at all with Kien. After a general silence she said: "Well, what about it? How much will you give me?" Kien blushed. Fischerle went for her at once. "Don't talk so silly! I won't have my friend insulted. He's got a head on his shoulders. He doesn't talk nonsense. Every word he turns over in his head a hundred times before he says it. If he says something it's worth saying. He's interested in my stipendium and is going to make a voluntary contribution of twenty schillings." "Stipendium? Whatever's that?" "'Stipendium' is a refined word!" Fischerle bawled. "It comes from the French and means the same as 'capital' in Jewish!" "Capital? Who says I got capital?" His wife simply didn't catch on. Why on earth had he used a French word? He was determined to be in the right. He looked at his wife long and gravely, indicated Kien with his nose, and declared pompously: "He knows everything." "Everything?" "That we're saving up for my chess championship." "I wouldn't dream of it! I don't earn that much. My name isn't Mizzi and you're not Ferdy. What do I get out of you? More kicks than ha'pence. You know what you are, do you? You're a cripple! Go and beg if you don't like it!" She called Kien to witness the crying injustice of it. "The cheek of it! You wouldn't hardly credit it. A cripple like him! He ought to think himself lucky!"

Fischerle shrank down, he gave his game up for lost and only said mournfully to Kien: "You be thankful you're not a married man. First we scrape and save twenty years every brass farthing and now she's blued the whole bloody stipendium with her fancy boys." For a moment this shameless lie took his wife's breath away. "I swear," she screamed as soon as she had recovered herself, "in all these twenty years I haven't had a single man, only him!" Fischerle opened his hands to Kien in a gesture of resignation: "A whore who never had a man!" At the word "Whore" he raised his eyebrows. At this insult his wife burst into noisy crying. Her words grew incomprehensible but one had the impression that she was sobbing about a regular income. "Now you can see yourself, she's admitting it." Fischerle was regaining courage. "Where do you think she gets a regular income from? From a gentleman who turns up every Monday. In my flat. Listen, a woman *always* tells lies, and why does a woman always tell lies? Because she's a liar! Now I ask you: Could you tell a lie? Could I tell a lie? Out of the question! And why? because we've got heads on our shoulders. Have you ever seen a man with a head on his shoulders who tells lies? I haven't!" His wife sobbed more and more loudly.

Kien agreed with all his heart. In his terror he had never asked himself whether Fischerle was telling the truth or lying. Since the woman had sat down at the table, he was relieved by every hostile gesture in her direction wherever it came from. Since she had asked him for a present he knew who it was he had before him; a second Therese. He knew nothing about the rituals of the place, but one thing he recognized clearly—this stainless spirit in a wretched body had struggled for twenty years to lift itself out of the mire of its surroundings. Therese would not allow it. He was forced to impose enormous sacrifices on himself, never losing sight of his glorious goal—a free mind. Therese, no less determined, dragged him forever back into the slime. He saves, not out of meanness, his is a generous soul; she wastes it again, so that he shall never escape her. He has clutched at one tiny corner of the world of the spirit and clings to it like a drowning man. Chess is his library. He only talks about rackets because any other kind of speech is forbidden here. But it is significant that he regards the book racket with such esteem. Kien pictured to himself the battle this downtrodden man fought for his own flat. He takes a book home to read it secretly, she tears it in pieces and scatters it to the winds. She forces him to let her use his home for her unspeakable purposes. Possibly she pays a servant, a spy, to keep the house clear of books when she is out. Books are forbidden, her own way of life is permitted. After a long struggle he succeeds in wringing from her the concession of a chessboard. She has confined him to the smallest room in the house. There he sits through the long nights and handling those wooden chessmen recovers his human dignity. He almost feels released when she is receiving these visits. During these hours he might be dead for her. Things must reach this pass with her before she will stop torturing him. But even then he listens unwillingly lest she should reappear, the worse for drink. She stinks of alcohol. She smokes. She flings open the door and with her clumsy foot kicks over the chessboard. Mr. Fischerle weeps like a little child. He had just reached the most interesting part of his book. He picks up the letters scattered all over the floor and turns his face away so that she shall not rejoice over his tears. He is a little hero. He has character. How often does the word "Strumpet!" spring to his lips. He swallows it, she would not understand. She would long since have turned him out of the house, but she is waiting until he makes a will in her favor. Probably he is not rich. All the same he has enough for her to want to rob him of it. He has no intention of making this final sacrifice. Defending himself he keeps his roof over his head. Did he but know that he owed that roof to her speculations on his will! He must not be told. He could do himself an injury. He is not made of granite. His dwarfish constitution . . .

Never before had Kien felt himself enter so deeply into the

mind of another man. He had been successful in freeing himself from Therese. He had struck at her with her own weapons,
outwitted her, and locked her in. Here she was again, sitting at
his very table, making the same demands as before, nagging as
before, and—the only alteration in her—had this time adopted
a suitable profession. But her destructive activity was not directed at him, she took little notice of him, all her attention was
directed at the man opposite, whom nature by a mistaken etymology had, moreover, fashioned as a cripple. Kien felt himself
deeply indebted to this man. He must do something for him.
He respected him. Had Mr. Fischerle not been of so delicate a
sensibility he would have offered him money direct. No doubt
he could make use of it. But he was as anxious not on any account to hurt his feelings, as he was anxious not to hurt his own.
Possibly he might steer the conversation back to that point at
which, with a woman's shamelessness, Therese had interrupted
them?

He drew out his wallet, still crammed full of valuable
banknotes. Holding it unusually long in his hand, he extracted
from it all the banknotes and placidly counted them all over.
Mr. Fischerle was to be persuaded by this that the offer about
to be made to him was by no means a great sacrifice. When he
reached the thirtieth hundred-schilling note Kien looked down
at the little fellow. Possibly he was already mellowed enough for
the offer to be dared, for who enjoys counting money? Fischerle
was looking stealthily all about him; the only person for whom
he had no eyes at all was Kien counting his money, surely out
of the delicacy of his feelings and his repulsion from filthy lu-
cre. Kien was not to be discouraged, he went on counting, but
loudly now in a clear high voice. Secretly he apologized to the
little man for his insistence, for he noticed how much he hurt his
ears. The dwarf wriggled restlessly on his chair. He laid his head

down on the table so as to stop up at least one ear, the sensitive
creature, then he pushed his wife's bosom about, what was he
doing that for, he was making it broader, it was broad enough
already, he was obscuring Kien's views. The woman let him do
as he liked, she was silent now. Doubtless she was counting on
the money. But she was making a mistake there. Therese would
get nothing. When Kien had got to forty-five the little fellow's
agonies had reached their peak. Imploringly he whispered: "Pst!
Pst!" Kien softened. Should he spare him the gift after all, no,
no, later he would be glad of it all the same, perhaps he would
run away with it and rid himself of this Therese. At the number
fifty-three Fischerle clutched his wife's face and croaked out like
a madman: "Can't you keep quiet? What are you after, you silly
bitch? What d'you know about chess? I'll chessboard you! I'll
eat you alive! Scram!" With every new figure he said something
else; the woman seemed bewildered and made as if to go. This
did not suit Kien at all. She had to be there when he gave the
little fellow his present. She had to be angry at getting nothing
herself, or her husband wouldn't enjoy it. Money alone meant
little to him. He must hand it over to him before she went.

He waited for a round figure—the next was sixty—and broke
off his counting. He rose to his feet and took out a hundred schilling note. He would rather have selected several at once but he
was not going to hurt the dwarf's feelings with either too large or
too small a sum. For a moment he stood there, tall and in silence,
to heighten the solemnity of his proposal. Then he spoke; they
were the most courteous words of his life:

"Honored Mr. Fischerle! It is impossible for me to repress
any longer a request which I have to address to you. Pray do
me the honor of accepting toward your stipendium, as you are
pleased to call it, this token of my esteem!"

Instead of "thank you," the little fellow whispered "Pst!

Have it your own way," and went on screaming at his wife; he was evidently bewildered. His furious words and looks almost knocked her under the table. He cared so little for the money offered that he did not even look at it. Not to hurt Kien's feelings he simply stretched out his arm and clutched at the note. Instead of the single note he grasped the entire bundle, but in his excitement didn't even notice it. Kien nearly smiled. From sheer modesty the man acts like the greediest thief. As soon as he notices it he will be painfully embarrassed. To spare him embarrassment, Kien exchanged the bundle for the single note. The dwarf's fingers were hard and sensitive, they clawed themselves, doubtless against the will of their owner, round the bundle; they still did not feel anything even when Kien detached them one after another from the packet, but closed themselves automatically again over the single hundred schilling note which remained. Playing chess has hardened his hands, thought Kien; Mr. Fischerle is used to grasping the pieces firmly, they alone keep him alive. In the meantime he had sat down again. His beneficence made him happy. Therese too, smothered in injuries, her face aflame, had got up and left the table in earnest. She might as well go, he had no further use for her. She could expect nothing from him. It was his duty to help her husband to his victory over her, and in that he had succeeded.

In the tumult of his happy sensations, Kien did not hear what was going on about him. Suddenly he felt a heavy blow on his shoulder. It made him jump and he looked round. A vast hand lay there, and a voice zoomed: "What about me?" At least a dozen fellows were seated round about, since when? He had not noticed them before. Fists were piled up on the table, more fellows were coming along, those standing at the back leaned over those in front who were sitting. A girl's voice called out plaintively: "Let me out, I can't see a thing." Another one, shrilly:

"Ferdy, your motorbike's in the bag!" Someone held the open briefcase in the air, shook it, found nothing, and wailed, disillusioned: "Go to hell with your paper." You couldn't see the room anymore for the people in it. Fischerle was croaking. No one listened to him. His wife was there again. She was screaming. Another woman, fatter still, struck out right and left and forced her way through the men shouting: "I'll have something too!" She was covered with all those scraps of rags that Kien had seen behind the bar. The stars shook. Chairs collapsed. An angel's voice was crying with joy. Just as Kien understood what it was all about, he was crowned with his own briefcase. He saw and heard no more, he only felt that he was lying on the floor while his pockets, and the very seams and holes in his suit were being searched by hands of every shape and weight. He trembled all over, not for himself, only for his head; they might throw his books about. They are going to kill him but he won't betray his books. We want the books! they will order him, where are your books? But he won't give them up, never, never, never, he is a martyr, he is dying for his books. His lips move, they want to say how strong he is in his resolution, but they dare not speak aloud, they move only as though they had spoken.

But it occurs to no one to ask him. They prefer to find out for themselves. Several times he is pushed around over the floor. They all but undress him to the skin. Whichever way they twist and turn him, they find nothing. Suddenly he realizes that he is alone. All the hands have vanished. Stealthily he feels for his head. As a protection against the next attack he leaves his hand up there. The second hand follows it. He tries to stand up without taking his hands away from his head. His enemies are watching for this moment to snatch at the defenseless books; careful, careful! He succeeds. He is lucky. Now he is standing. Where are these creatures? Better not look round; he may be noticed. His glance, cautiously directed to the furthest corner of the room, falls on a heap of people at work on each other with knives and fists. Now, too, he hears their wild screams. He will not understand them. If he did they might understand him. On tiptoe, on his long legs he creeps out. Someone clutches at his back. Running even, he is too cautious to look round. He squints backward, holding his breath, pressing his hands with all his strength to his head. But it is only the door curtains. In the street he draws a deep breath. What a pity he can't close those doors. The library is saved.

A few doors off the dwarf was waiting for him. He handed his briefcase back to him. "The paper's there too," he said, "I'll show you the kind of man I am." In his distress Kien had forgotten that a person called Fischerle existed in the world. He was all the more overcome by this incredible proof of his devotion. "The paper too," he faltered, "how can I thank you . . ." He had not mistaken his man. "That's nothing," declared the little fellow. "Now will you kindly step in here with me." Kien obeyed, he was deeply moved and would gladly have embraced the little man. "Do you know what a reward is?" asked the dwarf as soon as they were inside a porch hidden from passersby. "You must know what that is. Ten percent. In there they are killing each other, men and women, and I've got it." He drew out Kien's wallet and handed it over to him like a ceremonial presentation. "I'm not a fool! I'm not going to be locked up to save their throats." Since his most precious possessions had been in danger, Kien had forgotten all about the money too. He laughed aloud at so much conscientiousness, took the wallet back mainly because he was so pleased with Fischerle, and repeated: "How can I thank you! How can I thank you!" "Ten percent," said the dwarf. Kien plunged into the packet of notes and offered a large portion to Fischerle. "You count first of all," he yelled. "Business is business. All of a sudden you'll be saying I robbed you." It was all very well for Kien to count. Had he an idea how much there had been before? Fischerle on the other hand knew exactly how many notes he had already set aside. His demand that Kien should count referred to the reward alone. But to please him Kien counted it all carefully through. When for the second time today, he reached the figure sixty, Fischerle saw himself locked up. He decided to make off at once—for this contingency he had already extracted his own reward—but quickly he tried one last attempt. "There you are, it's all safe!" "Of course," said Kien, pleased not to have to do any more counting. "Count out the reward now and we're quits." Kien began again and got as far as nine, he would have gone on counting forever. "Stop! Ten percent!" cried Fischerle. He knew exactly how much there had been in all. While he was waiting for Kien he had swiftly and thoroughly been through the wallet.

When the deal was finished, he gave Kien his hand, looked sadly up at him, and said: "You ought to know what I've done for you! It's all over with the Stars of Heaven for me. You don't think I can ever go in there again, do you? They'd find all this money on me and kill me dead. Because where does Fischerle get the money from? And how am I to tell them where I got it from? If I say I got it from the gentleman in the book racket they'll smash me to smithereens and steal the money out of my pockets while I lie there. If I say nothing they'll take it from me while I'm still alive. You see how it is, if Fischerle lives, then he's nothing left to live for, and if he dies, well he's dead. That's what you get for being a friend." He was still hoping for a tip.

Kien felt obliged to help this person, the first worthy object he had found in his life, to a better and more dignified existence. "I am not a tradesman, I am a man of learning and a librarian," he said and bowed condescendingly to little dwarf. "You may enter my service and I will look after you."

"Like a father," completed the little fellow. "Just as I thought. Very well, off we go!" He marched boldly out. Kien ambled after him. He cast about for work to give to his new *famulus*. A friend must never suspect that he is being given presents. He could help him in the evenings to unload and pile up the books.

Chapter II: The Hump

A few hours after he had started on his new job Fischerle was fully enlightened as to the desires and peculiarities of his master. On taking up their quarters for the night he was presented to the hotel porter as "my friend and colleague." Fortunately the porter recognized the openhanded Owner of a Library who had already spent a night in that hotel; otherwise both the gentleman and his colleague would have been thrown out. Fischerle took pains to follow what Kien was writing on the registration form. He was too small, he couldn't contrive to poke his nose into these matters. His fears were on account of the second registration form which the porter had ready for him. But Kien, who was making up in one night for the lack of delicacy of a lifetime, considered how difficult the little fellow would find it to write and included him on his own form under the heading "accompanied by . . ." He handed the second form back to the porter with the words, "This is unnecessary." Thus he spared Fischerle not only the difficulty of writing, but, more important still in his eyes, the humiliating admission of his status as a servant.

As soon as they reached their rooms upstairs, Kien took out the brown paper and began to smooth it out. "True, it's all

crumpled," he said, "but we have no other." Fischerle seized the
occasion to make himself indispensable, and worked carefully
over each sheet which his master regarded as already perfected.
"I was to blame, with that slapping," he declared. His success
was the measure of the enviable nimbleness of his fingers. Next
the paper was spread out over the floor in both rooms. Fischerle gamboled from side to side, lay flat down and crawled—a
peculiar, squat, hump-backed reptile—from corner to corner.
"We'll soon have it all shipshape, that's nothing!" he panted
again and again. Kien smiled, he was not accustomed to this
cringing nor to the hump and rejoiced at the personal honor
which the dwarf was showing him. The impending explanation
however filled him with a certain anxiety. Possibly he overesti-
mated the intelligence of the manikin, almost as old as he, who
had lived countless years in exile without books. He might well
misunderstand the task which was intended for him. Perhaps he
would ask: "Where are the books?" even before he had grasped
where they were safely kept during the day. It would be best to
leave him crawling about on the floor a little longer. Meanwhile
some popular simile might occur to Kien with which he could
enlighten this uneducated brain. Even the little fellow's fingers
disquieted him. They were in constant motion; they kept on
smoothing out the paper far too long. They were hungry, hungry fingers want food. They might demand the books, which
Kien was determined no one should touch, no one at all. Also
he feared to come into collision with the little fellow's thirst for
education. He might reproach him, with some appearance of
justice, for letting his books lie fallow. How was he to defend
himself? Fools rush in where wise men fear to tread. There was
the fool already standing in front of him saying: "All done!"

"Then please will you help me unpack the books!" said Kien
blindly, and was astonished at his own boldness. To cut short

any unwelcome questions he immediately lifted a packet out of his head and held it out to the little fellow. The latter managed to take it up cleverly in his long arms and said: "So many! Where shall I put them down?" "Many?" shouted Kien, indignantly. "That isn't the thousandth part."

"I get you. A tenth percent. Do you want me to stand about here another year? I can't manage it much longer with all this to carry. Where shall I put them down?" "On the paper. Begin in the corner over there, then we won't fall over them later on."

Fischerle slid carefully over to the corner. He avoided any violent movement which would have endangered his burden. In the corner he knelt down, laid the packet carefully on the floor, and straightened its sides so that no irregularity should shock the eye. Kien had followed him. He was already holding out the next packet toward him: he distrusted the little fellow, it seemed to him somehow as if he was being mocked. In Fischerle's hands the work went forward swimmingly. He took packet after packet, his nimbleness grew with practice. Between the piles he left always a few inches where he could conveniently insert his hands. He thought of everything, even of the repacking in the morning. He allowed only a moderate height to each pile and tested them when he had got so far by gently passing the tip of his nose over them. Although he was quite absorbed in his measuring, he said every time: "Beg pardon, sir!" Higher than his nose he would not let them be. Kien was doubtful: it seemed to him that if the piles were to be built thus low the available space would be used up too soon. He had no desire to sleep with half the library still in his head. But for the present he said nothing and let his *famulus* do as he wished. He had half taken him to his heart already. He forgave him the disdain contained in his exclamation: "So many!" He rejoiced to think of the moment when, the floor space available in both rooms being completely used up, he would look down at the little fellow with mild irony and ask: "And now where?"

After an hour Fischerle was in the greatest difficulty on account of his hump. Twist and turn as he would he collided with books everywhere. Except for a narrow path from the bed in one room to the bed in the other, everything was evenly covered with books. Fischerle was in a sweat and no longer dared to pass the tip of his nose over the topmost layer of the piles of books. He tried to draw in his hump but couldn't manage it. This physical exertion was almost too much for him. He was so tired he felt like spitting on the books and going to sleep. But he carried on until, however much he tried, he couldn't discover the tiniest empty space and then crumpled up half dead. "In all my born days I never see such a library," he growled. Kien's smile spread over his entire face. "You haven't seen half of it," he said. Fischerle had not reckoned with this. "We'll finish the rest in the morning," he asserted, threateningly. Kien felt caught out. He had boasted. In fact a good two-thirds of the books were already unloaded. What would the little man think of him if he found out. Accurate people do not like to be accused of exaggeration. He must take care to sleep tomorrow in a hotel where the rooms were smaller. He would give him smaller packets at a time, two packets made up one pile precisely, and if Fischerle, with the help of his nose, were to notice anything, he would say to him simply: "People's noses are not always on the same level. There are many things you will have to learn from me." He could not allow any more unpacking tonight, the little man was tired enough already. He must be permitted a well-earned rest. "I respect your fatigue," he said; "what we do for books, is well done. You can go to bed now. We will continue in the morning." He treated him considerately, but as a servant. The work which he had just performed reduced him to that rank.

When Fischerle was in bed and had rested himself a little, he called out to Kien: "Bad beds!" He felt so comfortable—in all his born days he had never lain on such a soft mattress—he had to say something about it.

Kien was in China; he was there every night before he fell asleep. The extraordinary happenings of the day gave his imaginings a different form. He conceived without an immediate revulsion the idea of a popularization of his learning. He felt that the dwarf understood him. He conceded that like-minded human beings might exist. If it were possible to infuse these with a little education, a little humanity, this would certainly be an achievement. The first step is always the hardest. Moreover no encouragement should be given to arbitrary action. Through daily contact with so vast a quantity of learning the little man's hunger for it would grow greater and greater; suddenly he would be caught secreting a book and trying to read it. This must not be allowed, it would be harmful to him, it would destroy what little intelligence he had. How much could the poor fellow possibly absorb? He would have to be prepared for it orally. There was no hurry for him to begin reading on his own. Years would pass before he would be fluent in Chinese. But he would become familiar with the ideas and the interpreters of the Chinese cultural world long ere this. To awaken his interest in these things they must be associated with the experiences of every day. Under the title "Mencius and Us" a very pretty essay might be put together. What would he be able to make of it? Kien recollected that the dwarf had just said something; what it was he did not know, but in any case he must still be awake.

"What have we to learn from Mencius?" he called loudly. That was a better title. It was clear from it at once that Mencius was a human being. A man of learning is naturally anxious to avoid gross misunderstandings.

"Bad beds, say I!" Fischerle called back even louder.

"Beds?"

"Yeh, bugs!"

"What! Go to sleep at once and let me have no more jokes! You have much to learn in the morning."

"I tell you what, I've learned quite enough today."

"That's only an idea of yours. Go to sleep, I shall count up to three."

"Sleep, indeed! And suppose someone steals the books and we're ruined. I'm not taking any risks. Do you suppose I shall sleep a wink? You may, seeing you're a rich man. Not me!"

Fischerle was really afraid of going to sleep. He was a man of habits. Should he dream he would be perfectly capable of stealing all Kien's money. In his sleep he had not the least idea what he was doing. A man dreams of the things which mean something to him. Fischerle was happiest rolling in heaps of banknotes. When he got tired of rolling, and if he knew for dead certain that not one of his false friends was anywhere about, he would sit down on top of them and play a game of chess. There was an advantage in sitting up so high. He could do two things at once this way; he could see a long way off anyone coming to steal them, and he could hold the chessboard. That was the way great men managed their affairs. With the right hand you pushed the pieces about, with the left you rubbed the dirt off your fingers onto the banknotes. The trouble was there were too many of them. Say—millions. What should we do with all these millions? Giving them away wouldn't be a bad idea, but who could trust himself to do it? They'd only have to see that a small man had got anything, that lot, and they'd snatch it away. A small man wasn't allowed to get above himself. He'd got the money all right, but he mustn't use it. What had he got to be sitting up there for, they'd say. It's all very well, but where was a small man to put all those millions when he hadn't anywhere to keep them? An operation would be the sensible thing. Dangle a million in front of the famous surgeon's nose. Sir, you said, cut off my hump and that's for you. For a million a man would become an artist. Once the hump had gone, you said: dear sir, the million was a forgery, but here's a couple of thou'. The man might even thank you. The hump was burnt. Now you might walk straight for the rest of your life. But a sensible person wasn't such a fool. He took his millions, rolled up all the banknotes small, and made a new hump out of them. He put it on. Not a soul noticed anything. He knew he was straight; people thought he was a poor cripple. He knew he was a millionaire; people thought he was a poor devil. When he went to bed he pushed the hump round onto his stomach. Great God, he'd love to sleep on his back, just once.

At this point Fischerle rolled over and lay on his hump and was thankful for the pain which jerked him out of his dozing. This mustn't go on he said to himself; all of a sudden he'd be dreaming that the heaps of money were just over there, he'd get up to fetch them and a fine mess he'd be in then. As though the whole lot didn't belong to him, anyway. The police were quite unnecessary. He could do without their interference. He'd earn it all honestly. The man in the other room was an idiot, the man in this one had got a head on his shoulders. Who was going to have the money in the end?

Fischerle might well argue with himself. Stealing had become a habit with him. For a little while he hadn't been stealing because where he lived there was nothing to steal. He didn't take part in expeditions far afield as the police had their eye on him. He could be too easily identified. Policemen's zeal for their duty knew no limits. Half the night he lay awake, his eyes forcibly held open, his hands clenched in the most complicated fashion.

He expelled the heaps of money from his mind. Instead he went
through all the rough passages and hard words he had ever experienced in police stations. Were such things necessary? And
on top of it all they took away everything you possessed. You
never saw a penny of it again. *That* wasn't stealing! When their
insults ceased to be effective and he was fed to the back teeth
with the police and already had one arm hanging out of bed, he
fell back on some games of chess. They were interesting enough
to keep him firmly fixed in bed; but his arm remained outside,
ready to pounce. He played more cautiously than usual, pausing before some moves to think for a ridiculously long time. His
opponent was a world champion. He dictated the moves to him
proudly. Slightly bewildered by the obedience of the champion
he exchanged him for another one: this one too put up with a
great deal. Fischerle was playing, in fact, for both of them. The
opponent could think of no better moves than those dictated to
him by Fischerle, nodded his head gratefully, and was beaten
hollow in spite of it. The scene repeated itself several times until
Fischerle said: "I won't play with such half-wits," and stretched
his legs out of bed. Then he exclaimed: "A world champion?
Where is there a world champion? There isn't any world champion here!"

To make sure, he got up and looked round the room. As
soon as they won the world's title people simply went and hid
themselves. He could find no one. All the same he could have
sworn the world champion was sitting on the bed playing chess
with him. Surely he couldn't be hiding in the next room? Now
don't you worry. Fischerle would soon find him. Calm as calm,
he looked through the next room; the room was empty. He
opened the door of the wardrobe and made a pounce with his
hand, no chess player would escape him. He moved very softly,
who wouldn't? Why should that long creature with the books

be disturbed in his sleep only because Fischerle had to track down his enemy? Quite possibly the champion wasn't there at all, and for a mere whim he was throwing his beautiful job away. Under the bed he grazed over every inch with the tip of his nose. It was a long time since he'd been back under any bed and it reminded him of the old days at home. As he crawled out his eyes rested on a coat folded up over a chair. Then it occurred to him how greedy world champions always were for money, they could never get enough; to win the title from them one had to put down heaps of money in cash, just like that, on the table; there was no doubt the fellow was after the money, and was lurking about somewhere near the wallet. He might not have found it yet, it ought to be saved from him; a creature like that could manage anything. Tomorrow the money'd be gone and the flagpole would think Fischerle took it. But you couldn't deceive him. With his long arms he stretched for the wallet from below, pulled it out, and withdrew himself under the bed. He might have crawled right out, but why should he? The world champion was larger and stronger than he, sure as fate he was standing behind that chair, lurking for the money, and would knock Fischerle out because he'd got in first. By this skillful maneuver no one noticed anything. Let the dirty swindler stay where he was. Nobody asked him to come. He could scram. That would be best. Who wanted him?

Soon Fischerle had forgotten him. In his hiding place right at the back under the bed he counted over the beautiful new notes, just for the pleasure of it. He remembered exactly how many there were. As soon as he had done he started again at the beginning. Fischerle is off now to a far country, to America. There he goes up to the world champion Capablanca, and says: "I've been looking for you!" puts down his caution money, and plays until the fellow is beaten hollow. On the next day Fischerle's picture is in all the papers. He does pretty well out of it all. At home, under the Stars of Heaven, that lot wouldn't believe their eyes, his wife, the whore, begins to howl and yell if she'd only known it she would have let him play all he wanted; the others shut her up with a couple of smacks—serve her right—that's what happens when a woman won't bother to learn about the game. Women'll be the end of men. If he'd stayed at home, he'd never have made good. A man must cut loose, that's the whole secret. None but the brave deserve to be world champion. And people have the nerve to say Jews aren't brave. The reporters ask him who he is. Not a soul knows him. He doesn't look like an American. There are Jews everywhere. But where does this Jew come from, who's rolled in triumph over Capablanca? For the first day he'll let people guess. The papers would like to tell their readers, but they don't know. Everywhere the headlines read: "Mystery of the new World Champion." The police become interested, naturally. They want to lock him up again. No, no, gentlemen, not so fast this time; now he throws the money about and the police are honored to release him at once. On the second day, a round hundred reporters turn up. Each one promises him, shall we say, a thousand dollars cash down if he'll say something. Fischerle says not a word. The papers begin to lie. What else are they to do? The readers won't wait any longer. Fischerle sits in a mammoth hotel with one of those luxury cocktail bars, like on a giant liner. The head waiter brings the loveliest ladies to his table, not tarts mind you, millionairesses with a personal interest in him. He thanks them politely, but hasn't time, later perhaps . . . And why hasn't he time? Because he's reading all the lies about him in all the papers. It takes all day. How's he to get through it? Every minute he's interrupted. Press photographers ask for a moment of his time. "But gentlemen, a hump . . . !" he protests. "A world champion is a world champion, honored Mr. Fischerle. The hump is quite immaterial." They photograph him right and left, before and behind. "Why don't you retouch it," he suggests, "take the hump out. Then you'll have a nice picture for your paper." "Just as you please, most honored world champion!" But really, where's he had his eyes? His picture is everywhere, without a hump. It's gone. He hasn't one. But he worries a bit about his size. He calls the head waiter and points to a paper. "A bad picture, what?" he asks. The head waiter says: "*Well.*" In America people speak English. He finds the picture excellent. "But it's only the head," he says. That's right too. "You can go now," says Fischerle and tips him a hundred dollars. In this picture he might be a fully grown man. No one would notice he was undersized. He loses his interest in the articles. He can't be bothered to read all this in English. He only understands "Well!" Later on he has all the latest editions of the papers brought to him and looks hard at all his pictures. His head is everywhere. His nose is a bit long, that's true; can't help his nose. From a child up he's been all for chess. He might have taken some other idea into his head, football or swimming or boxing. But not he. It's a bit of luck really. If he were a boxing champion, now, he'd have to be photographed half naked. Everyone would laugh at him and he'd get nothing out of it. On the next day at least a thousand reporters turn up. "Gentlemen," he says, "I'm surprised to find myself called Fischerle everywhere. My name is Fischer. I trust that you will have this error rectified." They promise they will. Then they all kneel down in front of him—how small men are—and implore him to say something at last. They'll be thrown out, they'll lose their jobs, they cry, if they get nothing out of him today. My sorrow, he thinks, nothing for nothing, he gave the head waiter a hundred dollars, but he won't give the reporters anything. "What's your bid, gentlemen?" he cries boldly. A thousand dollars, shouts one. Cheek, screams another, ten thousand! A third takes him by the hand and whispers: a hundred thousand, Mr. Fischer. People throw money about like nothing. He stops his ears. Until they get into millions he won't even listen to them. The reporters go mad and begin tearing each other's hair, each one wants to give more than the other; all this fuss; auctioneering his private life! One goes up to five millions, and all at once there is absolute quiet. Not one dares offer more. World Champion Fischer takes his fingers out of his ears and declares: "I will now say something, gentlemen. What good will it do me to ruin you? None. How many of you are there? A thousand. Let each one of you give me ten thousand and I'll tell you all. Then I shall have ten millions and not one of you will be ruined. Agreed?" They fall on his neck and he's a made man. Then he clambers up on a chair, he doesn't really need to anymore but he does it all the same, and tells them the simple truth. As a world champion, he fell from Heaven. It takes a good hour to convince them. He was unhappily married. His wife, a Capitalist, fell into evil ways, she was—as they used to call it in his home, the Stars of Heaven—a whore. She wanted him to take money from her. He didn't know any way out. If he wouldn't take any, she used to say, she'd murder him. He was forced to do it. He had yielded to her blackmail and kept the money for her. Twenty long years he had to endure this. In the end he was fed up. One day he demanded categorically that she should stop or he'd become chess champion of the world. She cried, but she wouldn't stop. She was too much accustomed to doing nothing, to having fine clothes and lovely clean-shaven gentlemen. He was sorry for her but a man must keep his word. He goes straight from the Stars of Heaven to the United States, finishes off Capablanca, and here he is! The reporters rave about him. So does he. He founds a charity. He will pay a stipendium to every café in the world. In return the proprietors must undertake to put up on their walls every game played by the world champion. Any person defacing the notices will be prosecuted. Every individual person can thus convince himself that the world champion is a better player than he is. Otherwise some swindler may suddenly pop up, a dwarf or even a cripple, and brag he plays better. People may not think of checking up the cripple's moves. They are capable of believing him simply because he's a good liar. Things like that must stop. On each wall is a placard. The cheat makes one wrong move, everyone looks at the placard, and who then will blush to the very hump on his miserable back. The crook! Moreover the proprietor must undertake to fetch him a sock on the jaw for saying things about the world champion. Let him challenge him openly if he's got the money. Fischerle will put down a million for this foundation. He's not mean. He'll send a million to his wife so she needn't go on the streets anymore. In return she'll give it him in writing that she won't come to America and will keep mum about his former dealings with the police. Fischer's going to marry a millionairess. This will reimburse him for his losses. He'll have new suits made at the best possible tailor so that his wife'll notice nothing. A gigantic palace will be built with real castles, knights, pawns, just as it ought to be. The servants are in livery; in thirty vast halls Fischer plays night and day thirty simultaneous games of chess with living pieces which he has only to command. All he has to do is to speak and his slaves move wherever he tells them. Challengers come from all the chief countries of the world, poor devils who want to learn something from him. Many sell their coats and shoes to pay for the long journey. He receives them with hospitality, gives them a good meal, with soup, a sweet, and two veg, and pretty often a nice grilled steak instead of a cut from the joint. Anyone can be beaten by him once. He asks

nothing in return for his kindness. Only that each one should
write his name in the visitors' book on leaving and categorically
assert that he, Fischer, is the world champion. He defends his
title. While he does so his new wife goes out riding in her car.
Once a week he goes with her. In the castle all the chandeliers
are put out, lighting alone costs him a fortune. On the door he
pins up a notice: "Back soon. Fischer: World Champion." He
does not stay out two hours, but visitors are queueing up like in
the war when he gets back. "What are you queuing for?" asks a
passerby. "What, don't you know? You must be a stranger
here." Out of pity the others tell him who it is that lives here. So
that he shall understand each one tells him singly, then they all
shout in a chorus: "Chess Champion of the World, Fischer, is
giving alms today." The stranger is struck dumb. After an hour
he finds his voice again. "Then this is his reception day?" That
is just what the natives have been waiting for. "Today is not a
reception day or there would be far more people." Now all of
them begin talking at once. "Where is he? The castle is dark!"
"With his wife in the car. This is his second wife. The first was
only a simple Capitalist. The second is a millionairess. The car
belongs to him. It isn't just a taxi. He had it built specially."
What they are saying is the simple truth. He sits in his car, it
suits him very well. It is a little too small for his wife who has to
crouch all the time. But in return she's allowed to ride with him.
At other times she has her own. He doesn't go out in hers. It's
much too big for him. But his was the more expensive. The factory made his car specially. He feels inside it just as if he were
under the bed. Looking out of the windows is too boring. He
shuts his eyes tight. Not a thing moves. Under the bed he is
perfectly at home. He hears his wife's voice from above. He's
fed up with her, what does she mean to him? She doesn't understand a thing about chess. The man is saying something too. Is

he a player? He's obviously intelligent. Wait, now, wait; why should he wait? What's waiting to him? That man up there is talking good German. He's a professional man, sure to be a secret champion. These people are afraid of being recognized. It's with them like it is with crowned heads. They have to come to women incognito. That man's a world champion for sure, not just an ordinary champion! He must challenge him. He can't wait longer. His head bursts with good moves. He'll beat him into a cocked hat!

Fischerle crept swiftly and silently from under the bed, and reared himself on his crooked legs. They'd gone to sleep; he stumbled and clutched at the bedstead. The woman had vanished, all the better, she'd leave him in peace. A lanky stranger was lying alone on the bed, you might think he was asleep. Fischerle tapped him on the shoulder and asked loudly: "Do you play chess?" The stranger was really asleep. He must be shaken awake. Fischerle was about to grasp him with both hands by the shoulders when he noticed that he was holding something in his left hand. A little packet, it was in the way, throw it down, Fischerle! He flung his left arm about but his hand refused to let go. What's all this? Will you or won't you? he screamed. His hand clutched fast. It clung to the packet as if it were a conquered queen. He looked at it closer. The packet was a bundle of banknotes. Why should he throw them away? He could do with them, he was only a poor devil. Perhaps they belonged to the stranger? He was still asleep. But they belonged to Fischerle, because he was a millionaire. How did this person get here? A visitor? He might want to challenge him? People should read the notice on the entrance gate. A world champion and he couldn't even go for a quiet spin in his car? The stranger had a familiar look. A visitor from the Stars of Heaven? That wasn't a bad idea. Why, this was the chap in the book racket.

What did he want here, book racket, book racket . . . ? He used
to be in his service once. First he had to spread out brown paper
on the floor and then . . .

Fischerle grew even more crooked with laughing. While
laughing he woke up completely. He was standing in a hotel
bedroom, he ought to be sleeping next door, he had stolen the
money. Quickly, off with it. He must get to America. He ran
two or three steps in the direction of the door. Why did he laugh
so loud? Perhaps he had woken up the book racket. He slipped
back to the bed and made sure he was still asleep. The creature
would go to the police. He wasn't that mad; he'd go to the police. He took the same steps in the direction of the door; this
time he walked instead of running. How was he to get out of the
hotel? The room was on the third floor. He was bound to wake
the porter. The police would watch him in the morning, even
before he could get into a train. Why would they catch him? Because of his hump. His long fingers fondled it with repulsion. He
wouldn't be locked up again. Those swine took his chessboard
away. He had to touch the pieces or he got no pleasure out of
the game. They forced him to play in his head. Flesh and blood
couldn't stand that. He must make his fortune. He could do the
book racket in. Jews don't do things like that. What would he
do him in with? He could force him to give his word not to go
to the police. "Your word or your life!" he'd say to him. The
creature was sure to be a coward. He'd give his word. But who
could rely on such an idiot? Anyone could do what they liked
with him. He wouldn't break his word anyway; he'd break it
from pure silliness. Silly, Fischerle had got all the money in his
hand. America was a washout. No, he'd cut and run for it. Let
them find him if they could. If they couldn't then he'd become
chess champion of the world in America. If they could, he'd
hang himself. A pleasure. What the devil . . . He couldn't make a

go of it. He hadn't got a neck. Once he hanged himself by his leg but they cut him down. You didn't catch him hanging himself by the other leg. No!

Between the bed and the door Fischerle racked his brains for a solution. He was in desperation over his rotten luck. He could have cried out loud. But he mustn't for fear of waking the creature. It might be weeks before he got another chance. Weeks, weeks—he'd waited twenty years already! One foot in America and the other in a noose. Then let a fellow try and make up his mind. The American leg took a step forward, the hanged one a step back. What a filthy trick to play! He beat his hump, sticking the packet of notes between his legs. The hump was the root of all the trouble. Let it be hurt. It deserved to be hurt. If he didn't beat it he'd have to cry out loud. If he cried out loud, America was dead and buried.

Exactly in the middle between bed and door Fischerle stood rooted to a spot and beat his hump. Like whip-handles he raised his arms alternately and brought down his fingers, five double-knotted lashes, over his shoulders onto his hump. It did not budge. A pitiless mountain, it rose above the low foothills of his shoulders, proud in its rocky hardness. It didn't even scream, "I've had enough!" It was silent. Fischerle got into his stride. He saw the hump could take it. He prepared for a long-drawn ordeal. It wasn't a matter of expressing his anger but of seeing that the blows struck home. His long arms were much too short for him. He had to make do with them, though. The blows fell with regularity. Fischerle gasped. He needed music for this. There was a piano at the Stars of Heaven. He'd make his own music. His breath gave out; he sang. His voice sounded sharp and shrill with excitement. "That'll teach you—that'll teach you!" He beat the brute black and blue. Let it go to the police if it liked! Before each blow he thought: "Come down, you carrion!" The carrion didn't budge. Fischerle was running with sweat. His arms ached, his fingers were limp and tired. He persevered, he was patient, he swore, the hump was at its last gasp. Out of sheer spite, it pretended it didn't care. Fischerle knew it of old. He would look it in the face. He twisted his head round so as to leer in scorn at his enemy. So that was it, it was hiding—you coward—you abortion—a knife! a knife! he'd stab it dead, where was a knife? Fischerle frothed at the mouth, big tears gushed out of his eyes, he cried because he had no knife, he cried because the abortion wouldn't even answer him. The strength of his arms forsook him altogether. He crumpled up, an empty sack. It was all over, he'd hang himself. The money rolled to the floor.

Suddenly Fischerle leaped up again and yelled: "Checkmate!"

Kien was dreaming most of the time about falling books and trying to catch them with his body. He was as thin as a darning needle; to left and right the rarest books were cascading down; now the floor itself gave way and he woke up. Where are they, he whimpered, where are they? Fischerle had beaten the abortion, he picked up the bundle of notes at his feet, went up to the bed, and said: "Tell you what, you can talk of luck!"

"The books, the books!" Kien groaned.

"All of them saved. Here's the money. You've got a treasure in me."

"Saved—I dreamed . . ."

"Dreaming were you? And I was being beaten up."

"Then there was someone here!" Kien leaped up. "We must go over the books at once!"

"Don't upset yourself. I heard him at once. He hadn't even got in through the door. I crept into this room under your bed to see what he was up to. What do you think he was after? Money. He puts out his hand. I grab hold of him by it. He hits out at me, I hit back. He begs for mercy, I have none. He wants to go to America, I won't let him go. Do you think he touched one of the books? Not one. He had a head on his shoulders. But he was an ass all the same. In all his born days he'd never have got to America. Do you know where he'll have got to? Between ourselves, to the police court. He's off now."

"What did he look like?" asked Kien. He wanted to show his gratitude to the little fellow for so much vigilance. He was not in the least interested in the burglar.

"What shall I say? He was a cripple like me. I could have sworn a good chess player too. A poor devil."

"Well, let him go," said Kien, and cast an affectionate—or so he meant it—glance at the dwarf. Then both went back to bed.

III

Memoirs and Senses

8.

From *The Torch in My Ear*

Part II: "Storm and Compulsion" (Vienna, 1924–1925)

Translated by Joachim Neugroschel

Living with My Brother

In early April 1924, Georg and I moved into a room in Frau Sussin's apartment at 22 Praterstrasse, Vienna. It was the dark back room, with a window to the courtyard. Here we spent four months together, not a very long period. But this was the first time that I lived alone with my brother, and a great many things happened.

We became close. I took the place of a mentor with whom he conferred about everything, especially all moral problems. What one could do and what one should do, what one must despise under any circumstances, and also what one should find out, what one should get to know—almost every evening of those four months together, we discussed those things, in between our work at the large square table by the window, where we sat, each with his books and notebooks. We were at a ninety-degree angle to one another, we only had to raise our heads to see one another right in the face. Back then, although six years my junior, he was already slightly taller than I. When we sat,

we were nearly the same size. I had decided to begin studying
chemistry in Vienna (without being certain that I would stay
with it); the semester was to start in another month. Since I had
had no chemistry at school in Frankfurt, it was high time that
I acquired some knowledge in this field. In the remaining four
weeks, I wanted to make up for what I had missed. I had the
Textbook of Inorganic Chemistry in front of me; and since it was
theoretical, involving no practical tasks, it interested me, and I
made rapid headway.

But no matter how absorbed I was, no matter what the
topic, Georg was allowed to interrupt me at any time and ask
me questions. He attended the Realgymnasium in Stubenbastei
and, being thirteen, was in a lower year. He learned willingly
and easily, and had trouble only with drawing, which was taken
very seriously in his school. But he was as eager for knowledge as I had been at his age, and sensible questions crossed his
mind about every subject. They were seldom about something
he didn't understand; he easily understood everything he read.
What he asked about was details that he wanted to find out in
addition to the more general contents of the textbooks. I could
answer many of his questions on the spot without first thinking
about them or looking them up. It made me happy to trans-
mit information to him; previously, I had kept everything to
myself; there was no one for me to talk to about such things.
He noticed how glad I was about every interruption and that
there need be no limits to his questions. A lot of things came up
in just a few hours, and his questions enlivened chemistry for
me, which seemed a bit alien and threatening because I would
quite possibly be studying it for four years or longer. Thus he
asked me about Roman authors, about history (whereby I always turned the conversation to the Greeks, if I could), about
mathematical problems, about botany and zoology, and best

of all, in connection with geography, about countries and their people. He already knew that this was what he could hear most about from me, and sometimes I had to bring myself up short— that's how willingly and thoroughly I repeated to him the things I had learned from my explorers. Nor did I refrain from judging the behavior of people. When I got to the struggle against diseases in exotic lands, I was beside myself with enthusiasm. I still hadn't gotten over giving up medicine, and I passed my old wish on to him, naively and without restraint.

I loved his insatiableness. When I sat down to my books, I looked forward to his questions. I would have suffered more from his silence than he from mine. Had he been domineering or calculating, he could easily have put me in his power. An evening at our table without his questions would have crushed me and made me unhappy. But that was it: there was no ulterior motive to his questions, any more than there was to my answers. He wanted to know; I wanted to give him what I knew; everything he found out led automatically to new questions. It was amazing that he never embarrassed me. His insatiableness stayed within my limits. Whether our minds ran in the same channels or whether the energy of my mediation kept him away from other things, he only asked me questions that I could answer and he never humiliated me—which would have been easy, had he stumbled upon my ignorance. We were both completely open, holding nothing back from each other. During this period, we were mutually dependent; there was no one else close to us; we had only one demand to fulfill: not to disappoint one another. On no account would I have missed our joint "learning evenings" at the large, square table, which had been pushed over to the window.

Summer came, the evenings grew long, we opened the windows facing the courtyard. Two stories below, right underneath us, was Fink the tailor's shop; his windows were open, too, and the fine hum of his sewing machine wafted up to us. He worked until late at night; he worked all the time. We heard him when we ate supper at our square table, we heard him when we cleared up, we heard him when we settled down to read, and we forgot him only when our conversation got so exciting that we would have forgotten *anything* else. But then, when we lay in bed, tired because the day had begun early, we again heard the humming of his sewing machine until we fell asleep.

Our supper consisted of bread and yogurt, for a while just bread; for our living arrangement had commenced with a minor catastrophe, which was all my fault. Our allowance was scanty, but everything that we needed to live on had been calculated, and it would have sufficed for a somewhat more generous supper. I received the monthly allowance in advance, part of it from Grandfather, the rest from Mother. I carried the entire amount on my person, planning to administer it well. I was experienced in this respect; I had spent six months in Frankfurt with my little brothers and without Mother, and during the final, raging phase of the inflation, it hadn't been at all easy to do everything right and make ends meet. Compared with that period, Vienna seemed like child's play.

And it would have been child's play. But I hadn't reckoned with the Prater Amusement Park. It was very close by, not fifteen minutes away; and because of its overwhelming significance during my childhood in Vienna, the park seemed even closer. Instead of keeping my little brother away from its temptations, I took him along. One Saturday afternoon, I showed him the splendors, some of which had vanished. But even those I found again were rather disappointing. Georg had been five when we'd left Vienna the first time, and he had no memory of the amusement park; hence he was dependent on my stories, which

I embellished as temptingly as possible. For it was somewhat shameful that I, the seemingly omniscient big brother, who had told him about the Prometheus of Aeschylus, the French Revolution, the law of gravitation, and the theory of evolution, was now regaling him with, of all things, the Messina Earthquake in the Tunnel of Fun and the Mouth of Hell in front of it.

I must have painted it in dreadful colors, for when we finally found the Tunnel of Fun and stood in front of the Mouth of Hell, into which the devils were leisurely feeding sinners skewered on pitchforks, Georg looked at me in surprise and said: "And you were really scared of that?"

"I wasn't. I was eight already, but you two were scared; you were both still very little."

I noticed he was about to lose his respect for me. But he didn't feel right about it. He was very fond of our evening conversations, even though they had only just begun, and so he showed no desire to view the Earthquake of Messina, which had lured us here in the first place. I was relieved to get out of it. I didn't want to see the earthquake either now, and I pulled him away quickly. In this way, I could preserve my memory in all its old magnificence.

But I didn't get off the hook so easily; I had to offer him something to make up for the disappointment. So I threw myself into the games of chance in the amusement park, even though they had never really interested me. There were various kinds, but the ring-toss game caught our eye because we saw several people winning, one after the other. I let him try it; he had no luck. I tried it myself; every toss missed. I tried again; it was virtually hexed. I had soon gotten so caught up in the game that he started tugging at my sleeve, but I wouldn't give up. He watched our monthly allowance dwindling and was quite capable of gauging the consequences, but he said nothing. He

didn't even say he'd like to try it again himself. I believe he understood that I couldn't bear the shame in front of him for my
inexplicably bad marksmanship, and that I had to make up for it
with a series of lucky tosses. He stared paralyzed, pulling himself together now and then; he looked like one of the automaton
figures in the Tunnel of Fun. I tossed and tossed; I kept tossing
more and more poorly. The two shames blended, flowing into
one. It seemed like a brief time, but it must have been long, for
suddenly all our money for May was gone.

Had it involved me alone, I wouldn't have taken it so badly.
But it also concerned my brother, for whose life I was responsible, for whom I had to be a surrogate father, so to speak, whom
I gave the loftiest advice, whom I tried to fill with high ideals.
In the Chemical Laboratory, where I had just started to work, I
would think of things that I felt I had to tell him in the evening,
things that would impress him so deeply that he would never
forget them. I believed—precisely because of my brotherly love
for him, which had become my predominant emotion—that
every sentence carried responsibility, that a single false thing
I told him would make him go a crooked way, that he could
thereby waste his life—and now I had wasted the whole month
of May, and no one must find out about it, least of all the Sussin family with whom we were living—I was scared they would
give us notice.

Luckily, no one we knew had watched my fall from grace,
and Georg instantly understood how important silence was. We
comforted each other with manly resolves. We used to eat lunch
regularly right near the Carl Theater, at the Benveniste Restau-
rant, where Grandfather had introduced us. But we didn't have
to eat there. We would make do with a yogurt and a piece of
bread. For supper, a piece of bread would suffice. How I was

going to come up with money—at least for this food—was
something I didn't tell him: I didn't know myself.

This little misfortune that I had caused was, I believe, what
made us become close—even closer than the nightly question-
and-answer game. We led our exceedingly chary life for one
month. I don't know how we could have managed without the
breakfast that Frau Sussin brought us every morning. We waited,
absolutely famished, for the café au lait and two rolls each. We
woke up earlier, washed earlier, and were already seated at the
square table when she entered the room with the tray. We quelled
any jittery movements that would have betrayed our eagerness;
we sat there stiffly as though having to memorize something together. She set great store by a few morning phrases. We always
had to tell her how we'd slept, and it was lucky that she spared
us her own accounts of how she'd slept.

But every morning, she most emphatically mentioned her
brother, who was in a Belgrade prison. "An idealist!" That was
how she began, plunging right in, never mentioning him without first calling him "An idealist!" She didn't share his political
convictions, of course; but she was proud of him, for he was
friendly with Henri Barbusse and Romain Rolland. He was ill;
he had suffered from tuberculosis at an early age; prison was
poison for him; good and copious food would have been especially important. When she carried breakfast in to us, the
steaming coffee, she thought of his deprivation, and so naturally she spoke about him. "He started very early, in school.
At his age," she pointed at Georg, "he was an idealist. He gave
speeches at school and was punished. Even though his teachers
were on his side, they had to punish him." She didn't approve
of his stubbornness but she never uttered a word of reproof. She
and her unmarried sister, who lived with the Sussins, had heard

any number of things about their brother's convictions. Serbian royalists cared as little for his views as good Austrians. And so the sisters had once and for all made it a habit to understand nothing about politics and to leave them to men.

Moshe Pijade—that was their brother's name—had always considered himself a revolutionary and a writer. The fact that he had gotten somewhere in these capacities was vouchsafed by the names of his French friends. The prison, and especially her brother's illness and hunger, greatly preoccupied Frau Sussin. The breakfast she carried into our room was something she would have wanted to give him; and so it was the least she could do to remember him every morning. True, she thus delayed us in our ravenousness; but to make up for it, she strengthened us by talking about her brother's hunger. He would never have owned up to being hungry. Even as a boy at home, he had never noticed he was hungry, for he had always been busy with his ideals. In this way, he had become a pillar for us. And every morning, we waited no less for Frau Sussin's story than for the café au lait with the good rolls. This was also the first time that Georg heard about tuberculosis, which subsequently became the content of his life.

We left the apartment together. Right in the courtyard, to the left, we saw Herr Fink, the tailor; he had been sitting at his sewing machine for a long time already. It was the first sound we heard upon awakening in the morning, as well as the last sound before falling asleep at night. Now we walked past the window of his shop and greeted him, the taciturn man with the painful cheekbones. When I saw him with the needles in his mouth, he looked as if he'd stuck a long needle through his cheek and couldn't talk. When he did say something after all, I was surprised; the needles he held in his lips, they, too, were gone.

There, in the window of his shop, was his sewing machine,

which he never left—a young man who never went out. By the
time I got to know him better, it was summer; the window was
open, the hum of the machine was audible in the courtyard,
softly accompanying the laughter of his wife, whose black,
voluptuous beauty filled the shop. If you wanted to see Fink
about tailoring and you knocked at the door of the small room
in which he lived with his family, you hesitated briefly before
entering, in order to hear his wife's laughter a bit longer and
to believe it. You knew very well that the joy with which the
shop received you wasn't meant for you; it was the joy of her
brimming body, which imparted its scent to everything. The
scent and the laughter permeated one another, and there were
also the occasional calls to Kamilla, the three-year-old daughter.
This child preferred playing near the threshold, right behind the
door—another reason why you opened it hesitatingly. And the
first thing you heard amid the laughter was the sentence: "Kamilla, get out of the way, let the gentleman come in." She always
said "the gentleman," even though I wasn't yet nineteen; and
she also said it if I was inside and a woman was coming in. The
instant she saw it was a woman, she briefly stopped laughing,
but never altered her sentence; which didn't surprise me, for
Herr Fink was a gentlemen's tailor. He would quickly look up,
his needles in his mouth. A huge, dreadful needle had pierced
both his cheeks—how could he have spoken? The laughter
spoke in his stead.

Karl Kraus and Veza

It was natural that the rumors about both these people should
reach me at the same time; they came from the same source,
from which everything new for me came at that time. And had I

been entirely on my own after arriving in Vienna or dependent on the university (which I was about to start), then I would have had a hard time with my new life. Every Saturday afternoon, I visited Alice Asriel and her son Hans at their home on Heinestrasse near the Prater Star, and here I found out enough things to last me for years: names that were completely new, and suspect, if only because I had never heard them before.

But the name I heard most often from the Asriels was Karl Kraus. He was, I heard, the strictest and greatest man living in Vienna today. No one found grace in his eyes. His lectures attacked everything that was bad and corrupt. He put out a magazine, I heard, written entirely by himself. Unsolicited manuscripts were undesirable; he refused contributions from anyone else; he never answered letters. Every word, every syllable in *Die Fackel* (*The Torch*) was written by him personally. It was like a court of law. *He* brought the charges and *he* passed judgment. There was no defense attorney; a lawyer was superfluous: Kraus was so fair that no one was accused unless he deserved it. Kraus never made a mistake; he couldn't make a mistake. Everything he produced was 100 percent accurate; never had such accuracy existed in literature. He took personal care of every comma, and anyone trying to find a typographical error in *Die Fackel* could toil for weeks on end. It was wisest not to look for any. Kraus hated war, I was told, and during the Great War he had managed to print many antiwar pieces in *Die Fackel*, despite the censors. He had exposed corruption, fought against graft that everyone else had held their tongues about. It was a miracle he hadn't landed in prison. He had written an eight-hundred-page play, *The Last Days of Mankind*, containing everything that had happened in the war. When he read aloud from it, you were simply flabbergasted. No one stirred in the auditorium, you didn't dare breathe. He read all parts himself, profiteers and generals, the scoundrels and the poor wretches who were the victims of the war—they all sounded as genuine as if they were standing in front of you. Anyone who had heard Kraus didn't want to go to the theater again, the theater was so boring compared with him; he was a whole theater by himself, but better, and this wonder of the world, this monster, this genius bore the highly ordinary name of Karl Kraus.

I would have believed anything about him but his name or that a man with this name could have been capable of doing the things ascribed to him. While the Asriels belabored me with items about him—which both mother and son greatly enjoyed—they mocked my distrust, my offense at this plain name; they kept pointing out that it's not the name that matters but the person, otherwise we—she or I—with our euphonious names would be superior to a man like Karl Kraus. Could I possibly imagine anything so ridiculous, anything so absurd?

They pressed the red journal into my hands; and much as I liked its name, *Die Fackel*, *The Torch*, it was absolutely impossible for me to read it. I tripped over the sentences; I couldn't understand them. Anything I did understand sounded like a joke, and I didn't care for jokes. He also talked about local events and typographical errors, which struck me as terribly unimportant. "This is all such nonsense, how can you read it? I even find a newspaper more interesting. You can at least understand something. Here, you drudge away, and nothing comes of it!" I was honestly indignant at the Asriels, and I recalled my schoolmate's father in Frankfurt who, whenever I visited his home, read to me out of the local author Friedrich Stoltze and would then say at the end of a poem: "Anyone who doesn't like this deserves to be shot. This is the greatest poet who ever lived." I told the Asriels, not without scorn, about this poet of the Frankfurt dialect. I badgered them, I wouldn't let go, and I embarrassed them so greatly that they suddenly started telling me about the elegant ladies who attended every lecture given by Karl Kraus and were so carried away by him that they always sat in the first row so that he might notice their enthusiasm. But with these accounts, the Asriels missed the boat with me altogether: "Elegant ladies! In furs no doubt! Perfumed aesthetes! And he's not ashamed to read to such people!"

"But they're not like *that*! These are highly educated women! Why shouldn't he read to them? They understand every allusion. Before he even utters a sentence, they've already caught the drift. They've read all of English and French literature, not just German! They know their Shakespeare by heart, not to mention Goethe. You just can't imagine how educated they are!"

"How do you know? Have you ever talked to them? Do you talk to such people? Doesn't the smell of the perfume make you sick? I wouldn't spend one minute talking to someone like that. I just couldn't. Even if she were really beautiful, I'd turn my back on her and at most I'd say: 'Don't put Shakespeare on your lips. He'll be so disgusted he'll turn over in his grave. And leave Goethe in peace. *Faust* isn't for monkeys.'"

But now the Asriels felt they had gotten through to me, for both of them cried at once: "What about Veza! Do you know Veza? Have you ever heard of Veza?"

Now this was a name that surprised me. I liked it right off though I wouldn't admit it. The name reminded me of one of my stars, Vega in the constellation of Lyra, yet it sounded all the more beautiful because of the difference in one consonant. But I said gruffly: "What kind of a name is that again? No one's got a name like that. It *would* be an unusual name. But it doesn't exist."

"It does exist. We know her. She lives on Ferdinandstrasse with her mother. Ten minutes from here. A beautiful woman with a Spanish face. She's very fine and sensitive, and no one could ever say anything ugly in her presence. She's read more than all of us put together. She knows the longest English poems by heart, plus half of Shakespeare. And Molière and Flaubert and Tolstoy."

"How old is this paragon?"

"Twenty-seven."

"And she's read everything already?"

"Yes, and even more. But she reads intelligently. She knows why she likes it. She can explain it. You can't put anything over on her."

"And she sits in the front row to hear Karl Kraus?"

"Yes, at every lecture."

On April 17, 1924, the three-hundredth lecture of Karl Kraus took place. The Great Concert House Hall had been selected for the occasion. I was told that even this building would not be large enough to hold the multitude of fans. However, the Asriels ordered tickets in time and insisted on taking me along. Why always fight about *Die Fackel*? It was better to hear the great man in person for once. Then I could form my own verdict. Hans donned his most arrogant smirk; the thought that anybody, much less a brand-new high school graduate, fresh out of Frankfurt, could possibly resist Karl Kraus in person made not only Hans smirk: his nimble, delicate mother couldn't help smiling as she repeatedly assured me how greatly she envied me for this first experience with Karl Kraus.

She prepared me with a few well-turned bits of advice: I shouldn't be frightened by the wild applause of the audience: these weren't the usual operetta Viennese who assembled here, no Heuriger winos, but also no decadent clique of aesthetes à la Hofmannsthal. This was the genuine intellectual Vienna, the best and the soundest in this apparently deteriorated city. I'd

be amazed at how quickly this audience caught the subtlest allusion. These people were already laughing when he began a
sentence, and by the time the sentence was over, the whole auditorium was roaring. He had trained his public carefully; he
could do anything he wanted to with his people, and yet don't
forget, these were all highly educated people, almost all of
them academic professionals or at least students. She said she
had never seen a stupid face among them; you could look all
you liked, it was futile. Her greatest delight was to read the re-
sponses to the speaker's punchlines in the faces of the listeners.
It was very difficult for her, she said, not to come along this
time, but she greatly preferred the Middle Concert House Hall:
you could miss nothing there, absolutely nothing. In the Great
Hall—even though his voice carried very nicely—you did miss
a few things, and she was so keen on every word of his that she
didn't want to lose a single one. That was why she had given
me her ticket this time, it was meant more as an honor to him
to appear at this three-hundredth lecture, and so many people
were thronging to attend, that her presence really didn't matter.

I knew in what straitened circumstances the Asriels lived—
even though they never talked about it; there were so many
more important, namely intellectual things that totally absorbed
them. They insisted on my being their guest on this occasion,
and that was why Frau Asriel decided not to be present at the
triumphal affair.

I managed to guess one intention of the evening, which they
concealed from me. And as soon as Hans and I had taken our
seats way in back, I stealthily peered around the audience. Hans
did the same, no less stealthily; we both concealed from one
another whom we were looking for. It was the same person. I
had forgotten that the lady with the unusual name always sat
in the first row; and though I had never seen a picture of her, I

hoped I would suddenly come upon her somewhere in our row. It seemed inconceivable to me that I couldn't recognize her on the basis of the description they had given me: the longest English poem that she knew by heart was Poe's "The Raven," they said, and she looked like a raven herself, a raven magically transformed into a Spanish woman. Hans was too agitated himself to interpret my agitation correctly, he stubbornly gazed forward, checking the front entrances into the auditorium. Suddenly, he gave a start, but not arrogantly now, rather embarrassedly, and he said: "There she is, she just came in."

"Where?" I said, without asking whom he meant. "Where?"

"In the first row, on the far left. I figured as much, the first row."

I could see very little from so far away; nevertheless, I recognized her raven hair and I was satisfied. I quelled the ironic comments I had prepared, and I saved them for later. Soon, Karl Kraus himself came out and was greeted by an applause the likes of which I had never experienced, not even at concerts. My eyes were still unpracticed, but he seemed to take little notice of the applause, he hesitated a bit, standing still. There was something vaguely crooked about his figure. When he sat down and began to read, I was overwhelmed by his voice, which had something unnaturally vibrating about it, like a decelerated crowing. But this impression quickly vanished, for his voice instantly changed and kept changing incessantly, and one was very soon amazed at the variety that he was capable of. The hush in which his voice was at first received was indeed reminiscent of a concert; but the prevailing expectation was altogether different. From the start, and throughout the performance, it was the quiet before a storm. His very first punchline, really just an allusion, was anticipated by a laughter that terrified me. It sounded enthusiastic and fanatic, satisfied and ominous at once; it came before he had actu-

ally made his point. But even then, I couldn't have understood
it, for it bore on something local, something that not only was
connected to Vienna, but also had become an intimate matter
between Kraus and his listeners, who yearned for it. It wasn't
individuals who were laughing, it was many people together. If
I focused on someone cater-corner in front of me in order to
understand the distortions of his laughter, the causes of which I
couldn't grasp, the same laughter boomed behind me and a few
seats away from me on all sides. And only then did I notice that
Hans, who was sitting next to me and whom I had meanwhile
forgotten, was laughing, too, in exactly the same way. It was always many people, and it was always a hungry laughter. It soon
dawned on me that the people had come to a repast and not to
celebrate Karl Kraus.

I don't know what he said on this evening of my earliest
encounter with him. A hundred lectures that I heard later have
piled up on top of that evening. Perhaps I didn't know even
then, because the audience, which frightened me, absorbed me
so thoroughly. I couldn't see Kraus too well: a face narrow-
ing down to the chin, a face so mobile that it couldn't be pin-
pointed, penetrating and exotic, like the face of an animal, but
a new, a different face, an unfamiliar one. I was flabbergasted
by the gradations that this voice was capable of; the auditorium
was enormous, yet a quivering in his voice was imparted to
the entire space. Chairs and people seemed to yield under this
quivering; I wouldn't have been surprised if the chairs had bent.
The dynamics of such a mobbed auditorium under the impact
of that voice—an impact persisting even when the voice grew
silent—can no more be depicted than the Wild Hunt. But I believe that the impact was closest to this legendary event. Imagine the army of the Wild Hunt in a concert hall, trapped, locked

up, and forced to sit still, and then repeatedly summoned to its true nature. This image doesn't bring us much closer to reality; but I couldn't hit on a more accurate image, and thus I have to forgo transmitting a notion of Karl Kraus in his actuality.

Nevertheless, during intermission, I left the auditorium, and Hans introduced me to the woman who was to be chief witness to the effect I had just experienced. But she was quite calm and self-controlled, everything seemed easier to endure in the first row. She looked very exotic, a precious object, a creature one would never have expected in Vienna, but rather on a Persian miniature. Her high, arched eyebrows, her long, black lashes, with which she played like a virtuoso, now quickly, now slowly—it all confused me. I kept looking at her lashes instead of into her eyes, and I was surprised at the small mouth.

She didn't ask me how I liked the performance; she said she didn't want to embarrass me. "It's the first time you're here." She sounded as if she were the hostess, as if the hall were her home and she were handing everything to the audience from her seat in the first row. She knew the people, she knew who always came, and she noticed, without compromising herself, that I was new here. I felt as if she were the one who had invited me, and I thanked her for her hospitality, which consisted in her taking notice of me. My companion, whose forte was not tact, said: "A great day for him," and jerked his shoulder in my direction.

"One can't tell as yet," she said. "For the moment, it's confusing."

I didn't sense this as mockery, even though each of her sentences had a mocking undertone; I was happy to hear her say something so precisely attuned to my frame of mind. But this very sympathy confused me, just like the lashes, which were now performing lofty motions, as though they had important things to conceal. So I said the plainest and most undemanding thing that could be said in these circumstances: "It sure is confusing."

This may have sounded surly; but not to her, for she asked: "Are you Swiss?"

There was nothing I would have rather been. During my three years in Frankfurt, my passion for Switzerland had reached a boiling point. I knew her mother was a Sephardi, née Calderon, whose third husband was a very old man named Altaras; and so she must have recognized my name as being Ladino. Why did she inquire about the thing I would have most liked to be? I had told no one about the old pain of that separation; and I made sure not to expose myself to the Asriels, who, for all their satirical arrogance, or perhaps precisely because of Karl Kraus, plumed themselves on being Viennese. Thus, the beautiful Raven Lady couldn't have learned about my unhappiness from anyone, and her first direct question struck me to the quick. It moved me more deeply than the lecture, which—as she had accurately said—was confusing, for the moment. I answered: "No, unfortunately," meaning that unfortunately I wasn't Swiss. I thereby put myself completely in her hands. The word "unfortunately" betrayed more than anyone knew about me at that time. She seemed to understand, all mockery vanished from her features, and she said: "I'd love to be British." Hans, as was his wont, pounced upon her with a flood of chitchat, from which I could glean only that one could be very familiar with Shakespeare without having to be English, and what did the English today have in common with Shakespeare anyhow? But she paid as little attention to him as I, even though, as I soon saw, she missed nothing of what he said.

"You ought to hear Karl Kraus reading Shakespeare. Have you been to England?"

"Yes, as a child, I went to school there for two years. It was my first school."

"I often visit relatives there. You have to tell me about your childhood in England. Come and drop in on me soon!"

All preciousness was gone, even the coquettish way she paid homage to the lecture. She spoke about something that was close to her and important, and she compared it with something important to me, which she had touched quickly and lightly and yet not offensively. As we stepped back into the auditorium, and Hans, in the brief time remaining, quickly asked me two or three times what I thought of her, I pretended not to understand, and it was only when I sensed that he was about to pronounce her name that I said, in order to forestall him: "Veza?" But by now Karl Kraus had reappeared and the tempest broke loose and her name went under in the tempest.

Early Honor of the Intellect

The young people I associated with had one thing in common, no matter how varied they may have been otherwise: all they were interested in was intellectual matters. They knew about everything in newspapers, but they grew excited when it came to books. Their attention focused on just a few books; it would have been despicable not to know about these. But still, it cannot be said that they parroted some general or leading opinion. They read such books themselves; they read passages from them aloud to one another; they quoted them from memory. Criticism was not only permitted, it was desired; they tried to find vulnerable points that compromised the public reputation of a book, and they heatedly thrashed out these points, setting great store by logic, snappy comebacks, and wit. Except for everything ordained by Karl Kraus, nothing was definite; they loved rattling away at things that found acceptance too easily and too quickly.

The particularly important books were those allowing great scope for discussion. The heyday of Spengler's impact, which I had witnessed at the boardinghouse table in Frankfurt, seemed past. Or had his effect in Vienna not been so decisive? However, a pessimistic note was unmistakable here, too. Otto Weininger's *Sex and Character*, though published twenty years earlier, cropped up in every discussion. All the pacifist books of my wartime days in Zurich had been superseded by Karl Kraus's *The Last Days of Mankind*. The literature of decadence didn't count at all. Hermann Bahr was a has-been: he had played too many parts; none was now taken seriously. Particularly decisive for a writer's prestige was his conduct *during* the war. Thus, Schnitzler's name remained intact; he was no longer urgent, but he was never scorned, for unlike the others, he had never lent himself to war propaganda. Nor was it a propitious time for Old Austria. The monarchy, having crumbled, was discredited; the only monarchists left, I was told, were among the "candle women" (the old women who spent their days in churches, lighting candles). The dismemberment of Austria, the amazing survival of Vienna—now an oversized capital—as a "hydrocephalic" head, was on everyone's mind. But by no means did they relinquish the intellectual claim that is part of a metropolis. They were interested in everything in the world, as if the world might value what they thought, and they clung to the specific proclivities of Vienna, such as had developed through generations, especially music. Whether musical or not, they attended concerts, standing room. The cult of Gustav Mahler, a composer still unknown to the world at large, had reached its first high point here; his greatness was undisputed.

There was hardly a conversation in which Freud's name

did not pop up, a name no less compressed for me than that of Karl Kraus; yet the name Freud was more alluring because of its dark diphthong and the *d* at the end, as well as its literal meaning, "joy." A whole series of monosyllabic names was circulating; they would have sufficed for the most disparate needs. But Freud had become very special; some of his coinages had become everyday terms. He was still haughtily rejected by the leading figures at the university. Freudian slips, however, had become a sort of parlor game. In order to use this buzzword frequently, slips were produced in spates. During any conversation, no matter how animated and spontaneous it may have sounded, there arrived a moment when you could read on your interlocutor's lips: here comes a Freudian slip. And it was already out; you could already start analyzing it, uncovering the processes that had led to it, and thereby you could talk about your private life in tireless detail, without seeming overbearingly intimate, for you were involved in shedding light on a process of universal, even scientific, interest.

Nevertheless, as I soon realized, this portion of Freudianism was the most plausible. When slips were being discussed, I never got the feeling that something was being twisted to make a point, to fit into a never-changing and hence soon boring pattern. Also, each person had his own way of devising Freudian slips. Clever things came out, and sometimes there was even a genuine slip, which you could tell was unplanned.

Now, Oedipus complexes were an altogether different affair. People had fistfights over them, everybody wanted his own, or else you threw them at other people's heads. Anyone present at these social functions could bank on one thing: if he didn't bring up his Oedipus complex himself, then it was hurled at him by someone else, after a ruthlessly penetrating glare. In some way or other, everybody (even posthumous sons) got his Oedipus;

and eventually, the whole company sat there in guilt, everyone a potential mother-lover and father-killer, hazily wreathed with mythical names—all of us secret kings of Thebes.

I had my doubts about the matter, perhaps because I had known murderous jealousy since early childhood and was quite aware of its highly disparate motives. But even if one of the countless advocates of this Freudian theory had succeeded in convincing me of its universal validity, I would never have accepted this name for the phenomenon. I knew who Oedipus was, I had read Sophocles, I refused to be deprived of the enormity of this fate. By the time I arrived in Vienna, the Oedipus complex had turned into a hackneyed prattle that no one failed to drone out; even the haughtiest scorner of mobs wasn't too good for an "Oedipus."

Admittedly, however, they were still under the impact of the recent war. No one could forget the murderous cruelty they had witnessed. Many who had taken an active part in it were now home again. They knew what things they had been capable of doing—on orders—and they eagerly grabbed at all the explanations that psychoanalysis offered for homicidal tendencies. The banality of their collective compulsion was mirrored in the banality of the explanation. It was odd to see how *harmless* everyone became as soon as he got his Oedipus. When multiplied thousands of times, the most dreadful destiny crumbles into a particle of dust. Myth reaches into a human being, throttling him and rattling him. The "law of nature," to which myth is reduced, is nothing more than a little pipe for him to dance to.

The young people I associated with hadn't been to war. But they all attended Karl Kraus's lectures and knew *The Last Days of Mankind*—one could say: by heart. This was their chance to catch up with the war that had overshadowed their youth, and there can hardly be a more concentrated and more legitimate method for getting acquainted with war. It thus constantly remained before their eyes; and since they didn't wish to forget, since they hadn't been forced to escape the war, it haunted them incessantly. They did not investigate the dynamics of human beings as a crowd, in which people had devotedly and willingly gone into the war, remaining trapped in it—albeit in a different way—years after it was lost. Nothing had been said about this crowd, no theory of these phenomena existed as yet. Freud's comments about them were, as I soon found out myself, completely inadequate. So people contented themselves with the psychology of individual processes, such as Freud offered in unshakable self-assurance. Whenever I came out with anything concerning the enigma of the crowd, which I had been mulling over since Frankfurt, they found my remarks not worth discussing; there were no intellectual formulas for what I said. Anything that couldn't be reduced to a formula did not exist, it was a figment of the imagination, it had no substance; otherwise, it would have appeared in some way or other in Freud or Kraus.

The lacuna I felt here could not be filled for the time being. It wasn't long before the "illumination" came, during my first winter in Vienna (1924–1925): the "illumination" that determined the entire rest of my life. I have to call it an "illumination," for this experience was connected with a special light; it came upon me very suddenly, as a violent feeling of expansion. I was walking down a street in Vienna, with a quick and unusual energetic motion, which lasted as long as the "illumination" itself. I have never forgotten what happened that night. The illumination has remained present to me as a single instant; now, fifty-five years later, I still view it as something *unexhausted*. While its intellectual content may be so simple and small that its effect is inexplicable, I nevertheless drew strength from it as from a revelation—the strength to devote thirty-five years of my life, twenty of them full years, to the explanation of what a crowd really is, how power comes into being from a crowd and how it feeds back upon it. At the time, I was unaware of how much the manner of my enterprise owed to the fact that there was someone like Freud in Vienna, that people talked about him in such a way as if every individual could, by himself, of his own accord and at his own resolve, find explanations for things. Since Freud's ideas did not suffice for me, failing to explain the phenomenon that was most important to me, I was sincerely, if naively, convinced that I was undertaking something different, something totally independent of him. It was clear to me that I needed him as an adversary. But the fact that he served as a kind of model for me—this was something that no one could have made me see at that time.

The illumination, which I recall so clearly, took place on Alserstrasse. It was night; in the sky, I noticed the red reflection of the city, and I craned my neck to look up at it. I paid no attention to where I was walking. I tripped several times, and in such an instant of stumbling, while craning my neck, gazing at the red sky, which I didn't really like, it suddenly flashed through my mind: I realized that there is such a thing as a crowd instinct, which is always in conflict with the personality instinct, and that the struggle between the two of them can explain the course of human history. This couldn't have been a new idea; but it was new to me, for it struck me with tremendous force. Everything now happening in the world could, it seemed to me, be traced back to that struggle. The fact that there was such a thing as a crowd was something I had experienced in Frankfurt. And now I had experienced it again in Vienna. The fact that there was something that forces people to become a *crowd* seemed obvious and irrefutable to me. The fact that the crowd fell apart into individuals was no less evident; likewise, the fact that these individuals wanted to become a crowd again. I had no doubt about the existence of the tendency to become a crowd and to become an individual again. These tendencies seemed so strong and so blind that I regarded them as an instinct, and labeled them one. However, I didn't know what the crowd itself really was. This was an enigma I now planned to solve; it seemed like the most crucial enigma, or at least the most important enigma, in our world.

But how stale, how drained, how anemic my description now sounds. I said, "tremendous force," and that's exactly what it was. For the energy I was suddenly imbued with made me walk faster, almost run. I dashed along Alserstrasse, all the way to the Gürtel; I felt as if I'd gotten here in the twinkling of an eye. My ears were buzzing; the sky was still red, as though it would always be this color; I was still stumbling, but never falling; my stumbles were an integral part of my overall movement. I have never again experienced motion in this way; nor can I say that I would care to do so — it was too peculiar, too exotic, a lot swifter than is appropriate for me, an alien thing that came out of me, but that I didn't control.

Patriarchs

Everyone found Veza exotic. She drew attention wherever she went. An Andalusian who had never been in Seville, but spoke about it as though she had grown up there. You had encountered her in *The Arabian Nights*, the very first time you'd read any of the tales. She was a familiar figure in Persian miniatures. But despite this Oriental omnipresence, she was no dream personage; your conception of her was very definite; her image never melted, it never dissolved; it retained its sharp outline and its radiance.

Her beauty was breathtaking, and I threw up a resistance
to it. As an inexperienced creature, barely out of boyhood,
clumsy, unpolished, a Caliban next to her (albeit a very young
one), awkward, insecure, gross, incapable in her presence of the
one thing that may have been in my control, namely speech, I
cast about for the most absurd insults before seeing her, insults
to armor me against her; "precious" was the least; "saccharine,"
"courtly," a "princess"; able to use only half of language, the
elegant half; alien to anything real, inconsiderate, rigorous, relentless. But I only had to recall that lecture on April 17 to dis-
arm these accusations. The audience had cheered Karl Kraus not
for his elegance, but for his rigor. And when I was introduced
to her during intermission, she had seemed controlled and lofty,
and was not about to flee the second part of the program. Since
then, at every lecture (I now attended all of them), I had stealthily peered around for her and always found her. I had greeted
her across the auditorium, never daring to approach her. And I
was dismayed whenever she didn't notice me; mostly, however,
she returned my greeting.

Even here, she drew attention, the most exotic creature in
this audience. Since she always sat in the first row, Karl Kraus
must have noticed her. I found myself wondering what he
thought of her. She never clapped, it must have struck him. But
the fact that she was always back again, in the same place, was
a tribute that must have mattered even to him. During the first
year, when I didn't dare visit her despite her invitation, I felt
more and more irritated about her sitting in the front row. Failing to understand the nature of my irritation, I concocted the
most peculiar things. I felt it was too loud up there: how could
she stand the intensest parts? Some of the characters in *The Last
Days of Mankind* made you feel so ashamed, you just had to
sink into the ground. And what did she do when she had to cry,

during Hauptmann's *The Weavers*, during *King Lear*? How could she endure his watching her cry? Or did she want him to watch her? Was she proud of this reaction? Was she paying homage to him by weeping in public? She was certainly not devoid of shame; she struck me as being extremely modest, more than anyone else; and then there she sat, showing Karl Kraus everything he did to her. She never went over to the platform after the reading; many people tried to crowd up there, she merely stood and watched. Shaken and shattered as I was every time, I, too, remained in the auditorium for a long while, standing and applauding until my hands ached. In this state of mind, I lost sight of her; I wouldn't have found her again but for her conspicuously parted, blue-black hair. After the reading, she did nothing that I could have regarded as unworthy. She stayed in the auditorium no longer than others; when he took his bows, she wasn't among the very last to leave.

Perhaps it was her concurrence that I sought, for the excitement after these readings persisted on and on; whether he read *The Weavers*, *Timon of Athens*, or *The Last Days of Mankind*, these were high points of existence. I lived from one such occasion to the next; anything occurring in between belonged to a profane world. I sat alone in the auditorium, speaking to no one, making sure I left the building alone. I observed Veza because I was avoiding her; I didn't realize how deeply I longed to be sitting next to her. This would have been quite impossible so long as she sat in the first row, visible to all. I was jealous of the god I was imbued with. Even though I didn't try to barricade myself against him anywhere, at any point, even though my every pore was open to him, I begrudged him the exotic creature with black, parted hair, sitting near him, laughing for him and weeping and bending under his tempest. I wanted to be next to her, but not up front, where she was; it could only be where the god didn't see her, where we could exchange glances to communicate what he did to us.

Although steadfast in my proud resolution not to visit her, I was jealous of her and failed to realize that I was gathering strength to abduct her from the god. At home, while thinking I would suffocate under my mother's animosity, which my conduct provoked, I pictured the moment when I would ring Veza's doorbell. I shoved that instant away from me like a solid object, but it came closer and closer. To remain strong, I imagined how the flood of Asriel chitchat would smash over me. "How was it? What did she say? I thought so! She doesn't like that. Of course not." I could already hear the warnings of my mother, who would be told everything "hot off the press." In an imaginary repartee, I anticipated the conversations that eventually did take place. While painstakingly avoiding any closer contact with Veza and unable to figure out what I could say to her that wasn't too gross or too ignorant, I devised all the nasty, hateful things I would get to hear about her at home.

Notwithstanding my self-inflicted prohibitions, I always knew I would go there; and every lecture I saw her at made this realization more intense. But when the time came, one free afternoon, more than a year had passed since the invitation. No one learned that I was going; my feet found their own way to Ferdinandstrasse. I cudgeled my brain to come up with a plausible explanation that didn't sound immature or servile. She had said she wished she were English; what could be more obvious than asking her about English literature? I had recently heard *King Lear*, one of Karl Kraus's grandest readings; of all the Shakespeare plays, it was the one that absorbed me the most. I was haunted by the image of the old man on the heath. She must have known the play in English. There was something about

King Lear that I couldn't cope with. This was what I wanted to talk to her about.

I rang, she herself opened, greeting me as though she'd been expecting me. I had seen her just a few days earlier at the reading in the Middle Concert Hall. By chance, as I thought, I had come near her, applauding, on my feet with the others. I behaved like a lunatic, waving my arms, shrieking "Bravo! Bravo! Karl Kraus!" clapping. I wouldn't stop, no one stopped, I dropped my hands only when they ached. And then I noticed someone next to me, in a trance like myself, but not clapping. It was Veza; I couldn't tell whether she had noticed me.

Letting me into her apartment, she took me through the dark corridor to her room, where a warm radiance welcomed me. I sat down amid books and paintings, but I didn't take any closer look at them, for she sat opposite me at the table and said: "You didn't notice me. I was at *Lear.*"

I told her I had very much noticed her, and that was why I had come. Then I asked her why Lear has to die in the end. He was a very old man, granted, and had suffered terrible things. But I would gladly have gone away knowing he had overcome everything and was still there. He should always be there. If a different hero, a younger one, were to die in a play, I was ready to accept it, especially braggarts and fighters, the sort people called heroes; I didn't mind their dying, for their prestige was based on their causing the deaths of so many other people. But Lear, who had grown so old, ought to grow even older. We should never learn about his death. So many other people had died in this play. But someone should survive, and this someone was Lear.

"But why he of all people? Doesn't he deserve to have peace and quiet at last?"

"Death is a punishment. He deserves to live."

"The eldest? Should the eldest live even longer? While young people have preceded him into death and been deceived of their lives?"

"*More* dies with the eldest. All his years die. There is a lot more that perishes with him."

"Then you'd like people who are as old as the Biblical patriarchs?"

"Yes! Yes! Don't you?"

"No. I could show you one. He lives two rooms away. Perhaps he'll make his presence known while you're here."

"You mean your stepfather. I've heard about him."

"You couldn't have heard anything about him that approaches the truth. The only ones who know the truth are we, my mother and I."

It came too quickly for her, she didn't want to tell me about him right away. She had managed to protect her room, her atmosphere from him. Had I had an inkling of what it cost her, I would have avoided this subject of old people who ought to keep on living because they have grown so old. I had come to her blind, as it were, from *Lear*, and thankful that we had experienced something wonderful together. I had to talk about it. I was in Lear's debt, for he had driven me to her. Without him, I would surely have waited longer before coming; and now, here I sat, filled with him; how could I not have paid homage to him. I knew how much Shakespeare of all authors meant to her, and I was convinced there was nothing she would rather speak about. I didn't get to ask about her trips to England, and she didn't think about my childhood there. Originally, she had invited me over so that I might tell her about it. Now, I had struck her sorest point; for both of them, her mother and herself, life with this stepfather was a torment. He was almost ninety, and here I came and seemed to be saying if a man was that old, it was best that he keep on living.

I hurt her so deeply at my first visit that it was very nearly my last. She pulled herself together, because she was so visibly frightened; she felt as if she had to justify herself, and she told me—it was difficult enough for her—how she made herself at home in this hell.

The apartment in which Veza lived with her mother consisted of three fairly large rooms in a row, their windows facing Ferdinandstrasse. This apartment was in the mezzanine, not very high; it was easy to catch their attention from the street. A hallway led from the apartment door past the main rooms, which were left of the hallway; the kitchen and the other rooms were to its right. Behind the kitchen lay a small, dark maid's room, so out of the way that no one thought about it.

The first of the three left-hand rooms was the parents' bedroom; Veza's stepfather, a haggard old man of almost ninety, lay in bed or sat in a bathrobe, upright, in front of the fire in the corner. Next came the dining room, used mostly for company. The third room was Veza's room, which she had furnished to her own taste, in colors she liked, with books and paintings, unsettled and yet serious. It was a room that you entered with a sigh of relief and were sorry to leave, a room so different from the rest of the apartment that you thought you were dreaming when you stood at its threshold—a severe threshold to a blossoming place. Very few people were allowed to cross into it.

The occupant of this room reigned over the others with an unbelievable control. It was no reign of terror; everything occurred soundlessly; a raising of the eyebrows sufficed to drive intruders away from the threshold. Her chief enemy was her stepfather, Mento Altaras. In earlier days, before I came on the scene, the struggle had still been waged openly, the demarcation lines had not been drawn, and it was still uncertain whether peace would ever be concluded. Back then, the stepfather would suddenly slam open the door and bang his cane repeatedly and ominously on the threshold. The skinny, haggard man stood there in his bathrobe, his narrow, somber, emaciated head resembling that of Dante, whose name he had never heard. Momentarily pausing in his banging, he spouted dreadful Ladino curses and threats, and, alternately banging and cursing, he stood at the threshold until his wish, for meat or wine, had been fulfilled.

As an adolescent girl, the stepdaughter had tried to help herself by locking both her doors—to the dining room and to the hall—from the inside. Then, as she grew older and more attractive, the keys used to vanish; and when the locksmith brought new ones, these vanished, too. The mother would go out, the maid wasn't always around, and when the old man craved something, he had the strength of three despite his age and could have overcome his wife, his stepdaughter, and the maid. They had every reason to be scared. The mother and the daughter couldn't stand the thought of separating for good. In order to remain in her mother's apartment, Veza devised a tactic for taming the old man. Her tactic demanded a strength, insight, and persistence that were unheard of in an eighteen-year-old girl. What happened was that the old man would receive nothing if he left his room. He could knock, rage, curse, threaten, all to no avail. He got neither wine nor meat until he was back in his room; if he asked for them then, they were instantly brought. It was a Pavlovian method, thought up by the stepdaughter, who knew nothing about Pavlov. It took the old man several months to give in to his fate. He saw that he received juicier and juicier beefsteaks, older and older wines by skipping his assaults. If ever he did lose his temper again and appeared at the forbidden threshold, cursing and raging, he was punished and got nothing to eat or drink before evening.

He had spent most of his life in Sarajevo, where, as a child, he had peddled hot corn on the cob in the streets. People talked about these beginnings. That was back in the middle of the past century, and his origins had become the most important part of his legend, its commencement. You learned nothing about his later life. There was an enormous leap. Before retiring from his business in old age, he had become one of the richest men in Sarajevo and Bosnia. He owned countless houses (forty-seven was the number that you always kept hearing) and huge forests. His sons, who took over his business, lived in grand style; it was no surprise that they wanted to get the old man out of Sarajevo. He insisted that they live frugally and quietly and not flaunt their wealth. He was renowned for both his avarice and his harshness: he refused to donate to charities, which was considered scandalous. He showed up unannounced at the great festivities given by his sons and drove the guests out with a cane. They managed to get the widower, who was over seventy, to remarry in Vienna. A very beautiful widow, much younger than he, Rachel Calderon, was the bait he couldn't resist. The sons breathed a sigh of relief the instant he was in Vienna. The eldest son—and this was unusual back then—bought himself a private airplane, which greatly enhanced his prestige in their hometown. From time to time, he came to Vienna, bringing his father cash—thick packets of banknotes; the father demanded the money in this form.

During the first few years in Vienna, the old man still went out, refusing to let anyone accompany him. He donned worn-out trousers and a baggy, threadbare overcoat, and, in his left hand, he carried a raggedy hat, which looked as if it came from a garbage can. He kept the hat in a secret place and refused to let it be cleaned. No one understood why he took it along, since he never put it on.

One day, the maid came home all atremble and said she had just seen the master at a midtown street corner, the hat had lain open in front of him, and a passerby had tossed in a coin. No sooner was he back than his wife confronted him about it. He grew so furious that they were afraid he would kill her with the cane, with which he never parted. She was a gentle, terribly kind person and normally stayed out of his way; but this time, she wouldn't let up. She grabbed the hat and threw it away. Without the hat, he wouldn't go begging anymore. However, he continued to wear the worn-out trousers and the threadbare coat whenever he left the house. The maid was dispatched to observe him and followed him all the long way to Naschmarkt. She was so scared of him that she lost the trail. He returned with a bag of pears, holding them up triumphantly to his wife and his stepdaughter: he crowed that he had gotten them for free, from a market woman; and truly, he could look so famished and down-at-the-heels that even hard-boiled hawkers at Naschmarkt felt sorry for him and handed him fruit that wasn't even rotten.

At home, he had other worries: he had to hide the thick packets of banknotes somewhere in the bedroom, so that they'd always be at hand. The mattresses on both beds were bursting with them, a subcarpet of paper money had accumulated between the rug and the floor; of his many shoes, he could only wear one pair: the others were chock full of cash. His dresser contained a good dozen pairs of socks, which no one was allowed to touch, and whose contents he frequently checked. Only two pairs, which he wore alternately, were used by him. His wife received a weekly amount of household money, carefully counted out; it had been established by his son in an agreement with her. The stepfather had tried to cheat her out of part of it, but this affected his wine and meat, of which he devoured enormous quantities; so he then paid the stipulated amount.

He ate so much that they feared for his health. Nor did he stick to the usual meals. At breakfast, he already asked for meat and wine, and for the midmorning snack, long before lunch, he asked for the same. He wanted nothing else. When his wife tried to satisfy his appetite with side dishes, rice and vegetables, to keep him from devouring so much meat, he scornfully sent the food back. And when she tried again, he angrily dumped it on the carpet, ate only the meat in one gulp, and demanded more, saying they had given him far too little. There was no coping with his raging hunger, which concentrated on this one bloody food. The wife summoned a doctor, sedate, experienced, himself a native of Sarajevo, informed about the old man, speaking his language, and able to converse with him fluently. Nevertheless, the old man refused to be examined. He said there was nothing wrong with him, he had always been skinny, his only medicine was meat and wine, and if he didn't get as much of them as he wanted, he would go into the streets and *beg* for them. He had noticed that nothing horrified his family so deeply as his lust to beg. They took his threat as seriously as he meant it. The doctor warned him that if he kept on eating like that, he'd be dead within two years; to which the old man replied with a terrible curse. He wanted meat, nothing else. He had never eaten anything else, he said; he had no intention of becoming an ox at the age of eighty. That was that, *ya basta!*

Two years later, instead of him, it was the doctor who died. The old man was always delighted when people died. But this time his joy kept him awake for several nights, and he celebrated with meat and wine. The next doctor they tried it with, a man in his late forties, sturdy and very much of a meat-eater himself, had even less luck. The old man turned his back on him, refused to say a word, and dismissed him without cursing him. The doctor died like his predecessor; but this time it took longer. The old man took no notice of his death. Survival had now become second nature for him; meat and wine were nourishment enough, and he needed no more doctors as victims. One more attempt was made when his wife fell ill and lamented *her* complaint to the doctor. She said she wasn't getting enough sleep: her husband would wake up in the middle of the night and ask for his feed. Since he was going out less, it had become worse. The physician, a daredevil—perhaps he didn't know about his predecessors' fate—insisted on having a look at the old man, who was devouring his bloody beefsteak in the next bed, unconcerned about his sick wife. The doctor grabbed the plate and scolded him: What did he think he was doing? This was mortally dangerous! Did he realize he was going blind? The old man got scared for the first time; but the reason for his fright didn't come out until later.

Nothing changed about his food intake; but he totally gave up going out; now and then, he locked himself up in his bedroom for an hour or two—something he had never done before. He wouldn't respond to any knocks. They heard him poking around in the fire, and since they knew he liked the fire, they assumed he was sitting in front of it lost in thought; he would surely respond as soon as he got hungry for the usual. This always happened. But one day, the stepdaughter, accustomed to the hide-and-seek game with her own keys, took the key for the door between the dining room and the bedroom and suddenly opened it when she heard him poking around the fire. She found him clutching a packet of banknotes, which he was tossing into the fire before her very eyes. A few packets lay next to him on the floor, others had already turned to ashes in the fire.

"Leave me," he said. "I don't have time. I'm not done." And he
pointed to the unburned packets on the floor. He was burning
his money so as not to leave it to anyone; but enough was still
left, the room was brimming with packets of banknotes.

It was the first symptom of senility: old Altaras was burning
money. This third physician—who hadn't even been summoned
for him, whom he received disinterestedly, as though it were
no concern of his, to whom he wanted to show, by means of
his usual food, his indifference to his wife and her complaints—
this physician had impressed and frightened him with his gross-
ness. Perhaps he now felt doubts that things could always go
like this; in any case, the threat about his eyes had confused him.
He gazed at money and fire as often as possible; and more than
anything, he loved it when one was consumed by the other.

Having been found out, he didn't lock himself in anymore;
he sat down openly to his occupation. It would have taken the
strength of several men to hinder him. The helpless wife was at
her wit's end. She brooded about it for a while and then wrote
to the eldest son, in Sarajevo, who, for all his generosity, was so
indignant at this willful destruction of money that he instantly
came to Vienna and hauled the old man over the coals. Neither mother nor daughter ever found out what he threatened
him with. It must have been something that he feared more than
the rare announcements of the doctor—perhaps he was told
he would be legally dispossessed and thrown into a sanatorium,
where there would be an end to the usual quantities of meat and
wine. At any rate, the threat worked. He kept whatever was left
of the banknotes in his hiding places, but he burned them no
more and had to put up with the family's entering the bedroom
regularly to check up on him.

Veza was marked by saving her own atmosphere from the
banging cane, the threats and curses of this sinister man; she had

succeeded in doing so at the age of eighteen. It now seldom happened that he appeared at her threshold. He would tear her door
open at most every few weeks, and stand there, tall and haggard,
in front of her visitors, but always at a distance; and they were
more astonished than frightened. He did clutch the cane, but he
didn't bang it, he didn't curse, he didn't threaten. He came for
help. It was fear that now drove him to the forbidden door. He
said: "They've stolen my money. It's burning." No one could
endure him, and so he spent a lot of time alone, and the anxieties
that overcame him were always connected with money. Since he
could no longer burn it, he was being robbed: the flames leaped
into his room to obtain forcibly what was no longer sacrificed
to them voluntarily.

He never came when Veza was alone, but only when he
heard voices from her room. His hearing was still good, he always heard when she had company: the ringing of the doorbell,
the footsteps past his room, the lively voices in the hall and then
in her room, speaking a language he didn't understand—seeing
nothing of all this, he got scared that a secret attack on his money
was being plotted. Thus I witnessed his appearance two or three
times during my early visits. I was struck by his resemblance to
Dante.

It was as if the Italian poet had risen from the grave. We were
just talking about the *Divine Comedy*, when suddenly the door
flew open, and he stood there, as though draped in white sheets,
raising his cane not in defense but in lament: "*Mi arrobaron las
paras*—They've stolen my money!" No, not Dante. A figure
from hell.

9.

From *Earwitness: Fifty Characters*

Translated by Joachim Neugroschel

The Earwitness

The earwitness makes no effort to look, but he hears all the better. He comes, halts, huddles unnoticed in a corner, peers into a book or a display, hears whatever is to be heard, and moves away untouched and absent. One would think he was not there for he is such an expert at vanishing. He is already somewhere else, he is already listening again, he knows all the places where there is something to be heard, stows it nicely away, and forgets nothing.

He forgets nothing, one has to watch the earwitness when it is time for him to come out with everything. At such a time, he is another man, he is twice as large and four inches taller. How does he do it, does he have special high shoes for blurting things out? Could he possibly pad himself with pillows to make his words seem heavier and weightier? He does nothing else, he says it very precisely, some people wish they had held their tongues. All those modern gadgets are superfluous: his ear is better and more faithful than any gadget, nothing is erased, nothing is blocked, no matter how bad it is, lies, curses, four-letter words, all kinds of indecencies, invectives from remote and little-known languages, he accurately registers even things he does not understand and delivers them unaltered if people wish him to do so.

The earwitness cannot be corrupted by anybody. When it comes to this useful gift, which he alone has, he would take no heed of wife, child, or brother. Whatever he has heard, he has heard, and even the Good Lord is helpless to change it. But he also has human sides, and just as others have their holidays, on which they rest from work, he sometimes, albeit seldom, claps blinders on his ears and refrains from storing up the hearable things. This happens quite simply, he makes himself noticeable, he looks people in the eye, the things they say in these circumstances are quite unimportant and do not suffice to spell their doom. When he has taken off his secret ears, he is a friendly person, everyone trusts him, everyone likes to have a drink with him, harmless phrases are exchanged. At such times, people have no inkling that they are speaking with the executioner himself. It is not to be believed how innocent people are when no one is eavesdropping.

The Blind Man

The blind man is not blind by birth, but he became blind with little effort. He has a camera, he takes it everywhere, and he just loves keeping his eyes closed. He walks about as though asleep, he has seen absolutely nothing as yet, and already he is shooting it, for when all things lie next to one another, equally small, equally large, always rectangular, orderly, cut off, named, numbered, proven, and demonstrated, then you can see them much better in any event.

The blind man saves himself the trouble of viewing anything beforehand. He gathers the things he would have seen and piles them up and enjoys them as though they were stamps. He travels all over the world for the sake of his camera, nothing is far enough, shiny enough, strange enough—he gets it for the camera. He says: I was there, and he points to it, and if he could not point at it he would not know where he had been, the world is confusing, exotic, and rich, who can retain it all?

The blind man does not believe anything that was not shot. People chatter and boast and talk through their hats, his motto is: Get out the photos! Then you know what a man has really seen, then you hold it hard in your hand, then you can put your finger on it, then you can also calmly open your eyes instead of senselessly squandering them beforehand. Everything in life has its season, too much is too much, save your eyesight for photos.

The blind man loves to project enlargements of his photos on the wall and treat his friends to the show. Such a festival lasts two or three hours, silence, explanations, indications, interpretations, advice, humor. The jubilation when something has been inserted upside down, the *savoir-faire* when you realize that something is being shown for the second time! There is no saying how good a man feels when the shots are big and the show goes on long enough. At last the reward for the unswerving blindness of a whole trip. Open up, open up, you eyes, now you may see, now it's time, now you've been there, now you have to prove it.

———

The blind man is sorry that other people can also prove it, but he proves it better.

The Name-licker

The name-licker knows what is good, he can smell it a thousand miles away and spares no effort to get near the name that he plans to lick. Nowadays that is an easy matter by car or by plane, the effort is not all that great, but it must be said that he would make more of an effort if it were necessary. His cravings arise when he reads the newspapers, anything that is not in the newspapers is not his cup of tea. If a name recurs frequently in the newspapers and even appears in the headlines, his craving becomes irresistible and he hastily gets underway. If he has enough money for the trip, then fine; if he does not, he borrows it and pays with the glory of his grand goal. It always makes an impression when he speaks about it. "I have to lick N.N.," he says, and it sounds as the discovery of the North Pole once sounded.

He knows how to pay a surprise visit whether citing someone else or not, he always sounds as though he were about to perish. It flatters names that a craving for them could make someone die of thirst, the whole world a desert and they the only well. And so, not without first complaining in detail about their lack of time, they agree to receive the name-licker. One might even say that they wait for him somewhat impatiently. They put their best parts aright for him, wash them—and only them—thoroughly and polish them to a high shine. The name-licker appears and is dazzled. Meanwhile his lust has grown and he does not hide it. He walks up impudently and seizes the name.

After licking and licking it thoroughly, he photographs it. He has nothing to say, perhaps he stammers something that sounds like veneration, but no one falls for it, they know that all he cares about is the contact of his tongue. "With my very own tongue," he announces later on, sticking it out and receiving an awe such as has never been imparted to any name.

The Fame-tester

Since his birth, the fame-tester has known that nobody could be better than he. He may have known it earlier, but he could not say so back then. Now he is eloquent and tries to show how awful the world is. Every day he skims through the newspapers, looking for new names, what's this one doing there, he shouts indignantly, it wasn't there yesterday! There's something fishy going on, how can anybody suddenly sneak into the papers? He grabs it between his thumb and forefinger, sticks it between his teeth, and bites. It is incredible how woefully the new stuff yields. Ugh! Wax! And it thinks it's metal!

It gives him no peace, he investigates the matter, he is a fair man; if there is *anything* he takes seriously, it is the public, he won't be taken in by fraudulent practices and he'll show that dirty new name a thing or two. From the first moment of discovery, he follows every stirring of that scum. Here he has said something wrong and there he can't spell. Where did he go to school anyway? Did he really go to college or is he simply pretending? Why didn't he ever get married? And what does he do in his spare time? How come no one ever heard of him? The old days lasted long enough, and where was he then? If he's old, it certainly took him a long time; if he's young, then he ought to get his diapers washed. The fame-tester looks him up in all available reference books but, to his satisfaction, he finds him nowhere.

One may say that the fame-tester lives with the deceiver, he talks and dreams about him incessantly. He feels pestered by him and persecuted, and he stubbornly refuses to fill out a good-conduct certificate for him. When he comes home and finally wants his peace, he deposits him in a corner and says: "Down, boy!" and threatens him with a whip. But the sly new name is patient and waits. He exudes a peculiar smell, and when the fame-tester is asleep, the smell cuts into his nose.

The Fun-runner

The fun-runner would once have come with the wind, now he comes faster. No sooner has his airplane landed in Bangkok than he checks the takeoff times for Rio and instantly makes a mental reservation for Rome. The fun-runner lives in the tempest of towns. There is something to buy everywhere, there is something to experience everywhere.

He enjoys living today, for what was it like in the past? Where did people really get to and how dangerous and bothersome traveling was! Now you can travel without the slightest effort. You name a city and you've already been there. Perhaps you get there again at some point; if it works out in the fun-runner, then anything is possible. People believe that he's been everywhere, but he knows better. New airports are built, new airlines spring into life. Doddery old men may dream of calm ocean voyages, he hopes they have a good time in their deck chairs, but that's nothing for him, he's in a hurry.

———————

The fun-runner has his own language. It consists of names of cities and currencies, exotic specialties and clothes, hotels, beaches, temples, and nightclubs. He also knows where a war happens to be taking place, that can be bothersome. But if you're near it, life can be extremely wild, and if it's not too dangerous, he gets woolly, he goes to see the war for two or three days, and then hurries off somewhere else for contrast, where there is the opposite of war.

The fun-runner has no prejudices. He finds that people are alike everywhere, for they always want to buy something. Whether it's clothes or antiques, they crowd into shops. There is money everywhere, even if it's different, it is exchanged everywhere. Just show him a place anywhere in the world without manicurists and slums. If it doesn't take too long, then nothing human is alien to him, he feels sympathy for and interest in everything. A fun-runner who is not interfered with has no ill-will toward anyone; the world would be a much better place if everybody were like him. Everybody will be like him, but it is better to live in the meantime. The mass fun-runner will be no picnic. He sighs quickly, forgets all about it, and hops the next plane.

The Never-must

The never-must will not be forced to do anything by anyone, just try. He will not listen to the right, he will not listen to the left, can he hear at all? He understands very well what you want from him, but he already shakes his head and shoulders before he understands it. In place of a backbone, he has a powerful *No!* more reliable than bones.

———

The never-must spits out. Orders whirl about in the air and even though a man may avoid them like the plague, something does remain in him after all. He has a special handkerchief for things like that, and before it's full of spit he burns it.

The never-must never goes to any window for service. Those barred faces nauseate him, you can't tell them apart. He'd rather go straight to vending machines, get what he needs from them, and save himself the nausea. Nor is he yelled at by them, and he doesn't have to beg and plead. He just throws in the coin when he feels like it, presses the button, gets what he wants, and overlooks what he doesn't.

The never-must hates having buttons on him, he adjusts everything loosely and wears no trousers. Ties are the devil's handiwork for him, just right for strangling. "I'm not going to hang myself," he says when he sees a belt, and he is amazed at the unsuspecting innocence of its wearer.

The never-must moves in knight's gambits and has no address. He forgets where he is in order not to say it. If he is stopped and asked where to find a street, he says: "I'm a stranger here myself." The trick is that he is not only a stranger here, the trick is that he is a stranger everywhere. At times, he has left a house without realizing that he has spent the night there. A knight's gambit is all it takes and he is off to the side, everything has a different name and a different look; instead of hiding, he leaps away.

The never-must speaks only if he absolutely must. Words exert a pressure on him, other people's words and his own. What a state one is in when one is alone after a conversation and all words repeat themselves! They do not stop, one cannot get rid of them, they squeeze and squeeze, you gasp for air, where can you escape from the words? There are some words that repeat themselves with terrible, diabolical stubbornness, while others gradually yield and seep away. One can elude that affliction only with premeditation: one simply does not say the words, one lets them sleep.

The never-must has finally discarded his name and will not let himself be named. He springs away on his chessboard, cunningly and easily, and no one can call him.

10.

From *The Play of the Eyes*

Parts III and IV: "Chance" and "Grinzing"

Translated by Ralph Manheim

Musil

Musil was always—though one wouldn't have noticed it—
prepared for defense and offense. In this posture he found safety.
One thinks of armor plate, but it was more like a shell. He hadn't
built the barrier he put between himself and the world, it was
an integral part of him. He eschewed interjections and all words
charged with feeling. He looked with suspicion on mere affabil-
ity. He drew boundaries between objects as he did around himself. He distrusted amalgamations and alliances, superfluities
and excesses. He was a man of solids and avoided liquids and
gases. He was well versed in physics; not only had he studied
it, it had become part and parcel of his mind. It seems doubtful
that any other writer has been so much a physicist and remained
so in all his lifework. He took no part in vague conversation;
when he found himself surrounded by the windbags it was impossible to avoid in Vienna, he withdrew into his shell. He felt
at home and seemed natural among scientists. A discussion, he
felt, should start from something precise and aim at something

precise. For devious ways he felt contempt and hatred. But he did not aim at *simplicity*; he had an unerring instinct for the inadequacy of the simple and was capable of shattering it with a detailed portrait. His mind was too richly endowed, too active and acute to content itself with simplicity.

No company made him feel inferior; although in company he seldom went out of his way to pick a quarrel, he did interpret every controversy as a fight. The fighting started later, when he was alone, sometimes years later. He forgot nothing. He remembered every confrontation in all its details, and since it was an innermost need with him to triumph in all of them, this in itself made it impossible for him to complete a work intended to encompass them all.

He avoided unwanted contacts. He was determined to remain master of his body. I believe he disliked shaking hands. In his avoidance of handshaking, he was at one with the English. He kept his body supple and strong and took good care of it. He paid more attention to it than was usual among the intellectuals of his day. To him sports and hygiene were one, they governed his daily schedule, and he lived in accordance with their requirements. Into every character he conceived he injected a healthy man, himself. In him extreme eccentricity contrasted with awareness of health and vitality. Musil, who understood a great deal because he saw with precision and was capable of thinking with even greater precision, never lost himself in a character. He knew the way out, but liked to postpone it because he felt so sure of himself.

To stress his competitiveness is not to diminish his stature. His attitude toward men was one of combat. He did not feel out of place in war, in war he sought to prove himself. He was an officer, and tried by taking good care of his men to make up for what he regarded as the brutalization of their life. He had a natural or, one might call it, a traditional attitude toward survival and was not ashamed of it. After the war, competition took its place; in that he resembled the Greeks.

A man who put his arm around him as around all he wished to appease or win over became the most long-lived of his characters and was not saved by being murdered. The unwanted touch of this man's arm kept him alive for another twenty years.

Listening to Musil speak was a particular pleasure. He had no affectations. He was too much himself to put one in mind of an actor. As far as I know, no one ever surprised him playing a role. He spoke rather rapidly but never in a rush. One could never tell from his way of speaking that several ideas were pressing in on him at once. Before expounding them, he took them apart. There was a winning orderliness in everything he said. He expressed contempt for the frenzied inspiration that was the principal boast of the expressionists. To his mind inspiration was too precious to use for exhibitionistic purposes. Nothing so sickened him as Werfel's foaming at the mouth. Musil had delicacy, he made no display of inspiration. In unexpected, astonishing images he suddenly gave rein to it, but checked it at once by the clear progression of his sentences. He was hostile to torrents of language, and when to the general surprise he submitted to someone else's, it was with the intention of swimming resolutely through the flood and demonstrating that the muddiest waters have a far shore. He was glad when there was an obstacle to overcome, but he never showed his determination to take up a fight. Suddenly he was standing self-reliant in the midst of the subject, and one lost sight of the battle, one was captivated by the subject matter, and even when the victor stood supple but firm before one, the argument itself had become so important that one forgot how eminently victorious *he* had been.

But this was only one aspect of Musil's public behavior. His self-assurance went hand in hand with a sensibility I have never seen outdone. To come out of himself, he had to be in company that recognized his rank. He did not function everywhere, he needed certain ritual circumstances. There were people against whom his only defense was silence. He had something of the turtle about him, there were many people who knew only his shell. When his surroundings didn't suit him, he didn't say a word. He could go into a café and leave it again without having uttered a single sentence. I don't think that was easy for him; though you couldn't tell it by his face, he felt offended throughout this silent time. He was right not to recognize anyone's superiority; among those who passed as writers in Vienna, or perhaps in the whole German-speaking world, there was none of his rank.

He knew his worth, in this one decisive point he was untroubled by doubt. A few others knew it too, but not well enough for his liking, for to give their support of him greater force, they would mention one or more other names in the same breath. In the last four or five years of Austrian independence, during which Musil returned from Berlin to Vienna, the avant-garde trumpeted three names: Musil, Joyce, and Broch, or Joyce, Musil, and Broch. Today, fifty years later, it is not hard to understand why Musil was not particularly pleased at that odd triad. He categorically rejected *Ulysses*, which by then had appeared in German. The atomization of language went against his grain; if he said anything about it, which he did reluctantly, he called it old-fashioned, on the ground that it derived from association psychology, which according to him was obsolete. In his Berlin period he had frequented the leaders of Gestalt psychology, which meant a good deal to him; he probably identified his book with it. The name of Joyce was distasteful to him; what that man did had nothing to do with him. When I told him how

I had met Joyce in Zurich at the beginning of 1935, he grew irritable. "You think that's important?" I counted myself lucky that he changed the subject instead of leaving me flat.

But he found it absolutely insufferable to hear Broch's name mentioned in connection with literature. He had known Broch a long time, as industrialist, as patron of the arts, as late student of mathematics, and he refused to take him seriously as a writer. Broch's trilogy struck him as a copy of his own undertaking, which he had been working on for decades, and it made him very suspicious that Broch, having scarcely begun, had already finished. Musil didn't mince matters in this connection and I never heard him say a kind word about Broch. I can't remember the details of what he said about Broch, possibly because I was in the difficult situation of thinking highly of them both. Tensions between them, let alone a quarrel, would have been more than I could bear. I had no doubt that they belonged to the small group of men who made writing hard for themselves, who did not write for the sake of popularity or vulgar success. At the time that may have meant even more to me than their works.

It must have given Musil a strange feeling to hear about this triad. How was he to believe that somebody recognized the importance of his work if that somebody mentioned him in the same breath with Joyce, who to his mind represented the antithesis of what he was trying to do? And even when Musil, who had no existence for the readers of the then popular literature, from Zweig to Werfel, was glorified, he found himself in what he regarded as unfit company. When friends told him that someone had praised *The Man Without Qualities* to the skies and would be overjoyed to meet him, Musil's first question was "Whom else does he praise?"

His touchiness has often been held against him. Though I was to be its victim, I would like to defend it on the strength of

my profound conviction. He was in the midst of his great undertaking, which he was determined to complete. He could not
know that it was destined to be endless in two senses, immortal
as well as unfinished. There has been no comparable undertaking in all German literature. Who would have ventured to resur-
rect the Austrian Empire in a novel? Who could have presumed
to understand this empire, not through its peoples, but through
its center? Here I cannot even begin to say how much else this
work contains. But the awareness that he himself, he alone more
than anyone else, was this defunct Austrian Empire gave him a
very special right to his touchiness, which no one seems to have
appreciated. Was he to let this incomparable material that he was
be buffeted this way and that? Was he to let it suffer any ad-
mixture that would sully it and mar its transparence? Touchiness
concerning one's person, which seems ridiculous in Malvolio, is
not ridiculous when it relates to a special, highly complex, richly
developed world which a man bears within himself and which,
until he succeeds in bringing it forth, he can protect only by
being touchy.

His touchiness was merely a defense against murkiness and
adulteration. Clarity in writing is not a mechanical aptitude that
can be acquired once and for all; it has to be acquired over and
over again. The writer must have the strength to say to himself:
This is how I want it and not otherwise. And to keep it as he
wants it, he must be firm enough to bar all harmful influences.
The tension between the vast wealth of a world already acquired
and the innumerable things that demand to enter into it is enormous. Only the man who carries this world within himself can
decide what is to be rejected, and the late judgments of others,
especially of those who bear no world whatever within themselves, are paltry and presumptuous.

This touchiness made him react against the wrong kind of

food. And here it should be said that a reputation, too, must be constantly fed if it is to steer the project of the man who bears it in the right direction. A growing reputation requires its own sort of food, which it alone can know and decide on. As long as a work of such richness is in progress, a reputation for touchiness is best.

Later on, when the man who has preserved himself by being touchy is dead and his name is displayed in every marketplace, as ugly and bloated as stinking fish, then let the snoopers and know-it-alls come and draw up rules for proper behavior, then let them diagnose touchiness as monumental vanity. No matter, the work is there, they can impede its progress no longer, and they themselves with all their impertinence will seep away without trace.

Some people ridiculed Musil's helplessness in practical matters. The first time I mentioned Musil to Broch, who was well aware of his worth and not inclined to malice, he said to me: "He's king of a paper empire." He meant that Musil was lord of people and things only when at his writing desk, and that otherwise, in practical life, he was defenseless against things and circumstances, bewildered, dependent on other people's help. Everyone knew that Musil couldn't handle money, that he even hated to touch it. He was reluctant to go anywhere alone; his wife was almost always with him, it was she who bought the tickets on the streetcar and who paid at the café. He carried no money on him, I never saw a coin or banknote in his hand. It may be that money was incompatible with his notions of hygiene. He refused to think of money, it bored and upset him. He was quite satisfied to let his wife shoo money away from him like flies. He had lost what he had through inflation, and his financial situation was very difficult. His means were hardly equal to the long-drawn-out undertaking he had let himself in for.

When he returned to Vienna, some friends founded a Musil Society, the purpose of which was to enable him to work on *The Man Without Qualities*. Its members obligated themselves to monthly contributions. He had a list of contributors and reports were given him about the regularity with which they paid up. I don't think the existence of this Society shamed him. He believed, quite correctly, that these people knew what they were doing. They felt honored at being permitted to contribute to his work. It would have been even better if more people had felt the urge to join. I always suspected that he regarded this Musil Society as a kind of secret society, membership in which was a high honor. I often wondered if he would have barred persons he regarded as inferior. It took a sublime contempt for money to keep up his work on *The Man Without Qualities* under such circumstances. When Hitler occupied Austria, the jig was up; most members of the Musil Society were Jews.

In the last years of his life, when he was living in utter poverty in Switzerland, Musil paid dearly for his contempt for money. Painful as it is for me to think of his humiliating situation, I wouldn't have wanted him any different. His sovereign contempt for money, which was not combined with any ascetic tendencies, his lack of any talent for moneymaking, which is so commonplace that one hesitates to call it a talent, partook, it seems to me, of his innermost essence. He made no fuss about it, did not affect to rebel against it, and never spoke of it. He took a serene pride in ignoring its implications for his own life, while keeping well in mind what it meant to others.

Broch was a member of the Musil Society and paid his dues regularly. I found this out from others, he himself never mentioned it. Musil's harsh rejection of him as a writer—in a letter Musil accused him of having in his *Sleepwalkers* trilogy copied the plan of *The Man Without Qualities*—must have irked him, and one is inclined to forgive him for calling Musil "king of a paper empire." This ironic characterization is without value in my mind. Even now—long after their deaths—I feel the need of rejecting it. Broch, who had suffered sorely under his father's commercial heritage, died in exile in just such poverty as Musil. He had no wish to be a king and he was not one. In *The Man Without Qualities*, Musil *was* a king.

Joyce Without a Mirror

The year 1935 began for me amid ice and granite. In Comologno, high above the beautifully ice-clad Val Onsernone, I tried for several weeks to collaborate on a new opera with Wladimir Vogel. It was foolish of me, no doubt, to attempt anything of the kind. The idea of subordinating myself to a composer, of adjusting to his needs, didn't appeal to me at all. Vogel had told me that this would be an entirely new kind of opera, in which composer and writer would function as equals. This proved to be impossible: I read Vogel what I had written, he listened patiently, but I felt humiliated by his supercilious way of expressing approval with a nod of the head and the one word "Good," followed by words of encouragement: "Just keep it up." It would have been easier on me if we had quarreled. His approbation and his words of encouragement soured my enthusiasm for that opera.

I've kept some of my notes; nothing could have come of our collaboration. As I was leaving Comologno, he honored me with one more "Just keep it up," sensing, I'm sure, that he would never receive another word from me. I would have been ashamed to tell him so—what reason could I have given for my lack of enthusiasm? It was one of those puzzling situations that have occurred time and again in my life; I was offended in my pride, though the "offender" couldn't possibly have guessed what had happened. Perhaps he had given me an almost imperceptible impression that he felt superior to me. But if I was to subordinate myself to anyone, it had to be of my own free will. And it was for me to decide to whom. I chose my own gods and steered clear of anyone who set himself up as a god, even if he really was one; I regarded such a person as a threat.

Yet my weeks in Comologno were not fruitless. One sunny winter's day I read my *Comedy of Vanity* to Vogel and my hosts in the open air, and found a better audience than at the Zsolnays'. From then on my hosts were well disposed toward me; they suggested that on my way home I should give a reading at their home in Zurich. They had a fine auditorium suitable for such purposes, and all the intellectuals would be sure to come. The outcome, in January, was my first reading of *The Comedy of Vanity* to a large but select audience. It was there that I met James Joyce.

I read the first part of the play in unadulterated Viennese dialect. As it never occurred to me that many of those present would not understand this language, I provided no explanatory introduction. I was so pleased with the rigorous consistency of my Viennese characters that I failed to notice the none too friendly atmosphere in the hall.

In the intermission I was introduced to Joyce. "I," he said gruffly, "shave with a straight razor and no mirror"—a risky business in view of his impaired vision, he was almost blind. I was stunned. His tone was as hostile as if I had attacked him personally. The idea of prohibiting mirrors was central to the play; it occurred to me that this must have exasperated him because of his weak eyes. For a whole hour he had been exposed to Viennese dialect which, despite his linguistic virtuosity, he did not understand. Only one scene had been spoken in literary German, and that was where he had caught the bit about shaving in front of mirrors. This is what his wretched comment had referred to.

Evidently the linguist's frustration at failing to understand Viennese exacerbated his annoyance, in the one scene he understood, with the idea that mirrors were indispensable. This section, to which he seemed to object on moral grounds, he took personally and reacted by assuring me that *he* needed no mirror for shaving, that even though he used a straight razor, there was no danger of his cutting his throat. His outburst of male vanity might have been taken from the play. How stupid of me, I thought uncomfortably, to inflict *this* play on him. It was what I *wanted* to read, but I should have warned my hosts. Instead, I was glad when Joyce accepted their invitation and realized only when it was too late what havoc I had wreaked with my mirrors. His "no mirror" was a declaration of war. To my own consternation I felt ashamed for him, for his compulsive sensibility, which lowered him in my esteem. He left the auditorium at once; perhaps he thought the mirror play would be continued after the intermission. Someone in the audience told me to take it as an honor that he had come in the first place, and assured me that he had been expected to make some cutting remark.

I was introduced to several distinguished people, but the intermission was not long and I didn't catch the prevailing mood. My impression was that the people had shown and were still showing curiosity, and that they had not yet made up their minds. I pinned my hopes on the second part of my reading, for which I had chosen the "Kind Father" chapter from the novel that was soon to be titled *Die Blendung* (*Auto-da-Fé*). I had often read this chapter in Vienna, to both small and larger groups, and I felt as sure of it as if it had been an integral part of a generally known and widely read book. But as far as the public was concerned, that book did not yet exist, and while in Vienna there was already some talk of it, here it hit the audience with the shock of the totally unknown.

I had hardly spoken the last sentence when Max Pulver, who had come in a dinner jacket, bobbed up like a jack-in-the-box and sang out merrily: "Sadism at night is a bit of all right." The spell was broken, after that everyone felt free to express his distaste. The guests stayed awhile, I met almost all of them, and each in his own way told me how much the second part in particular had riled him. The more kindly souls represented me indulgently as a young writer, not entirely devoid of talent, but needful of guidance.

Wolfgang Pauli, the physicist, whom I greatly respected, was one of these. He gave me a benevolent little lecture, to the effect that my ideas were aberrant. Then, rather more sternly, he bade me listen to him, since after all he had listened to me. It is true that I hadn't been listening and consequently cannot repeat what he said, but the reason why my ears were closed to him was something he could never have guessed: he reminded me of Franz Werfel, though only in appearance of course, and in view of what Werfel had put me through exactly a year before, the resemblance was bound to shake me. But the manner of speaking was quite different, benevolent rather than hostile; I think—I may be mistaken—that he was trying to educate me along Jungian lines. After his admonition I managed to get hold of myself. I listened with apparent attention to the end, I even thanked him for his interesting observations, and we parted on the best of terms.

Bernard von Brentano, who had been sitting in the first row, exposed to the full force of my acoustic masks, seemed disgruntled. All he said, in his toneless way, was "I could never do that, stand up and act in front of all those people." The vitality of the characters had got on his nerves, he thought me an exhibitionist and exhibitionism was offensive to his secretive nature.

One after another was at pains to acquaint me with his disapproval; since many of these people were famous, the proceedings amounted to a sort of public trial. Each of them thought it important to demonstrate that he had been present, and since this was an established fact and could not be denied, to demonstrate his rejection in his own way. The hall had been full; there would be many names to mention; if I knew that any one among them was still alive I would mention him and at least clear him of any imputation of premature approval. The host, who felt sorry for me, finally led me to a gentleman whose name I have forgotten, a graphic artist, and said to me on the way: "You'll be pleased with what he has to say. Come." It was then that I heard the one positive statement of the evening. "It makes me think of Goya," said the artist. But there was no need of this consolation, which I mention only for fairness's sake, for I didn't feel shattered or even dejected. I was overpowered by the characters of my *Comedy*, their ruthlessness, their—I can find no other way of saying it—their truth; and as always after such a reading, I felt buoyant and happy. All the disapproval I had been subjected to merely intensified this feeling; I had felt surer of myself than ever before, and to this feeling the presence of Joyce, in spite of his absurd remark, actually contributed.

During the social part of the evening, which went on for some time, the mood changed for the better. Some erstwhile listeners even managed to talk about themselves so well that they became centers of attraction after all. The most striking of these was Max Pulver, who had already distinguished himself by being the only dinner-jacketed gentleman present and by his little quip about my sadism. He had a few confidential communications to make that attracted general attention. As a writer, he could not have meant much to this distinguished gathering, but for some time he had been busying himself with graphology. His recently published *The Symbolism of Handwriting* was being much discussed; it was thought to be the most important work on graphology since Klages.

He asked me if I knew whose handwriting had been submitted to him for an opinion. I had no idea, but at the time I took an interest in graphology and showed a satisfactory amount of curiosity. He didn't keep me on tenterhooks for long; in a voice loud enough for all to hear, he said something about "world-political importance."

"I shouldn't talk about it," he went on, "but I will all the same. I have specimens of Goebbels's and Göring's handwriting at my place, and that's not all. Oh yes, there's yet another, you can imagine who, but it's a deep secret. Himmler sent them to me for my opinion."

I was so impressed that for a moment I forgot my reading and asked: "And what do they show?"

This was six months after the Röhm putsch. Hitler had been in power for two years. The naivete of my question matched the childlike pride of his announcement. His tone was unchanged in his answer to my question, which sounded affable rather than boastful, with something almost Viennese about it (he had lived for a time in Vienna).

"Very interesting, really," he said apologetically. "I'd be glad to tell you. But I'm pledged to strictest secrecy. Like a doctor, don't you know."

By then the whole company had been alerted to the dangerous names he had mentioned. The lady of the house joined our group. She knew what was going on and she said with a nod of the head in Max Pulver's direction: "He's going to talk himself into trouble one of these days."

Whereupon he declared that he was well able to keep his mouth shut, or they wouldn't send him such things.

"No one will ever get anything out of me."

I would give more today than I would have then to know how he worded his analyses.

The list of persons invited included C. G. Jung and Thomas Mann, neither of whom had come. I wondered if Pulver would have boasted to Thomas Mann of the handwriting specimens the Gestapo had commissioned him to analyze. The presence of refugees didn't seem to trouble him. There were many in the hall: Bernard von Brentano was thought to be one, and Kurt Hirschfeld of the Schauspielhaus was there. I even had the impression that their presence had prompted Pulver to make his "revelations." I was tempted to throw his "sadism" back in his face, but I was too shy and too unknown.

The actual star of the evening was the lady of the house. Her friendship with Joyce was well-known. There was hardly a writer, painter, or composer of repute who didn't come to her house. She was intelligent, one could talk to her, she understood something of what such men said to her, she was able without presumption to talk to them. She took an interest in dreams; that brought her close to Jung, and it was said that even Joyce told her some of his dreams. She had made herself a home in Comologno, a refuge for artists, who could go there to work. Very much a woman, she did things that were not merely calculated to further her own glory. I compared her in my thoughts with the noisy, witless woman in Vienna, who dominated the scene through boasting, greed, and liquor. True, I knew that one better, I'd known her for years, and it's amazing how much you find out when you've known someone a long time. Still, I feel justified in comparing her with my hostess of that evening to the latter's advantage, and if my hostess is still alive, I hope she gets wind of my good opinion.

It was at her house that evening, among her guests who listened to me with disapproval, possibly because they only half understood me, that I recovered my self-confidence. Only a few days before, I had been ashamed to subordinate myself to a composer. Though I respected him, I had reason to doubt that he regarded me as an equal. At the house of this woman in Val Onsernone I had felt this to be a humiliation, though no one was to blame. Now in her Zurich town house she gave me an opportunity to read my latest work, which meant a great deal to me, to people more than one of whom I admired, and to suffer a defeat which was all my own and against which I could pit all my strength and conviction.

High Authority

In mid-October 1935 *Auto-da-Fé* appeared. In September we had moved to Himmelstrasse, halfway up the vine-clad slopes above Grinzing. It was a relief to be up here, away from the gloom of Ferdinandstrasse and at the same time to hold in my hands this novel sprung from the darkest aspects of Vienna. Himmelstrasse [Heaven Street] led to a hamlet known as Am Himmel [In Heaven], and I was so amused at the name that when Veza had stationery printed for me she gave the address as "Am Himmel 30" instead of "Himmelstrasse 30."

To her, our move and the publication of my novel meant escape from the world of the novel, which had depressed her. She knew that I would never break away from it, and as long as I had the thick manuscript in my house, she saw it as a threat. She was convinced that while I was working on it something had snapped inside me and that *The Comedy of Vanity*, which she preferred to my other works, gave a better idea of what I could do. Tactfully, thinking I didn't notice, she made it her business to find out to whom I was sending autographed copies of *Auto-da-Fé*. She saw I was sending only a few, hardly more than a dozen, and she was glad of that. She thought it inevitable that the critics would massacre me, but hated to see me alienate friends who thought well of me—there weren't many—by giving them this depressing novel to read.

She expatiated on the difference between public readings and reading to oneself. Apart from the obligatory "Kind Father," I had given readings of "The Morning Walk" (the first chapter) and some of the second part: "The Stars of Heaven" and "The Hump." The main character in these passages was Fischerle, whose manic exuberance was always infectious. But audiences were also moved by "The Kind Father," one could always feel pity for the tormented daughter. Some people might have been glad to read more, but the book was not in existence and thus they had been unable to subject themselves to the intolerably detailed presentation of the struggle between Kien and Therese. Having no reason for resentment against the author, they came to the next reading, which corroborated their previous opinion. Among the small groups of Viennese interested in modern literature, a deceptive reputation had been growing up; now, with the appearance of the book, it would receive a deathblow.

I myself had no fears, it was as if Veza had taken them all upon herself. My faith in the book had been reinforced by every publisher's rejection. I felt certain that the book would be a success, though perhaps not an immediate one. I don't know what gave me this certainty. Perhaps one defends oneself against the hostility of one's contemporaries by unhesitatingly appointing posterity as one's judge. That puts an end to all petty misgivings. One stops asking oneself what this one and that one are likely to say. Since it doesn't matter, one prefers not to think about it. Nor does one stop to recall what in times past contemporaries said about the books one loves. One sees them for themselves, detached from all the bothersome trivia in which their authors were involved in their lifetime. In some cases the books themselves have become gods, which means not only that they will always be around but also that they always have been around.

One cannot be absolutely sure about this gratifying posterity. Here again there are judges, but they are hard to find, and some unfortunate writers may never meet the man whom they can with a good conscience appoint as their posterity expert. I had met such a man, and after long talks with him over a period of a year and a half my respect for him was so great that if he had sentenced *Auto-da-Fé* to death I would have accepted his verdict. I lived for five weeks in expectation of his sentence.

I had inscribed his copy with words which no one else could have understood.

"For Dr. Sonne [Sun], to me still more. E.C."

In the copies I had sent to Broch, Alban Berg, and Musil, I was not chary of expressions of esteem; I wrote clearly and plainly what I felt, in terms intelligible to all. With Dr. Sonne it was different. Since an "intimate" word had never been spoken between us, I had never dared tell him how greatly I honored him. I never mentioned his name to anyone without the "Dr." This should not be taken to mean that the title meant anything to me, practically everyone you met in Vienna called himself "Dr." The word merely served as a kind of buffer. One didn't just come out with the man's name, I prepared the way with a neutral, colorless word, which made it clear that I was not entitled to intimacy, that the name would always keep its distance. And it was thanks to this distancing title that so sacred a word as *Sonne*, luminous, searing, winged, source and (as still believed at that time) end of all life, did not for all its roundness and smoothness become a household word. I didn't even *think* the name without the title; whether I was alone or with others, it was always "Dr. Sonne," and only now after almost fifty years has the title begun to seem too stiff and formal. I shall not use it very often from now on.

At that time only the man to whom my inscription was addressed could understand that he meant more to me than the sun. For no one else did I reduce my own name to initials. The handwriting—witness the size of the letters—remained incorrigibly self-assured; this was not a man who wanted to disappear; with this book, which for years had existed only in secret, he was at last challenging the public. But he wished to disappear in the presence of *him*, the man who was concerned not with himself but only with ideas.

One afternoon in mid-October, at the Café Museum, I handed Dr. Sonne the book which he had never seen in manuscript, which I had never mentioned to him, of which he had heard only an isolated chapter at a reading. He may have heard more about it from others, perhaps from Broch or Merkel. Broch's opinion in literary matters may well have meant something to him, but he would not have taken it on faith. He trusted only his own judgment, though he would never have dreamed of saying so. After that I saw him as usual every day. Every afternoon I went to the Museum and sat down with him, he made no secret of the fact that he was waiting for me. The conversations to which I owed my rebirth at the age of thirty continued. Nothing changed; true, every conversation was new, but not new in a *different way*. His words offered no indication that he had been reading my novel. On that subject he remained obstinately silent, and so did I. I burned to know if he had *begun*, at least *begun*, but I never once asked him. I had learned to respect every corner of his silence, for only when he began unexpectedly to speak of something was he at his true level. His independence, which he maintained quite openly, but always with tact and gentleness, taught me the meaning of an independent mind, and in my dealings with him I was certainly not going to disregard what I had learned from him.

Week after week went by. I kept my impatience under control. A rejection from him, however fully documented, however compellingly reasoned, would have destroyed me. It was to him alone that I accorded the right to pass an intellectual death sentence on me. He kept silent, and evening after evening when I came home to Himmelstrasse, Veza, from whom I couldn't very well conceal anything so all-important, asked me: "Did he say anything?" I replied: "No, I don't think he's had time to look at it." "What! He hasn't had time? When every day he spends two hours at the café with you." I would affect indifference and toss out lightly: "We've talked about dozens of 'auto-da-fés,'" or try to divert her in some other way. Then she would lose her temper and cry out: "You're a slave. That's what he's done for you. I'd never have expected you to choose a master! At last the book is out, but you've turned into a slave!"

No, I was not his slave. If he had done or said something contemptible, I would not have gone along with him. From him least of all would I have accepted anything base or contemptible. But I was absolutely sure that he was incapable of doing anything stupid or base. It was this absolute, though open-eyed trust that Veza regarded as slavery. It was a feeling she knew very well, because it was how she felt about me. In this feeling she now felt justified by three valid works. But what works had Dr. Sonne ever produced? If any, he had known how to conceal them. Why would he do that? Did he think them un- worthy of the few people with whom he associated? She was well aware that what Broch, Merkel, and others most admired in him was his self-abnegation. But it seemed inhuman that he should carry self-abnegation so far as to keep silent for weeks about my book, though we saw each other every day. She didn't mince words. She attacked him in every way. Her usually ready wit seemed to forsake her when she spoke of him. Since she herself didn't feel sure about the book, she was afraid his silence meant condemnation and she knew what an effect that would have on me.

One afternoon at the Café Museum—we had just exchanged greetings and sat down—Sonne said without preamble, without apology, that he had read my novel; would I like to know what he thought of it? And he proceeded to talk for two hours; that af- ternoon we spoke of nothing else. He illuminated the book from every angle, he established connections I had not suspected. He dealt with it as a book that had existed for a long time and would continue to exist. He explained where it came from and showed where it would inevitably lead. If he had contented himself with vague compliments, I would have been pleased after waiting for five weeks, for I would have known his approval was sincere. But he did far more. He brought up particulars which I had in- deed written but could not explain and showed me why they were right and could not have been different.

He spoke as though taking me with him on a voyage of dis- covery. I learned from him as if I were someone else, not the au- thor; what he set before me was so startling I would hardly have recognized it as my own. It was amazing enough that he had every slightest detail at his command, as though commenting on some ancient text before a classroom. The distance he thus created between me and my book was greater than the four years during which the manuscript had lain in my drawer. I saw before me an edifice thought out in every detail, which carried its dignity and justification within itself. I was fascinated by every one of his ideas, each one came as a surprise, and my only wish was that he would never stop talking.

Little by little, I became aware of the intention behind his words; he knew the book would have a hard life and he was arming me against the attacks that were to be expected.

After a number of observations that had no bearing on this purpose, he began to formulate the criticisms for which we should be prepared. Among other things, he said, it would be attacked as the book of an old and sexless man. Very meticulously he proved the contrary. It would be argued that my portrayal of the Jew Fischerle lent itself to misuse by racist propaganda. But, said Sonne, the character was true to life, as true to life as the narrow-minded provincial housekeeper or the brutal janitor. When the catastrophe had passed, the labels would fall from these characters, and they would stand there as the types that had brought about the catastrophe. I am stressing this particular, because in the course of subsequent events I often felt uneasy about Fischerle. And then I found comfort in what Sonne had said that day.

Far more important were the profound connections he revealed to me. Of these I say nothing. In the fifty years that have elapsed many of these have been discussed in print. It would seem as though *Auto-da-Fé* contained a reservoir of secrets, which would be tapped little by little until all were drawn off and explained. This time, I'm afraid, has not yet come. I still preserve intact within me a good part of the treasure Sonne gave me then. Some people are surprised that I still respond with wonderment to every new reaction. The reason is to be sought in this treasure, the one treasure in my life that I like to keep an eye on and that I knowingly administer.

The attacks I still get from outraged readers do not really touch me, even when they are made by friends whom I love for their innocence and whom for that reason I had warned against reading the book. Sometimes I succeed with earnest pleas in keeping someone away from it. But even for close friends whom I have been unable to deter from reading it, I am no longer the same man. I have a feeling that they expect to find the evil the book is replete with in *me*. I also know that they don't find it, for it is not the evil I have in me now, but a different kind. I can't help them, for how can I possibly explain to them that on that afternoon Sonne relieved me of *that* evil by picking it before my eyes from every nook and cranny of the book and piecing it together again at a salutary distance from myself?

A Letter from Thomas Mann

It was a long handwritten letter in the careful, well-balanced style known to us from his books. It said things that were bound to surprise and delight me. Exactly four years earlier, I had sent Thomas Mann the manuscript of my novel in three black linen binders—a trilogy, he must have thought—accompanied by a long dry letter explaining my plan for a "Human Comedy of Madmen." It was a proud letter, containing hardly a word of homage, and he must have wondered why I had written it to him rather than someone else.

Veza loved *Buddenbrooks* almost as much as *Anna Karenina*; when her enthusiasm rose to such heights, it often deterred me from reading the book. I had read *The Magic Mountain* instead, its atmosphere was familiar to me from what my mother told me about the Waldsanatorium in Arosa, where she had spent two years. The book had made a deep impression on me, if only because of its reflections on death, and although I felt differently about these matters, I thought the book offered a scrupulous treatment of them. At that time, October 1931, I saw no reason not to appeal first to Thomas Mann. I hadn't read Musil yet, and my only possible objection might have been that I had already read some things by Heinrich Mann, who was more to my liking than his brother. The astonishing part of it, in any case, was my self-confidence. This first letter didn't include the slightest homage to Thomas Mann, though having read *The Magic Mountain*, I might well have expressed my admiration. But it seemed to me that one look at my manuscript would suffice, and he would *have* to go on reading; I was convinced that a pessimistic author—as I thought him to be—would find this book irresistible. But the enormous package was returned unread with a polite letter pleading lack of sufficient time and strength. It was a hard blow, for who else would consent to read so depressing a book if *he* declined? I had expected not mere approval, but something more like enthusiasm. I felt sure that the right kind of statement from him, betokening conviction rather than a mere desire to be helpful, would clear the way for my book. I saw no obstacle in my path, and that may be why I took so presumptuous a tone.

His letter declining to read my manuscript was his answer to my presumption; it was probably not unjust, for he had not read the book. For four years my manuscript went unpublished. It is not hard to imagine how that affected my outward circumstances. But it meant still more to my pride. I felt that by declining to read my book he had abased it, and I accordingly decided to make no further attempt to publish it. Then little by little, as I won a few friends for it with my readings, I was persuaded to try a publisher or two. These attempts were fruitless, just as I had expected after the blow Thomas Mann had dealt me.

But now in October 1935 the book had appeared and I was determined to send it to Thomas Mann. The wound he had dealt me was still open. He alone could heal it by reading the book and admitting that he had been wrong, that he had rejected something deserving of his esteem. The letter I wrote him now was not impertinent, I merely told him the whole story and thus effortlessly put him in the wrong. He wrote me a long letter in return. He was too conscientious and upright a man not to make amends for the "wrong" he had done. After all that had happened his letter made me very happy.

Just then a first review of the book appeared in the *Neue Freie Presse*. It was written in a tone of lavish enthusiasm, but by a writer whom I did not take seriously, who could not be taken seriously. Still, it had its effect, for when I went to the Café Herrenhof that same day (or possibly the day after), Musil came up to me. I had never seen him so cordial. He put out his hand, and instead of merely smiling he positively beamed, which delighted me because I had been led to believe that he didn't permit himself to beam in public. "Congratulations on your great success," he said, and added that he had only read part of the book, but that if it went on in the same way I *deserved* my success. The word "deserved" from his lips almost made me reel. He uttered a few more words of praise, which I shall not repeat because, in view of what happened next, he may have withdrawn them since. His praise deprived me of my reason. I suddenly realized how eagerly I had been waiting for his opinion, possibly no less than I had been for Sonne's. I was intoxicated and befuddled. I must have been very befuddled, for how otherwise could I have made such a gaffe as I did then?

The moment he stopped speaking, I said: "And just imagine, I've had a long letter from Thomas Mann." He changed in a flash, he seemed to jump back into himself, his face went gray. "Did you?" he said. He held out his hand partway, giving me only the tips of his fingers to shake, and turned brusquely about. With that I was dismissed.

Dismissed forever. He was a master of dismissal. He had ample practice. Once he had dismissed you, you stayed dismissed. When I saw him in company, which happened now and then in the next two years, he was polite but never addressed me, never entered into a conversation with me. When my name was mentioned in company, he said nothing, as though he didn't know who I was and had no desire to find out.

What had happened? What had I done? What was the unpardonable offense that he could never forgive? A moment after he, Musil, had accorded me his recognition I had uttered the name of Thomas Mann. I had spoken of a letter, a long letter, from Thomas Mann immediately after he, Musil, had congratulated me and explained his congratulations. He was bound to assume that I had sent the book to Thomas Mann, as I had to him, with a similar respectful inscription. He had no knowledge of what had gone before, he didn't know that I had sent Thomas Mann the book four years before. But even if he had known the whole story, he would have been no less offended. Musil was touchier in his self-esteem than anyone else I have known, and there can be no doubt that in my euphoric befuddlement I stepped on his toes. It was understandable that he should make me repent it. My penance was very painful to me, I never really got over his dismissal of me in the most exalted moment I had ever known with him. But because it was he who imposed my penance, I accepted it. I realized how deeply I had wounded him in the state of euphoria that goes hand in hand with sudden recognition, and I felt ashamed.

He must have thought that I held Thomas Mann in higher esteem than him. And this he could not accept from someone who had stated the contrary everywhere. As he saw it, respect had to be based on intellectual considerations, otherwise it could not be taken seriously. He always attached importance to a clear decision between himself and Thomas Mann. If someone like Stefan Zweig had been involved, someone who owed his reputation to sheer bustle, the question of a decision would never have arisen. But Musil knew quite well who Thomas Mann was, and what exasperated him most was that Thomas Mann's prestige was so much greater than his own. In his own way, he (unbeknownst to me) had courted Thomas Mann at about this time, but with the feeling that he himself had every right to *wrest* Thomas Mann's fame away from him. All Musil's letters suggesting help from Thomas Mann sound like *demands*. It was a very different matter when a young writer, who had assured him of his sincerest reverence, should, a moment after Musil had set his stamp of approval on this young writer's work, mention the name of the man whom Musil aspired to supplant, and whose entrenchments he was still trying in vain to storm. Such an action cast suspicion on all my previous expressions of reverence. I had committed a crime of lèse-majesté, and deserved to be punished by banishment.

It made me very unhappy to have Musil turn away from me. Seeing the purely physical act at the Herrenhof, I knew that something irreparable had happened.

After that I couldn't answer Thomas Mann's letter. Its effect on Musil paralyzed me. For a few days I couldn't even bring myself to pick it up. I delayed my thanks so long that to write a simple note of thanks seemed out of the question. Then I went back to the letter and read it with all the greater pleasure. As long as I failed to answer it, my pleasure remained fresh. Every day I felt as if I had just received it. Perhaps after waiting for four years I wanted to make Thomas Mann wait awhile too, but this is an idea that came to me only recently. Friends who had heard about Thomas Mann's letter asked me what I had written in answer, and all I could say was: "Not yet, not yet." A few months later they asked: "How will you explain yourself? What explanation will you give for waiting so long to reply to such a letter?" And again I knew no answer.

In April 1936, after more than *five months*, I read in the newspapers that Thomas Mann was coming to Vienna to deliver a lecture on Freud. This seemed the last chance to make good my omission. I concocted the most effusive letter I have ever written; how else could I account for what I had done? I think it would embarrass me to read that letter today. For by the time I got around to writing it, I had read the work of a writer who meant more to me than Thomas Mann: the first two volumes of *The Man Without Qualities* had appeared. I was really grateful to Thomas Mann, *that* wound had healed. He had said things in his letter that filled me with pride. Though I didn't admit it to myself, I had done the same as Thomas Mann: made good an omission. He had read *Auto-da-Fé* and given his opinion of it. I had replaced my presumptuous first letter with another, improving on the homage that I had owed him then.

I think it gave him pleasure. But the circle did not fully close. In my letter I wrote that I should be delighted to meet him during his stay in Vienna. He was invited to the Benedikts' for lunch. There he asked after me and said he would have been glad to see me. Broch, who was present, said I lived nearby and offered to run over and get me. I was out when he came, I had just gone to meet Sonne at the Café Museum. And so it came about that though I heard Thomas Mann lecture I never met him personally.

11.

From *The Voices of Marrakesh: A Record of a Visit*

Translated by J. A. Underwood

Encounters with Camels

I came into contact with camels on three occasions, and each occasion ended tragically.

"I must show you the camel market," said my friend soon after my arrival in Marrakesh. "It's held every Thursday morning by the wall near the Bab-el-Khemis. That's right on the other side of the city—I'd better drive you there."

Thursday came and we drove there. We had started late, and by the time we reached the large open square by the city wall it was already noon. The square was almost empty. At the far end, about two hundred yards from us, stood a group of people, but we could see no camels. The little animals these people were occupied with were donkeys, and the city was full of donkeys anyway; they carried all the burdens and were so badly treated we certainly had no desire to see any more of it. "We're too late," said my friend. "The camel market's over." He drove into the middle of the square to convince me that there was really nothing more to be seen.

But before he stopped we saw a knot of people scatter. In their midst, balanced on three legs, its fourth having been bound up, stood a camel. It was wearing a red muzzle. A rope had been threaded through its nostrils and a man standing at some distance was trying to pull the animal away. It ran forward a little way, stopped, and then made a surprising leap into the air on its three legs. Its movements were as unexpected as they were uncanny. The man who was supposed to be leading it gave way every time; he was afraid to approach too close to the animal, never quite sure what it would get up to next. But he drew the rope tight again after each surprise, and he did manage very slowly to drag the animal in a particular direction.

We stopped and wound down the windows of the car; begging children surrounded us, and above their voices as they asked for alms we could hear the camel shrieking. Once it jumped so violently to one side that the man who was leading it lost his hold on the rope. The onlookers, who were standing at some distance, ran off even farther. The air around the camel was charged with fear, most of it coming from the camel itself. The drover ran with it for a bit and snatched up the rope as it trailed along the ground. The camel leaped sideways into the air with an undulating movement but did not break loose again; it was dragged along farther.

A man we had not noticed appeared behind the children standing around our car, pushed them aside, and explained to us in broken French: "The camel has rabies. It is dangerous. It is being taken to the slaughterhouse. One has to be very careful." He pulled a serious face. Between each of his sentences we could hear the animal's shrieks.

We thanked him and drove away saddened. We often spoke of the rabid camel during the next few days; its despairing movements had made a deep impression on us. We had gone to the market expecting to see hundreds of these gentle, curvaceous beasts. But in that huge square we had found only one, on three legs, captive, living its last hour, and as it fought for its life we had driven away.

Some days later we were passing another part of the city wall. It was evening; the red glow on the wall was beginning to fade. I kept the wall in view for as long as I could, delighting in the way its coloring gradually changed. Then, in the shadow of the wall, I saw a large caravan of camels. Most of them had lowered themselves to their knees; others were still standing. Men with turbans on their heads went busily and yet quietly about among them. It was a picture of peace and twilight. The camels' coloring blended with that of the wall. We got out of the car and walked among the animals ourselves. They knelt in rings of a dozen or more around mountainous piles of fodder. They stretched their necks out, drew the fodder into their mouths, threw their heads back, and calmly worked their jaws. We looked at them closely and I tell you they had faces. They all looked alike and yet they were so different. They put one in mind of elderly English ladies taking tea together, dignified and apparently bored but unable entirely to conceal the malice with which they observe everything around them: "That one's my aunt, honestly," said my English friend when I tactfully pointed out this resemblance to his countrywomen, and we soon spotted other acquaintances. We were proud of having come across this caravan that no one had told us about, and we counted 107 camels.

A young lad approached us and asked us for a coin. His face was dark blue in color, as was his robe; he was a drover and, to judge from his appearance, one of the so-called "blue men" who live to the south of the Atlas. The dye in their clothing, we had been told, comes off on their skin, making them all, men and

women, blue — the only blue race. Our young drover was grateful for the coin and we tried to find out from him something
about the caravan. He knew only a few words of French, however: they were from Goulimime and they had been on the road
for twenty-five days. That was all we understood. Goulimime
was in the desert away down to the south, and we wondered
whether the camel caravan had crossed the Atlas. We would also
have liked to know where it was going, because here beneath the
walls of the city could hardly be its journey's end and the animals appeared to be fortifying themselves for exertions to come.

The dark-blue lad, unable to tell us any more, went out of
his way to be helpful by leading us to a tall, slender old man
who wore a white turban and was treated with respect. He
spoke French well and answered our questions fluently. The
caravan was from Goulimime and really had been on the road
for twenty-five days.

"And where is it going from here?"

"Nowhere," he said. "They will be sold here for slaughter."

"For slaughter?"

We were both of us shocked — even my friend, who at home
is an enthusiastic hunter. We thought of the long journey the
animals had behind them; of their beauty in the dusk; of their
ignorance of what lay in store for them; of their peaceful meal;
and perhaps, too, of the people they had reminded us of.

"Yes, for slaughter," the old man repeated. His voice had a
jagged quality, like the edge of a blunted knife.

"Do people eat a lot of camel meat here then?" I asked, trying with matter-of-fact questions to conceal how shocked I was.

"Masses of it!"

"What does it taste like? I've never had any."

"You've never had camel meat?" He broke into a thin, de-
risive chuckle and said again, "You've never had camel meat?"

Clearly he believed we were given nothing but camel meat, and he put on a very superior air as if we were eating it as his bidding. "It's very good," he said.

"What does a camel cost?"

"It varies a great deal. Anything from 30,000 to 70,000 francs. Here—I can show you. You have to know what you're doing." He led us over to a very beautiful, light-colored animal and touched it with his stick, which I noticed now for the first time. "This is a good animal. This one is worth 70,000 francs. The owner rode it himself. He could have gone on using it for years. But he preferred to sell it. With the money, you see, he can buy two young animals."

We saw. "Are you from Goulimime—did you come with the caravan?" I asked.

He rejected this suggestion in some annoyance. "I am from Marrakesh," he said proudly. "I buy animals and sell them to the butchers." He had nothing but scorn for the men who had come all that way, and our young drover he dismissed with the words: "He doesn't know a thing."

But he wanted to know where we were from, and we told him for the sake of simplicity that we were both "from London." He smiled and appeared to be slightly nettled. "I was in France during the war," he said. His age made it plain he was talking of the First World War. "I was with Englishmen. I didn't get on with them," he added quickly, dropping his voice a little. "But war isn't war anymore. It's not the man that counts nowadays—it's the machine." He said some more things about war that sounded very resigned. "It isn't war anymore." We agreed with him on this point and it seemed to help him get over the fact that we were from England.

"Are all the animals sold already?" I asked.

"No. They can't sell them all. The rest stay with them and go on to Settat. Do you know Settat? It's on the way to Casablanca, 160 kilometers from here. That's the last camel market. The rest will be sold there."

We thanked him and he dismissed us without ceremony. We stopped walking round among the camels; we did not feel like it anymore. It was almost dark when we left the caravan.

But the sight of those camels would not leave me. I thought of them with aversion, and yet it was as if they were something I had long been familiar with. The memory of their last meal merged with that conversation about war. The idea of visiting the next camel market remained with us till the Thursday. We determined to set out early in the morning, and possibly we hoped to gain a less somber impression of camel existence this time.

We came to the El-Khemis Gate. The number of animals we found there was none too great; they were lost in the expanse of the square, which would have been difficult to fill. On one side were the donkeys again. We did not go over to them but stayed with the camels. There were never more than three or four of them together at a time; sometimes there was just one young animal standing beside its mother. At first they all seemed to be quiet. The only sound came from small groups of men haggling fiercely. Yet it struck me that the men apparently did not trust certain of the animals; these they avoided approaching too closely except when they absolutely had to.

It was not long before our attention was drawn to a camel that appeared to be putting up some kind of resistance; it was grunting and growling and flinging its head about in all directions. A man was trying to force it to its knees, and because it would not obey he was backing up his efforts with blows of his stick. Of the two or three other people busying themselves at the animal's head one stood out particularly: a powerful, stocky man with a dark, cruel face. His stance was solid, his legs as if rooted in the ground. With brisk movements of his arms he was drawing a rope through a hole he had bored in the animal's septum. Nose and rope were red with blood. The camel flinched and shrieked, now and then uttering a great roar; finally it leaped to its feet again, having by now knelt down, and tried to tug itself free, while the man pulled the rope tighter and tighter. The others made a supreme effort to control the animal, and they were still at it when someone came up to us and said in broken French:

"It smells. It can smell the butcher. It has been sold for slaughter. It is going now to the slaughterhouse."

"But how can it smell that?" asked my friend, incredulous.

"That is the butcher standing in front of him," and he pointed to the burly, dark fellow who had caught our eye. "The butcher has come from the slaughterhouse and smells of camel blood. The camel does not like that. A camel can be very dangerous. When one has rabies it comes in the night and kills people in their sleep."

"How can it kill people?" I asked.

"When they are asleep the camel comes and kneels on them and suffocates them in their sleep. One has to be very careful. Before the people wake up they have suffocated. Oh yes, the camel has a very good nose. It lies beside its master at night and scents thieves and wakes its master up. The meat is good. One should eat camel meat. Ça donne du courage. A camel does not like to be alone. It will go nowhere alone. If a man wants to drive his camel to the city he must find another one to go with it. He must borrow one, otherwise he will never get his camel to the city. It does not want to be alone. I was in the war. I was wounded. Look—here," and he pointed to his chest.

The camel had calmed down a little and I turned to look at the speaker for the first time. His chest had a caved-in look and his left arm was stiff. The man struck me as familiar. He was small, thin, and very earnest. I wondered where I had seen him before.

"How are camels killed?"

"You sever the jugular vein. They have to bleed to death. Otherwise one is not allowed to eat them. A Moslem is not allowed to eat them unless they have bled to death. I cannot work because of this wound, so I do a bit of guiding here. I spoke to you last Thursday—do you remember the camel with rabies? I was in Safi when the Americans landed. We fought a bit against the Americans, but not much, and then I was taken into the American army. There were a lot of Moroccans in the American army. I was in Corsica and in Italy with the Americans. I went all over the place. The Germans are good soldiers. The Casino was worst. It was really bad there. That's where I got my wound. Do you know the Casino?"

It dawned on me that he meant Monte Cassino. He gave me an account of the fierce fighting there, and in doing so this otherwise calm and self-possessed man became as excited as if it had been a question of the murderous cravings of maddened camels. He was an honest fellow and believed what he said. But he had spotted a group of Americans in among the animals, and he very quickly switched his attentions to them. He disappeared as swiftly as he had appeared, and I had no objection; I had lost sight and sound of the camel, which had now stopped its roaring, and I wanted to see it again.

I soon found it. The butcher had left it where it was. It was kneeling again, still tossing its head from time to time. The blood from its nostrils had spread further. I felt something akin to gratitude for the few illusory moments for which it had been left alone. But I could not look at it for long; I knew its fate and stole away.

My friend had wandered off during the guide's recital in search of some English people he knew. I went looking for him and found him over on the other side of the square, back among the donkeys. Perhaps he felt less uncomfortable there.

During the rest of our stay in the "red city" we did not mention camels once.

The Donkey's Concupiscence

I liked to return from my evening strolls through the streets of the city by way of the Djema el Fna. It was strange, crossing that great square as it lay almost empty. There were no acrobats anymore and no dancers; no snake charmers and no fire-eaters. A little man squatted forlornly on the ground, a basket of very small eggs before him and nothing and no one else anywhere near him. Acetylene lamps burned here and there; the square smelled of them. In the cookshops one or two men still sat over their soup. They looked lonely, as if they had nowhere to go. Around the edges of the square people were settling down to sleep. Some lay, though most squatted, and they had all pulled the hoods of their cloaks over their heads. Their sleep was motionless; you would never have suspected anything breathing beneath those dark hoods.

One night I saw a large, dense circle of people in the middle of the square, acetylene lamps illuminating them in the strangest way. They were all standing. The dark shadows on faces and figures, edged by the harsh light thrown on them by the lamps, gave them a cruel, sinister look. I could hear two native instruments playing and a man's voice addressing someone in vehement terms. I went up closer and found a gap through which I could see inside the circle. What I saw was a man, standing in the middle with a stick in his hand, urgently interrogating a donkey.

Of all the city's miserable donkeys, this was the most pitiful. His bones stuck out, he was completely starved, his coat was worn off, and he was clearly no longer capable of bearing the least little burden. One wondered how his legs still held him up. The man was engaged in a comic dialogue with him. He was trying to cajole him into something. The donkey remaining stubborn, he asked him questions; and when he refused to answer, the illuminated onlookers burst out laughing. Possibly it was a story in which a donkey played a part, because after a lengthy palaver the wretched animal began to turn very slowly to the music. The stick was still being brandished above him. The man was talking faster and faster, fairly ranting now in order to keep the donkey going, but it sounded to me from his words as if he too represented a figure of fun. The music played on and on and the men, who now never stopped laughing, had the look of man-eating or donkey-eating savages.

I stayed only a short time and so cannot say what happened subsequently. My repulsion outweighed my curiosity. I had long before conceived an affection for the donkeys of the city. Every step offered me occasion to feel indignant at the way they were treated, though of course there was nothing I could do. But never had quite such a lamentable specimen as this crossed my path, and on my way home I sought to console myself with the thought that he would certainly not last the night.

The next day was a Saturday and I went to the Djema el Fna early in the morning. Saturday was one of its busiest days. Onlookers, performers, baskets, and booths thronged the square; it was a job to make one's way through the crowd. I came to the place where the donkey had stood the evening before. I looked, and I could hardly believe my eyes: there he was again. He was standing all by himself. I examined him closely and there was no mistaking him; it was he. His master was nearby, chatting quietly with a few people. No circle had formed round them yet. The musicians were not there; the performance had not yet begun. The donkey was standing exactly as he had the night before. In the bright sunshine his coat looked even shabbier than at night. I found him older, more famished, and altogether more wretched.

Suddenly I became aware of someone behind me and of angry words in my ear, words I did not understand. Turning, I lost sight of the donkey for a moment. The man I had heard was pressed right up against me in the crowd, but it became apparent that he had been threatening someone else and not me. I turned back to the donkey.

He had not budged, but it was no longer the same donkey. Because between his back legs, slanting forward and down, there hung all of a sudden a prodigious member. It was stouter than the stick the man had been threatening him with the night before. In the tiny space of time in which I had had my back turned an overwhelming change had come over him. I do not know what he had seen, heard, or smelled. But that pitiful, aged, feeble creature, who was on the verge of collapse and quite useless for anything anymore except as the butt of comic dialogue, who was treated worse than a donkey in Marrakesh, that being, less than nothing, with no meat on his bones, no strength, no proper coat, still had so much lust in him that the mere sight absolved me of the impression caused by his misery. I often think of him. I remind myself how much of him was still there when I saw nothing left. I wish all the tormented his concupiscence in misery.

IV

Crowds and Power

"I have the impression that you [Hermann Broch] like to talk about modern psychology because it originated in your own backyard, so to speak, in a particular segment of Vienna society. It appeals to a certain local patriotism in you. Maybe you feel that you yourself might have invented it. Whatever it says, you find in yourself. You don't have to look for it. This modern psychology strikes me as totally inadequate. It deals with the individual, and in that sphere it has undoubtedly made certain discoveries. But where the masses are concerned, it can't do a thing, and that's where knowledge would be most important, for all the new powers that are coming into existence *today* draw their strength from crowds, from the masses. Nearly all those who are out for political power know how to operate with the masses. But the men who see that such operations are leading straight to another world war don't know how to influence the masses, how to stop them from being misled to the ruin of us all. The laws of mass behavior can be discovered. That is the most important task confronting us today, and so far nothing has been done toward the development of such a science."

—ELIAS CANETTI, *The Play of the Eyes*

12.

From *The Torch in My Ear*

Part III: "The School of Hearing" (Vienna, 1926–1928)

The Fifteenth of July

A few months after I had moved into my new room, something occurred that had the deepest influence on my subsequent life. It was one of those not too frequent public events that seize an entire city so profoundly that it is no longer the same afterward.

On the morning of July 15, 1927, I was not at the Chemical Institute on Währingerstrasse as usual; I happened to be at home. I was reading the morning newspaper at the coffeehouse in Ober Sankt Veit. Today, I can still feel my indignation when I took hold of *Die Reichspost*: the giant headline said: "A JUST VERDICT." There had been shootings in Burgenland; workers had been killed. The court had declared the murderers not guilty. This acquittal had been termed, nay, trumpeted, as a "just verdict" in the organ of the government party. It was this mockery of any sense of justice rather than the verdict itself that triggered an enormous agitation among the workers of Vienna. From all districts of the city, the workers marched in tight formations to the Palace of Justice, whose sheer name embodied the unjust verdict for them. It was a totally spontaneous reaction: I could tell how spontaneous it was just by my own conduct. I quickly biked into the center of town and joined one of these processions.

The workers, usually well disciplined, trusting their Social Democratic leaders and satisfied that Vienna was administered by these leaders in an exemplary manner, were acting *without* their leaders on this day. When they set fire to the Palace of Justice, Mayor Seitz mounted a fire engine and raised his right hand high, trying to block their way. His gesture had no effect: the Palace of Justice was *burning*. The police were ordered to shoot; there were ninety deaths.

Fifty-three years have passed, and the agitation of that day is still in my bones. It was the closest thing to a revolution that I have physically experienced. Since then, I have known quite precisely that I would not have to read a single word about the storming of the Bastille. I became a part of the crowd, I fully dissolved in it, I did not feel the slightest resistance to what the crowd was doing. I am amazed that despite my frame of mind, I was able to grasp all the concrete individual scenes taking place before my eyes. I would like to mention one such scene.

In a side street, not far from the burning Palace of Justice, yet out of the way, stood a man, sharply distinguished from the crowd, flailing his hands in the air and moaning over and over again: "The files are burning! All the files!"

"Better files than people!" I told him, but that did not interest him; all he could think of was the files. It occurred to me that he might have some personal involvement in the files, be an archivist. He was inconsolable. I found him comical, even in this situation. But I was also annoyed. "They've been shooting down people!" I said angrily. "And you're carrying on about files!" He looked at me as if I weren't there and wailed repeatedly: "The files are burning! All the files!" He was standing off to the side, but it was not undangerous for him; his lament was not to be missed—after all, I too had heard him.

In the following days and weeks of utter dejection, when you could not think of anything else, when the events you had witnessed kept recurring over and over again in your mind, haunting you night after night even in your sleep, there was still *one* legitimate connection to literature. And this connection was Karl Kraus. My idolization of him was at its highest level then. This time it was gratitude for a specific public deed; I don't know whom I could ever be more thankful to for such an action. Under the impact of the massacre on that day, he put up posters everywhere in Vienna, demanding the voluntary resignation of Police Commissioner Johann Schober, who was responsible for the order to shoot and for the ninety deaths. Kraus was alone in this demand; he was the only public figure who acted in this way. And while the other celebrities, of whom Vienna has never had a lack, did not wish to lay themselves open to criticism or perhaps ridicule, Kraus alone had the courage of his indignation. His posters were the only thing that kept us going in those days. I went from one poster to another, paused in front of each one, and I felt as if all the justice on earth had entered the letters of Kraus's name.

Some time ago, I set down this account of July 15 and its aftermath. I have quoted it here verbatim. Perhaps, although brief, it can offer a notion of the gravity of what happened.

Ever since, I have often tried to approach that day, which may have been the most crucial day of my life after my father's death. I have to say "approach," for it is very hard to get at this day; it is an outspread day, stretching across an entire city, a day of movement for me too, for I biked all over Vienna. My feelings on that day were all focused in *one direction*. It was the most *unambiguous* day that I can remember, unambiguous only because one's feelings could not be diverted from the day as it went by.

I don't know *who* made the Palace of Justice the goal of the tremendous processions from all parts of the city. One could think that the choice was spontaneous, even though this cannot be true. Someone must have blurted out the words "to the Palace of Justice." But it is not important to know who it was, for these words were taken in by everybody who heard them; they were accepted without qualms, waverings, or deliberation, without delay or demur, and they pulled everybody in one and the same direction.

Perhaps the substance of July 15 fully entered *Crowds and Power*. If this is so, then it would be impossible to trace anything back completely to the original experience, to the sensory elements of that day.

There was the long bike ride into town. I cannot remember the route. I do not know where I first bumped into people. I cannot *see* myself clearly on that day, but I still feel the excitement, the advancing, and the fluency of the movement. Everything is dominated by the word "fire," then by actual fire.

A *throbbing* in my head. It may have been sheer chance that I did not personally see any attacks upon policemen. But I did see the throng being shot at and people falling. The shots were like whips. I saw people run into the side streets and I saw them reemerge and form into crowds again. I saw people fall and I saw corpses on the ground, but I wasn't right next to them. I was dreadfully frightened, especially of these corpses. I went over to them, but *avoided* them as soon as I got closer. In my excitement, they seemed to be *growing bigger*. Until the Republican Defense Corps arrived to carry them away, the corpses were surrounded by empty space, as if people expected bullets to strike here again.

The mounted Defense Corps made an extremely horrible impression, perhaps because they were frightened themselves.

A man in front of me spat and pointed his right thumb halfway back: "Someone's hanging there! They've pulled his pants off!" What was he spitting at? The victim? Or the murder? I couldn't see what he was pointing at. A woman in front of me shrieked: "Peppi! Peppi!" Her eyes were closed and she was reeling. Everyone began to run. The woman fell down. However, she hadn't been shot. I heard galloping horses. I didn't go over to the woman, who was lying on the ground. I ran with the others. I sensed that I had to run with them. I wanted to flee into a doorway, but I couldn't get away from the running throng. A very big, strong man running next to me banged his fist on his chest and bellowed as he ran: "Let them shoot me! Me! Me! Me!" Suddenly, he was gone. He hadn't fallen down. Where was he?

This was perhaps the eeriest thing of all: you saw and heard people in a powerful gesture that ousted everything else, and then those very people had vanished from the face of the earth. Everything yielded and invisible holes opened everywhere. However, the overall structure did not disappear; even if you suddenly found yourself alone somewhere, you could feel things tugging and tearing at you. The reason was that you *heard* something everywhere: there was something rhythmic in the air, an evil music. You could call it music; you felt elevated by it. I did not feel as if I were moving on my own legs. I felt as if I were in a resonant wind. A crimson head popped up in front of me, at various points, up and down, up and down, rising and dropping, as if floating on water. I looked for it as though I were to follow its directives; I thought it had red hair, then I recognized a red kerchief and no longer looked for it.

I neither met nor recognized anyone; any people I spoke to were unknown to me. However, there were few people I spoke to. I heard a great deal; there was always something to hear; most cutting of all were the boohs when the police fired into the throng and people fell. At such moments, the boohs were relentless, especially the female boohs, which could be made out distinctly. It seemed to me as if the volleys of gunfire were elicited by boohs. But I also noticed that this impression was wrong, for the volleys continued even when no more boohs could be heard. You could hear the gunfire everywhere, even farther away, whiplashes over and over.

The persistence of the crowd, which, driven away, instantly erupted from the side streets. The fire would not let the people go; the Palace of Justice burned for hours, and the time of the burning was also the time of utmost agitation. It was a very hot day; even if you did not see the fire, the sky was red for a great distance, and the air smelled of burned paper, thousands and thousands of files.

The Defense Corps, which you saw everywhere, recognizable by their windbreakers and armbands, contrasted with the police force: the Corps was unarmed. Its weapons were stretchers on which the wounded and the dead were carried off. Its eagerness to help was obvious; its members stood out against the fury of the boohs as though they were not part of the crowd. Also, they turned up everywhere; their emergence often signaled victims before these victims were seen by anyone else.

I did not personally see the Palace of Justice being set on fire, but I learned about it before I saw flames: I could tell by a change of tone in the crowd. People shouted at one another about what had happened; at first, I did not understand; it sounded joyous, not shrill, not greedy; it sounded liberated.

The fire was what held the situation together. You felt the fire, its presence was overwhelming; even if you did not see it, you nevertheless had it in your mind, its attraction and the attraction exerted by the crowd were one and the same. The salvoes of gunfire by the police aroused boohs, the boohs new salvoes. But no matter where you happened to be under the impact of the gunfire, no matter where you seemingly fled, your connection with others (an open or secret connection, depending on the place) remained in effect. And you were drawn back into the province of the fire—circuitously, since there was no other possible way.

This day, which was borne by a uniform feeling (a single, tremendous wave surging over the city, absorbing it: when the wave ebbed, you could scarcely believe that the city was still there)—this day was made up of countless details, each one etched in your mind, none slipping away. Each detail exists in itself, memorable and discernible, and yet each one also forms a part of the tremendous wave, without which everything seems hollow and absurd. The thing to be grasped is the wave, not these details. During the following year and then again and again later on, I tried to grasp the wave, but I have never succeeded. I could not succeed, for nothing is more mysterious and more incomprehensible than a crowd. Had I fully understood it, I would not have wrestled with the problem of a crowd for thirty years, trying to puzzle it out and trying to depict it and reconstruct it as thoroughly as possible, like other human phenomena.

Even were I to assemble all the concrete details of which this day consisted for me, bring them together hard and unadorned, neither reducing nor exaggerating—I could not do justice to this day, for it consisted of more. The roaring of the wave was audible all the time, washing these details to the surface; and only if this wave could be rendered in words and depicted, could one say: really, nothing has been reduced.

Instead of approaching individual details, however, I could speak about the effects that this day had on my later thinking. This day was responsible for some of my most important insights in my book on crowds. Anything I looked for in widely separate source works, repeating, testing, taking notes, reading, and then subsequently rereading in slow motion, as it were, I was able to compare with the memory of that central event, which remained fresh—notwithstanding subsequent events, which occurred on a greater scale, involving more people, with greater consequences for the world. For later years, when agitation and indignation no longer had the same weight, the isolation of the Fifteenth of July, its restriction to Vienna, gave it something like the character of a model: an event limited in both space and time, with an indisputable cause and taking a clear and unmistakable course.

Here, once and for all, I had experienced something that I later called an *open* crowd, I had witnessed its formation: the confluence of people from all parts of the city, in long, steadfast, undeflectable processions, their direction set by the position of the building that bore the name *Justice*, yet embodied injustice because of a miscarriage of justice. I had come to see that a crowd has to fall apart, and I had seen it fearing its disintegration; I had watched it do everything it could to prevent it; I had watched it actually see itself in the fire it lit, hindering its disintegration so long as this fire burned. It warded off any attempt at putting out the fire; its own longevity depended on that of the fire. It was scattered, driven away, and sent fleeing by attacks; yet even though wounded, injured, and dead people lay before it on the streets, even though the crowd had no weapons of its own, it gathered again, for the fire was still burning, and the glow of the flames illuminated the sky over the squares and streets. I saw that a crowd can flee without panicking; that mass flight and panic are distinguishable. So long as the fleeing crowd does not disintegrate into individuals worried only about themselves, about their own persons, then the crowd still exists, although fleeing; and when the crowd stops fleeing, it can turn and attack.

I realized that the crowd needs no *leader* to form, notwithstanding all previous theories in this respect. For one whole day, I watched a crowd that had formed *without a leader*. Now and then, very seldom, there were people, orators, giving speeches that supported the crowd. Their importance was minimal, they were anonymous, they contributed nothing to the formation of the crowd. Any account giving them a central position falsifies the events. If anything did loom out, sparking the formation of the crowd, it was the sight of the burning Palace of Justice. The salvoes of the police did not whip the crowd apart: they whipped it together. The sight of people escaping through the streets was a mirage: for even when running, they fully understood that certain people were falling and would not get up again. These victims unleashed the wrath of the crowd no less than the fire did.

During that brightly illuminated, dreadful day, I gained the true picture of what, as a crowd, fills our century. I gained it so profoundly that I kept going back to contemplate it anew, both compulsively and willingly. I returned over and over and watched; and even today, I sense how hard it is for me to tear myself away, since I have managed to achieve only the tiniest portion of my goal: to understand what a crowd is.

13.

From *Crowds and Power*

"The Crowd"

Translated by Carol Stewart

The Fear of Being Touched

There is nothing that man fears more than the touch of the unknown. He wants to *see* what is reaching toward him, and to be able to recognize or at least classify it. Man always tends to avoid physical contact with anything strange. In the dark, the fear of an unexpected touch can mount to panic. Even clothes give insufficient security: it is easy to tear them and pierce through to the naked, smooth, defenseless flesh of the victim.

All the distances which men create round themselves are dictated by this fear. They shut themselves in houses which no one may enter, and only there feel some measure of security. The fear of burglars is not only the fear of being robbed, but also the fear of a sudden and unexpected clutch out of the darkness.

The repugnance to being touched remains with us when we go about among people; the way we move in a busy street, in restaurants, trains, or buses, is governed by it. Even when we are standing next to them and are able to watch and examine them closely, we avoid actual contact if we can. If we do not avoid it, it is because we feel attracted to someone; and then it is we who make the approach.

The promptness with which apology is offered for an unintentional contact, the tension with which it is awaited, our violent and sometimes even physical reaction when it is not forthcoming, the antipathy and hatred we feel for the offender, even when we cannot be certain who it is—the whole knot of shifting and intensely sensitive reactions to an alien touch—proves that we are dealing here with a human propensity as deep-seated as it is alert and insidious; something which never leaves a man when he has once established the boundaries of his personality. Even in sleep, when he is far more unguarded, he can all too easily be disturbed by a touch.

It is only in a crowd that man can become free of this fear of being touched. That is the only situation in which the fear changes into its opposite. The crowd he needs is the dense crowd, in which body is pressed to body; a crowd, too, whose psychical constitution is also dense, or compact, so that he no longer notices who it is that presses against him. As soon as a man has surrendered himself to the crowd, he ceases to fear its touch. Ideally, all are equal there; no distinctions count, not even that of sex. The man pressed against him is the same as himself. He feels him as he feels himself. Suddenly it is as though everything were happening in one and the same body. This is perhaps one of the reasons why a crowd seeks to close in on itself: it wants to rid each individual as completely as possible of the fear of being touched. The more fiercely people press together, the more certain they feel that they do not fear each other. This reversal of the fear of being touched belongs to the nature of crowds. The feeling of relief is most striking where the density of the crowd is greatest.

The Open and the Closed Crowd

The crowd, suddenly there where there was nothing before, is a mysterious and universal phenomenon. A few people may have been standing together—five, ten, or twelve, not more; nothing has been announced, nothing is expected. Suddenly everywhere is black with people and more come streaming from all sides as though streets had only one direction. Most of them do not know what has happened and, if questioned, have no answer; but they hurry to be there where most other people are. There is a determination in their movement which is quite different from the expression of ordinary curiosity. It seems as though the movement of some of them transmits itself to the others. But that is not all; they have a goal which is there before they can find words for it. This goal is the blackest spot where most people are gathered.

This is the extreme form of the spontaneous crowd and much more will have to be said about it later. In its innermost core it is not quite as spontaneous as it appears, but, except for these five, ten, or twelve people with whom actually it originates, it is everywhere spontaneous. As soon as it exists at all, it wants to consist of *more* people: the urge to grow is the first and supreme attribute of the crowd. It wants to seize everyone within reach; anything shaped like a human being can join it. The natural crowd is the *open* crowd; there are no limits whatever to its growth; it does not recognize houses, doors, or locks and those who shut themselves in are suspect. "Open" is to be understood here in the fullest sense of the word; it means open everywhere and in any direction. The open crowd exists so long as it grows; it disintegrates as soon as it stops growing.

For just as suddenly as it originates, the crowd disintegrates. In its spontaneous form it is a sensitive thing. The openness which enables it to grow is, at the same time, its danger. A fore-boding of threatening disintegration is always alive in the crowd. It seeks, through rapid increase, to avoid this for as long as it can; it absorbs everyone, and, because it does, must ultimately fall to pieces.

In contrast to the open crowd which can grow indefinitely and which is of universal interest because it may spring up any-where, there is the *closed* crowd.

The closed crowd renounces growth and puts the stress on permanence. The first thing to be noticed about it is that it has a boundary. It establishes itself by accepting its limitation. It creates a space for itself which it will fill. This space can be com-pared to a vessel into which liquid is being poured and whose capacity is known. The entrances to this space are limited in number, and only these entrances can be used; the boundary is respected whether it consists of stone, of solid wall, or of some special act of acceptance, or entrance fee. Once the space is completely filled, no one else is allowed in. Even if there is an overflow, the important thing is always the dense crowd in the closed room; those standing outside do not really belong.

The boundary prevents disorderly increase, but it also makes it more difficult for the crowd to disperse and so postpones its dissolution. In this way the crowd sacrifices its chance of growth, but gains in staying power. It is protected from outside influ-ences which could become hostile and dangerous and it sets its hope on *repetition*. It is the expectation of reassembly which en-ables its members to accept each dispersal. The building is wait-ing for them; it exists for their sake and, so long as it is there, they will be able to meet in the same manner. The space is theirs, even during the ebb, and in its emptiness it reminds them of the flood.

The Discharge

The most important occurrence within the crowd is the *discharge*. Before this the crowd does not actually exist; it is the discharge which creates it. This is the moment when all who belong to the crowd get rid of their differences and feel equal.

These differences are mainly imposed from outside; they are distinctions of rank, status, and property. Men as individuals are always conscious of these distinctions; they weigh heavily on them and keep them firmly apart from one another. A man stands by himself on a secure and well-defined spot, his every gesture asserting his right to keep others at a distance. He stands there like a windmill on an enormous plain, moving expressively; and there is nothing between him and the next mill. All life, so far as he knows it, is laid out in distances—the house in which he shuts himself and his property, the positions he holds, the rank he desires—all these serve to create distances, to confirm and extend them. Any free or large gesture of approach toward another human being is inhibited. Impulse and counter impulse ooze away as in a desert. No man can get near another, nor reach his height. In every sphere of life, firmly established hierarchies prevent him touching anyone more exalted than himself, or descending, except in appearance, to anyone lower. In different societies the distances are differently balanced against each other, the stress in some lying on birth, in others on occupation or property.

I do not intend to characterize these hierarchies in detail here, but it is essential to know that they exist everywhere and everywhere gain a decisive hold on men's minds and determine their behavior to each other. But the satisfaction of being higher in rank than others does not compensate for the loss of freedom of movement. Man petrifies and darkens in the distances he has created. He drags at the burden of them, but cannot move. He forgets that it is self-inflicted, and longs for liberation. But how, alone, can he free himself? Whatever he does, and however determined he is, he will always find himself among others who thwart his efforts. So long as they hold fast to *their* distances, he can never come any nearer to them.

Only together can men free themselves from their burdens of distance; and this, precisely, is what happens in a crowd. During the discharge distinctions are thrown off and all feel *equal*. In that density, where there is scarcely any space between, and body presses against body, each man is as near the other as he is to himself; and an immense feeling of relief ensues. It is for the sake of this blessed moment, when no one is greater or better than another, that people become a crowd.

But the moment of discharge, so desired and so happy, contains its own danger. It is based on an illusion; the people who suddenly feel equal have not really become equal; nor will they *feel* equal forever. They return to their separate houses, they lie down on their own beds, they keep their possessions and their names. They do not cast out their relations nor run away from their families. Only true conversion leads men to give up their old associations and form new ones. Such associations, which by their very nature are only able to accept a limited number of members, have to secure their continuance by rigid rules. Such groups I call crowd crystals. Their function will be described later.

But the crowd, as such, disintegrates. It has a presentiment of this and fears it. It can only go on existing if the process of discharge is continued with new people who join it. Only the growth of the crowd prevents those who belong to it creeping back under their private burdens.

14.

From *Crowds and Power*

"The Entrails of Power"

The Hand

The hand owes its origin to life in trees. Its primary characteristic is the separation of the thumb. It is the thumb's powerful development, and the gap between it and the other fingers, which make it possible to use what was once a claw to grasp whole branches and thus make it easy and natural to move about in trees: we see from the monkeys how useful hands are in this respect. As is now generally recognized, this is the oldest function of the hand.

There is, however, a tendency to overlook the fact that the two hands have different functions in climbing; they do not do the same thing at the same time. While the one hand is reaching for a new branch, the other holds fast to the old one. This holding fast is of cardinal importance, for in rapid movement it alone prevents a fall. In no circumstances must the hand from which the weight of the body is suspended loosen its hold, and this teaches the hand a tenacity of grip which is quite different from the older grip on prey. In addition, as soon as the second hand has grasped the new branch, the first hand must loosen its grip on the old one. Unless this is done quickly the climbing creature cannot proceed. The hand thus acquires a new faculty: the ability to let go of something instantly. Prey was never relinquished except under extreme pressure and against all the habits and desires of the holder.

For each hand, therefore, the act of climbing consists of two consecutive stages: grasping, letting go; grasping, letting go. It is true that one hand does the same as the other, but a stage later. At any given moment each is doing the opposite of the other. What distinguishes monkeys from other animals is the quick succession of these two movements; grasping and letting go follow immediately on each other, and it is to this that they owe part of the marvelous nimbleness we admire in them.

The higher monkeys or apes, who have abandoned the trees for the ground, have retained this essential faculty by which the two hands, as it were, partner each other; and there is a widespread human occupation which, in the whole manner of its pursuit, clearly recalls it: this is *trading*.

The essence of trading is the giving of one object in exchange for another. The one hand tenaciously holds on to the object with which it seeks to tempt the stranger. The other hand is stretched out in demand toward the second object, which it seeks to have in exchange for its own. As soon as it touches this, the first hand lets go of its object; but not before, or it may lose both. The crudest form of cheating, when something is taken from someone without any return being made, corresponds, translated into the context of climbing, to falling from the tree. To prevent this the trader remains on his guard during the whole transaction and scrutinizes every movement of his opposite number. The profound and universal pleasure men take in trading is thus partly explained by the fact that trade is a translation into nonphysical terms of one of the oldest movement patterns. In nothing else today is man so near the apes.

After this sortie into a much later time let us return to the hand itself and its origins. Among the branches of trees the hand learned a mode of grasp which was no longer solely concerned with immediate food. The route from hand to mouth, which is short and scarcely susceptible of variation, was thus interrupted. A branch which broke off in the hand was the origin of the *stick*. Enemies could be fended off with a stick and space made for the primitive creature who perhaps no more than resembled man. Seen from a tree, the stick was the weapon which lay nearest to hand. Man put his trust in it and has never abandoned it. It was a cudgel; sharpened, it became a spear; bent and the ends tied together, a bow; skillfully cut, it made arrows. But through all these transformations it remained what it had been originally: an instrument to create distance, something which kept away from men the touch and the grasp that they feared. In the same way that the upright human stance still retains a measure of grandeur, so, through all its transformations the stick has never wholly lost its magical quality; as scepter and as sorcerer's wand it has remained the attribute of two important forms of power.

THE PATIENCE OF THE HAND

It is the violent activities of the hands which are thought of as the oldest. We not only think of the act of seizing with hostile intent, which is expected to be cruel and sudden, but automatically, and in spite of their technical complexity and the remoteness of their derivation, we add to the group many movements which in fact only developed later: hitting, stabbing, thrusting, throwing, shooting. The speed and precision of these movements may be greater, but in substance and in intent they have remained the same. They are important for hunters and soldiers, but they have added nothing to the special glory of the human hand.

The hand has found other ways to perfect itself and these, in all cases, are ways which renounce predatory violence. Its true greatness lies in its *patience*. It is the quiet, prolonged activities of the hand which have created the only world in which we care to live. The potter whose hands are skilled in shaping clay stands as creator at the beginning of the Bible.

But how did the hands learn patience? How did the fingers of the hand become sensitive? One of the earliest occupations we know of is the picking over of the fur of a friend which monkeys delight in. We imagine that they are searching for something and, as they often do undoubtedly find something, we have ascribed a purely practical and far too narrow purpose to this activity. In reality they do it principally for the agreeable sensation that the individual fingers receive from the hairs of the skin. It constitutes the most primitive "finger exercises" that we know. It was through them that the hand became the delicate instrument we marvel at today.

THE FINGER EXERCISES OF MONKEYS

Everyone who observes monkeys is struck by their solicitous mutual examination of each other's coats. The meticulous way in which they separate and observe each individual hair leads one to suppose that they are hunting for vermin. Their posture recalls that of men looking for fleas, and their hands go carefully to their mouths as though they had found something—so frequently and productively, in fact, that it seems to prove the necessity of such a search. This, therefore, has always been the popular interpretation of it. Only recently has the proceeding been more precisely explained by zoologists.

A coherent description and analysis of this monkey habit may be found in Zuckerman's book *The Social Life of Monkeys and Apes*. It is so revealing that I shall quote from it at length.

"Flea-catching," regardless of what the sociologists may have to say, is the most fundamental and basal form of social intercourse between Rhesus monkeys. Monkeys, and to a lesser extent apes, spend a great part of the day grooming one another. An animal will carefully examine a fellow's coat with its fingers, eating many of the odds and ends that it finds. These are carried to its mouth either by hand or sometimes, after licking a tuft of hair, by direct nibbling. The performance implies exceedingly well co-ordinated movements of the fingers, associated with exact accommodation and convergence of the eyes. This behavior is commonly misinterpreted as an attempt to remove lice. Actually vermin are rarely found on either captive or wild monkeys. The fruits of the search generally turn out to be small, loose, scaly fragments of skin, particles of skin secretion, thorns, and other foreign matter. When not engaged in other pursuits, monkeys react immediately to the presence of fur by "picking." The stimulus of hair is one to which a monkey responds as soon as it is born, and one which remains powerfully effective in all phases of its growth. In the lack of a companion, a healthy monkey will pick through its own fur. Two, and sometimes even three, monkeys may, as a group, pick over one of their fellows. Usually the one being cleaned is passive, except for movements which facilitate the investigations carried out by its grooms. Sometimes, however, it may simultaneously be engaged in picking through the coat of yet another animal. Monkeys do not confine their grooming activities to their own kind. Any hairy object, animate or inanimate, may form the subject of their investigations. They readily

pick over the hair of a human "friend." They may be
seen in captivity, and have been seen in the wild, picking
through the fur of animals belonging to different orders.
The performance seems to have sexual significance, not
only because of its gentle stimulation of numerous cu-
taneous end organs, but also because it is sometimes accompanied by direct sexual activity. For this reason and
because of its frequent expression, it is perhaps legitimate
to regard the picking reaction and the stimulus of hair as
factors involved in the maintenance of a social group of
sub-human primates.

The surprising thing in this account is Zuckerman's attribu-
tion of sexual significance. He speaks of two or three monkeys
together picking over the fur of a companion, and he stresses
the significance for them of all kinds of fur. Later in his book he
contrasts this "picking" with sexual activity and points out that
even in periods of sexual inactivity when they show little sign
of such interest, they still come to the bars of their cages to be
scratched. He also has a good deal to say about the early significance of fur for the young monkey.

The first external phenomenon of which a monkey has any
sensory experience is hair. As soon as a baby monkey or ape is
born it is pulled by its mother to her breast, and its fingers immediately clutch and hold her fur. "Unaided, the young animal
finds the nipple by 'trial and error.' For about the first month
of its life it lives entirely on milk, and is carried by its mother
wherever she goes. When the mother is sitting, the young animal is generally held close to her body, with its feet clutching at
the hair of her belly and its hands buried in the fur of her chest.
When she moves the baby hangs on in the same way, slung, as

it were, beneath her. Usually it holds on by its own unaided efforts, but sometimes the mother clasps it with one 'arm,' while
she hops along on three 'legs.' When she is sitting she may em-
brace her baby with both arms. The baby manifests a strong interest in fur. It crawls over its mother's fur; within a week it may
scratch its own body. I once observed a monkey, a week old,
vaguely exploring with its hands the fur of its father, who was
sitting close to its mother. Sometimes the mother monkey behaves as though she were irritated by having her fur clutched."
One monkey in the London Gardens persisted in pulling away
the hands and feet of her infant wherever they clasped.

The behavior of a nursing monkey does not alter when her
baby dies. She continues to press it to her breast and carries it
in her arms wherever she goes. "At first she never puts it down,
picking through its fur as she did when it lived. She examines
its mouth and its eyes, its nose and its ears. In a few days one
notices a change in her behavior. A slightly decomposing body
now droops over her arms. Except when moving, she no longer
presses it to her breast, and although she continues to groom the
body and to bite at the skin, she begins to lay it on the ground
more frequently. The body becomes yet more decomposed, and
mummification sets in, but her investigation of the skin and fur
continues. The dried-up body now begins to disintegrate. One
notices a leg missing, an arm missing, and it is soon a shriveled
bit of skin. The mother is more often seen biting off pieces—it
is unknown whether she swallows them. At about this stage she
may abandon of her own accord what is left of the shriveled
remains."

Monkeys often retain many kinds of furry and feathery
objects. Zuckerman observed a year-old baboon who seized a
young kitten, killed it, and kept it in her arms the whole day,

picking through its fur meanwhile, and protesting vigorously when it was removed in the evening. Monkeys in the London Zoo can be seen picking through the feathers of sparrows they have killed. Also recorded is the case of a captive monkey who mothered the dead body of a rat thrown to her as elaborately as the monkey described above mothered her own dead infant.

From the evidence he collected Zuckerman deduced that there are three factors which contribute to effective maternal behavior. The two primary ones are fundamentally of social significance: first, the mother's attraction to a small furry object, and second, the living baby's strong attraction to its mother's fur. The third factor is the sucking reflex of the young animal, whose operation relieves mammary tension in the mother.

The reaction to fur is thus a basic factor in social behavior. Its importance is indicated by the fact that a young primate will cling to its mother's fur even after her death; but its attraction is apparently not to the specific body, since it is equally soothed by the carcass of any other dead baboon. "The fundamental nature of the reaction to fur is perhaps also indicated by its ill-defined character and by the variety of the situations in which it is evoked. Feathers, brooms, mice, kittens are all adequate stimuli. It seems very likely that the social performance of grooming develops from this innate response to fur, and that it always remains one of the fundamental bonds holding monkeys together."

It will be seen from these lengthy extracts that Zuckerman himself does not really believe in the specific sexual significance of the grooming of the coat among primates. He is quite clear that fur, in itself, and in all circumstances, has a peculiar attraction for monkeys. The pleasure which the touch of hair

affords them must be of a quite particular kind, and they seek it
from any source, the dead as well as the living, and strangers as
well as their own kind. The size of the animal they tend does not
matter. For this purpose the baby means as much to the mother
as the mother to the baby. Mating couples and friends indulge
in it equally and several animals may occupy themselves simultaneously with the fur of one.

The pleasure is a pleasure of the *fingers*. They can never
have enough of hair; they can spend whole hours drawing their
fingers through it. And these are the animals whose liveliness
and inconsequent mobility are proverbial. There is an old Chinese tradition according to which monkeys have no stomachs
and digest their food by leaping around. Hence the contrast to
the endless patience they display in this kind of grooming is
all the more striking. Through it the fingers become more and
more sensitive. The feeling of many hair tips simultaneously en-
genders a particular sense of touch which is entirely different
from the crude sensation of snatching or grasping. One is ir-
resistibly put in mind of all those later occupations of mankind
which depend on the delicacy and patience of the fingers. The
as yet unknown ancestors of man, like all the apes, had a long
period of such finger exercises behind them. Without these our
hands would never have developed as far as they have. Various
factors may originally have given rise to this grooming; perhaps
the search for parasites and perhaps the early experiences of the
baby ape at the hairy breast of its mother. But the process itself, in the developed state in which it can be observed in all
monkeys, has a unified significance of its own. Without it we
should never have learned to *shape* anything, nor to sew, nor
to *stroke*. The real specific life of the hand begins with it. As a
man watched his hands at work, the changing shapes they fashioned must gradually have impressed themselves on his mind.

Without this we should probably never have learned to form symbols for things, nor, therefore, to *speak*.

THE HANDS AND THE BIRTH OF OBJECTS

The hand which scoops up water is the first vessel. The fingers of both hands intertwined are the first basket. The rich development of all kinds of intertwining, from the game of cat's cradle to weaving, seems to me to have its origin here. One feels that hands live their own life and their own transformations. It is not enough that this or that shape should exist in the surrounding world. Before early man could create it himself, his hands and fingers had to enact it. Empty fruit husks in the shape of cups, like coconut shells, may have existed for a long time, but were thrown away heedlessly. It was the fingers forming a hollow to scoop up water which made the cup real. One could say that objects in our sense, objects which have value because we ourselves have made them, first existed as signs made by hands. There seems to be an immensely important turning point where the nascent sign language for things first comprehends a desire to shape them oneself, long before this is actually attempted.

What man, with the help of his hands, enacted, was only *made* long afterward, when it had been enacted often enough. *Words* and *objects* are accordingly the emanations and products of a single unified experience: *representation by means of the hands*. Everything that a man can do, everything that represents his culture, he first incorporated into himself by means of transformation. Hands and face were the instruments of these transformations and their significance, compared with the rest of the body, became increasingly great. The specific life of the hands, in this its earliest sense, still retains its pristine force in gesticulation.

DESTRUCTIVENESS IN MONKEYS AND MEN

Destructiveness in monkeys and men can plausibly be regarded as "hardening exercises" of the hands and fingers. Life in trees brought the hands of the climbing monkey into constant contact with a material harder than themselves. To make use of the branches of trees he had to hold on to them, but he also had to know how to break them. The testing of his "ground" was a testing of branches and twigs; one that broke easily was a false basis for progress. The exploration of the tree world was a ceaseless confrontation of hardness. It still remained necessary for him to test it even when he had acquired considerable experience of it. The stick which, to him as to men, became the earliest weapon, was the first in the long series of *hard* instruments. The hardness of the hands was measured against it, as later against stones. Fruit and the flesh of animals was soft; softest of all was fur. The grooming and picking of the coat trained the delicacy of the fingers; the breaking of whatever they held their strength.

There is thus a separate destructiveness of the hand, not immediately connected with prey and killing. It is of a purely mechanical nature and mechanical inventions are extensions of it. Precisely because of its innocence it has become particularly dangerous. It knows itself to be without any intention to kill, and thus feels free to embark on anything. What it does appears to be the concern of the hands alone, of their flexibility and skill, their harmless usefulness. It is this mechanical destructiveness of the hands, now grown to a complex system of technology, which, whenever it is linked with a real intention to kill, supplies the automatic element of the resulting process, that empty mindlessness which is so particularly disquieting. No one actually intends anything; it all happens, as it were, of itself.

Privately, and on a small scale, everyone experiences the same process in himself whenever his fingers thoughtlessly break matches or crumple paper. The multiform ramifications which this mechanical urge to destroy exhibits among men are closely connected with the development of his tool-using technique. It was through it that he learned to master the hard with the hard. But, in the last resort, it is always the hands that matter. Their faculty of independent life has had tremendous consequences. In more than one respect, man's hands have been his destiny.

THE KILLERS ARE ALWAYS THE POWERFUL

It is not only the whole hand which has served as a model and stimulus. The individual fingers, and particularly the extended index finger, have also acquired a significance of their own. The tip of the finger is pointed and armored with a nail. It first provided man with the sensation of stabbing. From it developed the dagger, which is a harder and more pointed finger. The arrow is a cross between finger and bird; it was lengthened in order to penetrate further, and made more slender to fly better. Beak and thorn also influenced its composition; beaks in any case are proper to feathered objects. A pointed stick became a spear, an arm extended into a single finger.

All weapons of this kind are concentrated on a point. Man was himself stabbed by long, hard thorns and pulled them out with his fingers. The finger which detached itself from the rest of the hand and, acting like a thorn, passed on the stab is the psychological origin of this kind of weapon. The man who has been stabbed stabs back with his finger and with the artificial finger he gradually learns to make.

Not all the operations of the hand are invested with the same degree of power; their prestige varies greatly. Things which are particularly important for the practical existence of a group of

men may be highly valued, but the greatest respect is always accorded to anything which has to do with killing. That which can
kill is feared; that which does not directly serve killing is merely
useful. All that the patient skills of the hand bring to those who
confine themselves to them is subjection. It is those who devote
themselves to killing who have power.

15.

From *Crowds and Power*

"The Survivor"

The Escape of Josephus

Among the stories of the war between the Jews and the Romans, which took place during Domitian's youth, there is an account of an incident which perfectly illustrates the nature of the survivor. The Roman forces were commanded by Vespasian, the father of Domitian, and it was during this war that the Flavii achieved imperial power.

The Jews had been chafing under Roman rule for some time. When they finally rose against it in earnest, they appointed commanders in each district of the country, to collect troops and to prepare the defense of the towns so that there would be some chance of their being able to repel the inevitable attack of the Roman legions. Josephus, then barely thirty years old, was appointed commander in Galilee and he set to work zealously to accomplish his task. In his *History of the Jewish War* he describes the obstacles he had to contend with: dissensions among the townspeople; rivals who intrigued against him and collected troops on their own account; towns which refused to acknowledge his leadership, or later denied it again. But, with astonishing energy, he got together an army—though it was badly equipped—and fortified strongholds against the coming of the Romans.

And, in due course, they came. They were under the command of Vespasian, who had with him his son, Titus, a young man the same age as Josephus. (Nero was then still emperor in Rome.) Vespasian had distinguished himself in many theaters of war and was known as a general of long experience. He advanced into Galilee and surrounded Josephus and his army in the town of Jotapata. The Jews defended it stubbornly and bravely. Josephus was full of resource and knew how every attack should be met. The siege lasted for forty-seven days and the Romans suffered heavy losses in the course of it. When at last, and then only by treachery and at night, they succeeded in forcing their way in, the defenders were all asleep and did not realize that the Romans were among them until daybreak. Then they fell into terrible despair and many of them killed themselves.

Josephus escaped. I shall give in his own words his story of what happened to him after the capture of the town, for, as far as I know, there is in all literature no other comparable account of a survivor. With curious self-awareness and with an insight into the very nature of survival, he describes everything that he did in order to save his life. It was comparatively easy for him to be honest, for he did not write his account until later, when he already stood high in the favor of the Romans.

> After the fall of Jotapata, the Romans searched everywhere for Josephus—among the dead and in all the secret hiding places of the city—partly because the soldiers themselves were incensed against him, and partly because their commander was set on his capture, thinking that it might de-

termine the whole course of the war. Josephus, however, as if helped by divine providence, had managed to slip through the enemy during the fighting and had jumped down into an underground cistern which opened on one side into a large cave, invisible from above. In this cave he found forty men of importance concealed, who had provided themselves with food for several days, and here he lay hid in the daytime, for the enemy were all around, but emerged at night to search for a way of escape and to see where sentries were posted. But the whole neighborhood was so closely guarded on his account that there was no possibility of escape, and so he retreated into the cave again. For two days he eluded his pursuers in this way, but on the third day a woman who had been among those in the cave was captured, and she betrayed him. Vespasian immediately dispatched two Tribunes with instructions to promise Josephus his safety and to persuade him to come out of the cave.

The Tribunes arrived and spoke courteously to him and guaranteed his life; but to no purpose, for he knew, or thought he knew, what he had to expect in return for all the injuries the Romans had suffered at his hands. The gentle bearing of those who spoke to him in no way altered his estimate of the fate that awaited him. He could not rid himself of the fear that the Romans were only trying to entice him out of the cave in order to execute him. Finally, Vespasian sent a third messenger, the Tribune Nicanor, who was well-known to Josephus; in fact, they had formerly been friends. Nicanor described the leniency with which the Romans treated their vanquished foes. He explained, too, that the generals admired Josephus for his courage more than they hated him, and

that Vespasian had no intention of having him executed.
If he wished, he could kill him without his leaving the
cave; but, in fact, what he wanted was to save the life of
a brave man. He added that it was unthinkable that Vespasian should maliciously send Josephus's friend to him
to trap him, covering a breach of faith with the mask of
friendship; nor would he, Nicanor, ever have lent himself
to such a betrayal of friendship.

As even Nicanor, however, failed to bring Josephus to
a decision, the soldiers in their fury prepared to set fire to
the cave; but Nicanor held them back, for he was determined to take Josephus alive. Surrounded thus by hostile,
threatening soldiers, and with Nicanor still urging him
to surrender, Josephus remembered suddenly the terrible
dreams in which God had revealed to him the impending disasters of the Jewish people and the fates of the Roman Emperors; for he was skilled in the interpretation of
dreams. A priest himself, and the son of a priest, he was
familiar with the prophecies of the Holy Scriptures and
could expound those that were obscure. At this very moment he was filled with inspiration, the terrors of those
dreams rose up before him and silently he prayed to
God, thus: "Since Thou art resolved to humble the Jewish people, whom Thou didst create; since all good fortune is passed to the Romans; and since Thou hast chosen
my spirit to make known the things that are to come, I
yield myself to the Romans; but Thou art my witness
that I go, not as a traitor, but as Thy servant."

After he had prayed, he told Nicanor he would go
with him. When the Jews who had been with him in hiding saw that he had decided to yield to the enemy's per-
suasion, they crowded round him and reproached him

vehemently. They reminded him of all who, on his per-
suasion, had died for freedom; of his own reputation for
courage, which had been so great, yet now he wanted to
live a slave. They asked what mercy he, supposed to be so
wise, thought he would obtain from those he had fought
so stubbornly. They said he had wholly forgotten himself
and that his care for his own life was an outrage to God
and to the Laws of their fathers. *He* might be dazzled by
the good fortune of the Romans; *they* were still mind-
ful of the honor of their people; their right hands and
their swords were his to command if he died willingly
as leader of the Jews; if he refused, he should die unwillingly as a traitor. They drew their swords and threatened
to cut him down if he gave himself up to the Romans.

Josephus was very frightened, but it seemed to him
that he would be betraying the commands of God if he
died before proclaiming them, and in his urgent need he
began to reason with his companions. He said that it was
indeed noble to die in war, but then it must be according
to the custom of war, that is, by the hand of the victor.
It was cowardly in the extreme to kill oneself. Suicide
was both repugnant to the very nature of all living beings and an outrage against God the Creator. God gave
men life and to God must men commit their end. Those
who turned their hands against themselves were hateful
to God, and he would punish both them and their descendants. To all that they had suffered in this life, they
must not now add sin against their Creator. If deliverance should come, they should not refuse it. It would
not be shameful in them to accept their lives, for they
had sufficiently proved their courage by their deeds. But
if they had to die, then they should die at the hands of

their conquerors. He had no thought of going over to
the Romans and so becoming a traitor himself; he hoped
rather for treachery on *their* part. If, in spite of their
given word they killed him, he would die joyfully. Their
broken faith, which God would punish, would be to him
a greater consolation than victory itself.

Thus Josephus put forward every possible argument
to dissuade his companions from suicide. But despair had
made them deaf. They had long dedicated themselves to
death and his words served only to increase their frenzy.
They accused him of cowardice and pressed round him
with drawn swords, as if ready to strike him down. In
danger of his life, and torn by conflicting emotions, Josephus called one man by name, fixed another with a
stare of command, took a third by the arm, pleaded with
a fourth, and so, in each case, succeeded in averting the
sword of death. He was like a wild animal at bay, turning
to face each successive assailant; and as they still, even
in this last extremity, respected him as their commander,
their arms were as if paralyzed, their daggers slipped
from their hands, and many who had drawn their swords
against him sheathed them again of their own free will.

In spite of his desperate position, Josephus's presence
of mind did not fail him. On the contrary, putting his trust
in God, he staked his life on a gamble and addressed his
companions thus: "Since we are resolved to die, and will
not be turned from it, let us draw lots and kill each other
accordingly. The first man on whom the lot falls shall be
killed by the second, and he, in turn, by the third; and so
on, as chance decides. In this way, all shall die, but no one
will have been compelled to take his own life, except the

last man. It would be unfair if he, after the death of his companions, changed his mind and did not kill himself."

With this proposal Josephus won their confidence again, and when they had all declared their agreement, he drew lots with the rest and each man on whom the lot fell offered himself to be killed by the next, for each imagined that a moment later his general would die too; and death with Josephus seemed sweeter than life. At last—let us say that it was either by chance or by divine providence—only Josephus was left with one other man.* Since he did not want to risk the lot falling on him, nor, supposing he escaped it, to stain his hands with the blood of a fellow Jew, he persuaded this man that they should both give themselves up to the Romans and so save their lives.

Having thus come safely through two wars—one with the Romans and one with his own people—Josephus was brought by Nicanor before Vespasian. All the Romans crowded to see the commander of the Jews and pressed shouting round him, some exulting in his capture, some threatening him, and others thrusting their way forward to see him close. Those at the back clamored for his execution; those nearer him remembered his deeds and marveled at the change in his fortunes. Among the officers, though, there were none who, in spite of their former hatred, were not moved by the sight of him. Titus, in particular, was impressed by his steadfast bearing in misfortune, and moved by fellow feeling for his youth—he

---

* In the Slavonic version of *The Jewish War*, which, according to some scholars, is based on an earlier text, there is a strikingly different sentence instead: "After saying this, he counted the numbers cunningly and so deceived them all."

was the same age as Josephus. He wanted to save his life
and pleaded strenuously for him with his father. Vespasian, however, put Josephus under strict guard, proposing
to send him immediately to Nero.

When Josephus heard this, he asked to speak to Vespasian alone. Vespasian ordered everyone to withdraw,
except his son, Titus, and two close friends, and Josephus
then spoke thus:

"You think, Vespasian, that I am simply a prisoner of
war who has fallen into your hands. But you are mistaken: I stand before you as harbinger of great events.
I, Josephus, am sent by God to declare this message to
you. Were this not so, I would not be here, for I know
the Jewish law and how a general should die. You want to
send me to Nero. Why? He and his successors who will
ascend the throne before you will not rule for long. You
yourself, Vespasian, shall be Caesar and Emperor, you
and your son here. Fetter me more securely and guard me
for yourself till that time comes. For you will be Caesar
and master, not only over me, but over land and sea and
the whole human race. Let me be closely watched and, if
I have taken the Name of God in vain, then kill me as I
shall have deserved."

At first Vespasian did not really trust Josephus; he
thought he was lying to save his life. Gradually, however,
he began to believe what he said, for God Himself had already awoken in him imperial ambitions, and he had also
received other signs of future power. He discovered, too,
that Josephus had prophesied truly on other occasions.
One of those who had been present at his private inter-
view with Vespasian expressed surprise that he had not
predicted either the fall of Jotapata or his own capture,

and suggested that what he put forward now was a fable
to ingratiate himself with his enemies. But Josephus replied that he had predicted to the people of Jotapata that
the town would fall after forty-seven days and that he
himself would be taken alive by the Romans. Vespasian
had secret inquiries made among the other prisoners, and
when they confirmed what Josephus had said, he began
to believe the predictions about himself. It is true that he
still kept Josephus fettered and in prison, but he gave him
a splendid robe and other valuable presents and, from
then on, thanks to Titus, treated him with kindness and
consideration.

Josephus's struggle falls into three distinct acts. First, he escapes the slaughter after the fall of Jotapata. The defenders of the
town either kill themselves or are killed by the Romans; a few
are taken prisoner. Josephus escapes by hiding in the cave by the
cistern. Here he finds forty men, whom he expressly describes
as "important." They, like himself, are all survivors. They have
provided themselves with food and hope to remain hidden from
the Romans until some way of escape offers.

But the presence of Josephus, who is the man the Romans are
actually searching for, is betrayed to them by a woman. There-
upon, the situation changes radically and the second, and by far
the most interesting act, begins; one may say that it is unique in
the frankness with which events are described by the chief actor.

The Romans promise Josephus his life. As soon as he believes
them, they cease to be enemies. It is, in the deepest sense, a question of faith. At precisely the right moment, he remembers a
prophetic dream he once had. In it he had been warned that
the Jews would be conquered. They are conquered, though at
first, it is true, only in the fortress of Jotapata which he had

commanded. Fortune is on the side of the Romans. The vision in which this had been revealed to him came from God and God would also help him to find the way to the Romans. He commends himself to God and turns to his new enemies, the Jews who are with him in the cave. They want to commit suicide, so as not to fall into the hands of the Romans. He, their leader, who had spurred them on to fight, should be the first to welcome this form of annihilation. But he is determined to live. He pleads with them and with a hundred arguments seeks to take from them their desire for death. But he does not succeed. Everything he says against death increases their blind passion for it, and also their anger against himself, who shuns it. He sees that he can only escape if they all kill each other and he is the last to remain alive. He therefore makes a show of agreeing with them and hits upon the notion of drawing lots.

The reader will have his own ideas about the way in which these lots were drawn; it is difficult not to suspect fraud. It is the one point in his narrative where Josephus is obscure. He ascribes the extraordinary outcome of this gamble on death either to God or to chance, but he also, as it were, leaves it open to the reader to guess the real course of events. For what follows is monstrous: his companions butcher each other before his eyes. But not simultaneously. Each killing follows the other in due order, and between each the lots are drawn again. Each man has with his own hand to kill one of his comrades and then himself be killed by the next on whom the lot falls. The religious scruples that Josephus advanced against self-murder evidently do not apply to murder. As each man falls, his own hope of deliverance grows. Individually and collectively, he wants them all dead. For himself he wants nothing but to live. They die gladly, believing that their commander dies with them. They cannot suppose that he will be the last left alive. It is unlikely that they even envisage the possibility. But since one of them has to be the last, Josephus forearms himself against this thought too. He tells them that it would be very unfair if the last man changed his mind after the death of his companions, and so saved his life. This, precisely, is what he intends to do. What could least be done after the death of comrades is what he himself wants to do. Pretending in this last hour to be wholly with them, to be one of them, he sends them all to their deaths and, by doing so, saves his own life. They are all caught in the same fate and believe him caught too. But he stands outside it, and destines it only for them. They die so that he may live.

The deception is complete. It is the deception of all leaders. They pretend that they will be the first to die, but, in reality, they send their people to death, so that they themselves may stay alive longer. The trick is always the same. The leader wants to survive, for with each survival he grows stronger. If he has enemies, so much the better; he survives *them*. If not, he has his own people. In any event he uses both, whether successively or together. Enemies he can use openly; that is why he has enemies. His own people must be used secretly.

In Josephus's cave the trick is made manifest. Outside are the enemy, but their former threats have turned to a promise. Inside the cave are his friends. They still hold firmly to their leader's old convictions, convictions with which he himself had imbued them, and they refuse to take advantage of this new hope. Thus the cave which Josephus had intended as his refuge becomes the place of his greatest danger. He dupes the friends who want to lay violent hands both on him and on themselves, and consigns them to a common death. From the very beginning, he has had no thought of sharing it; nor does he share it when it comes. He is left in the end with one sole companion and since, as he says, he has no wish to stain his hands with the blood of a fellow

Jew, he persuades this man to surrender. One man alone he can persuade to live. Forty had been too many for him. The two of them give themselves up to the Romans.

Thus he emerges safely from the war against his own people. This is precisely what he brings the Romans: the enhanced sense of his own life, feeding on the deaths of those he had led. The transmission of this newly won power to Vespasian is the third act of the struggle. It is embodied in a prophetic promise. The Romans were perfectly familiar with the Jews' stubborn belief in God. They knew that the last thing a Jew would do was to take the name of God in vain. Josephus had strong reasons for wanting to see Vespasian emperor in place of Nero. Nero, to whom Vespasian proposed sending him, had not promised him his life; Vespasian had. He knew, too, that Nero despised Vespasian, who was much older than himself, and fell asleep in public when he sang. He had often treated him harshly and had only called again on his military experience when the insurrection of the Jews had begun to assume dangerous proportions. Vespasian thus had every reason to mistrust Nero. A promise of future power must have been welcome to him.

Josephus may himself have believed that the message he gave Vespasian was from God. Prophecy was in his blood; he believed that he was a true prophet and, in prophesying, he brought the Romans something that they themselves lacked. He did not take the gods of the Romans seriously; to him they were superstition. But he knew that he had to convince Vespasian of the importance and authenticity of his message; and Vespasian, like every other Roman, despised the Jews and their religion. He was one man alone among enemies on whom he had inflicted terrible injuries, enemies who but lately had been cursing him, yet he faced them confidently, he expressed himself with force, and he believed in himself more strongly than in anything else.

This belief he owed to the fact that he had survived his own people. The power which he had achieved in the underground cave he transmitted to Vespasian, so that the latter survived not only Nero, his junior by thirty years, but also no less than three of Nero's successors. Each of these died, in effect, by the hand of the other, and Vespasian became Emperor of the Romans.

16.

From *The Human Province, The Secret Heart of the Clock*, and *The Agony of Flies*

Notes, 1942–1993

From *The Human Province*
Translated by Joachim Neugroschel

1942

The word "freedom" serves to express an important, perhaps *the* most important tension. People always want to get *away*, and if the place they want to get to has no name, if it is uncertain and they can't see any borders in it, they call it freedom.

The spatial expression of this tension is the vehement wish to cross a frontier as if it didn't exist. Freedom in flying—for the old, the mythical feeling, reaches as high as the sun. Freedom in time is the triumph over death, and people are quite content just to shove it further and further away. Freedom among *objects* is the liquidation of prices; and the ideal spendthrift, a very free man, desires nothing so much as an incessant changing of prices, undetermined by any rules, an aimless up and down, as though caused by the weather, beyond influence and not even really predictable. There is no freedom "to something," its blessing and its fortune are the tension of the man who wants to disregard barriers, and he always seeks the worst barriers to fulfill this wish. The man who wants to kill has to deal with the dreadful threats accompanying the shalt-not of killing, and if these threats hadn't so deeply tormented him, he would have certainly charged himself with happier tensions. The origin of freedom, however, lies in *breathing*. Anyone can draw breath from any air, and the freedom to breathe is the only one that has not really been destroyed to this day.

1945

A man who can never be neutral. In wars that do not involve him, he is on both sides.

The false foreigner: Someone takes an oath to live disguised as a foreigner in his country until someone recognizes him. He dies, deeply embittered, as a foreigner.

I would like to become tolerant without overlooking anything, persecute no one even when all people persecute me; become better without noticing it; become sadder, but enjoy living; become more serene, be happy in others; belong to no one, grow in everyone; love the best, comfort the worst; not even hate myself anymore.

1949

Crowds and outshouting. A significant function of the crowd is to outshout dangers: whether earthquakes or enemies. People get together in order to shout *louder*. When the other, the earthquake or the enemy, has gone silent, then the crowd has won. It is important to bear in mind that the *ocean* will not be outshouted. For even if a strong crowd succeeded in being louder than the sea for an instant, it would nonetheless never silence the sea.

Hence, in the minds of those who know it, the sea has remained the greatest crowd, which no one can ever equal.

1950

This urge of mine to know everything about all people, no matter when or where they lived, as though my salvation were contingent on each one, his peculiarity, uniqueness, the course of his life, and then what they should be together.

1952

The psychiatric observation of people has something wounding, which lies more in classifying the abnormal than in merely establishing it. There is really no such thing as a norm anymore; people having judgment and experience are now convinced that everyone and everything is abnormal in some way. The value of this insight is in the feeling of the uniqueness of every person that this insight helps; one would thus like to love, respect, and protect every single one, even if his behavior is neither understandable nor predictable. The psychiatrist, however, who creates categories of the abnormal, who aims at classifying and then curing, robs the frequently humiliated man of his uniqueness too. This power, of *grouping* others, is felt to be painful not only by its victim; it is also oppressive for the involved observer to see this power functioning and to be unable to reverse it.

I want to keep smashing myself until I am whole.

1967

He prides himself on being concerned for *all* people, not just for those in a few countries, since death makes no distinction between people, he too makes none.

He does wonder, how he would feel if the earth were suddenly faced with an alien invasion. Would he hate the aliens he does not know as bitterly as the old nations hated one another in that antediluvian age before the atom bomb? Would he say: "Destroy them no matter what they're like, all means are fine, *we* are the best in any event"?

Any expansion one exults in already contains the new narrowness that will make others suffocate.

1971

I am reading Ovid's *Metamorphoses* as though for the first time. It is not the speeches and feelings of the characters that impress me: they are too artistic, their rhetoric passed into European literature from the beginning and was purified into a better truth by later writers. But the inspiration of the poem, its subject matter, is metamorphosis, and Ovid thereby anticipated something that has profoundly interested writers until the present day. He is not content with *naming* metamorphoses, he tracks them down, he describes them, they become graphic processes. He thus detaches the very essence of myth from its usual context and gives it a conspicuousness that it never loses again. He is concerned with *all* metamorphoses, not just this one or that one, he gathers them, he lines them up, each single one of them is investigated in all its ramifications, and even where they still bear common traits by their very nature, they nevertheless seem like fresh, believably seized miracles.

Often it is the metamorphoses of flight, but they are unique; often it is those of pain. Their definitive character is what constitutes their earnestness. If there are rescues, they are dearly purchased; the freedom of the transformed being is lost forever. But the wealth and variation of the series of metamorphoses helps to maintain the mythic fluidity as a whole.

What he has thereby salvaged for the Christian world is

invaluable: the very thing that was most lost to its consciousness. Into its hierarchically paralyzed doctrine, its cumbersome system of virtues and vices, he breathed the older, more liberating breath of metamorphosis. He is the father of a modernism that always existed; its traces could still be readily demonstrated today.

From *The Secret Heart of the Clock:*
Notes, Aphorisms, Fragments, 1973–1985
Translated by Joel Agee

1974

More and more I believe that convictions arise from crowd experiences. But are people guilty of their crowd experiences? Don't they fall into them completely unprotected? What does a person have to be like to be able to defend himself against them?

That is what really interests me about Karl Kraus. Does one have to be capable of forming crowds of one's *own* in order to be impervious to others?

1980

A whale full of believers.

A mob of yawners.

1983

What is appealing in the idea of reincarnation is the notion that animals can thereby acquire souls and achieve a high rank (though not as high as human beings, for it is a punishment for a soul to be incarnated in an animal body).

It is less acceptable that by reincarnating as an animal, the soul turns into a completely different creature and then *remains* that creature for the rest of that life. The transformation, attractive in itself, should be free and not compulsory. Above all, one should always have the option of returning to oneself the way one is now in this life. So the main accent, for me, is always on this life now, it is a center of the world that I would like to see preserved as a center, I cannot accept its transience; not even if the soul, burdened with its actions, were to continue its existence. But when I say "center," I certainly do not see it as the only or most important center, but as one among countless others, of which each is important.

My "obstinacy" consists of not being able to consign a single life to extinction; to me each one is sacred. But this has nothing to do with the merit, the brilliance, the respect someone may have acquired in the course of his life. The notion according to which souls of a lower order must serve as nourishment for higher ones strikes me as despicable.

The hope must be sustained and nourished that *every* soul is of value not only for itself but might also, in some way that can never be foreseen, acquire significance for others or even for all others.

As soon as reincarnation is connected with karma, it becomes a predetermined order, none of the transformations still lying ahead is free, it is a compulsion of ceaseless dismemberment forever. But what makes true transformation wonderful and invaluable for human beings is its freedom. Since it is possible to be transformed into anything, i.e., in all directions, it is impossible to predict where one will go. You stand at a crossroad that opens out in a hundred directions and—this is the most important thing—you have no idea which one you will choose.

The planning nature of man is a very late addition that violates his essential, his transforming nature.

1984

The elimination of concepts becomes a necessity when one has heard them too often: expectorations of the mind. —That's how you feel these days about fetish, Oedipus, and other abominations. That's how others will feel about crowd, pack, and sting.

1985

A would-be man of power who cannot be powerful and is therefore a historian.

He needs the forms of animals in order not to lose faith in all forms.

   He does not want to know how these forms came about. They are blurred by transitions. He needs the leaps.

Immigrations. One and the same person immigrating to the same place again and again. He never finds himself, disappears, and always comes back again.

**From *The Agony of Flies: Notes and Notations*
Translated by H. F. Broch de Rothermann**

That which has no form cannot transform itself.

The pleasure of playing new roles in the presence of an audience who knows you very well, to slip, so to speak, surreptitiously out of its grasp—that pleasure is so great that the writing of new characters, as practiced by writers and playwrights, by comparison seems quite boring. This undoubtedly is the reason why some of the best such imagined characters never reach posterity. You wish to *be* these characters with such intensity as to have an immediate effect on others, magically and visibly—instead of merely recording and preserving them on paper. It is liberating when your old hands speak in new languages which a short while ago you had never heard of. And it is blissful to enter a new face and to slip the old one over it like a mask.

"Ready to be anything, in the ecstasy of being ever." *Sir Thomas Browne*

Dismantling knowledge without damaging its component perceptions.

To say no with open arms.

Man cannot improve himself by anything that he suppresses. The only path to change leads through the transformations he discovers for his evil traits. But these transformations must work, they must surprise, or else they merely will provoke new evil. In most cases, one bad trait merely supplants another, and so the game continues merrily along, undetected.

Much is being forgiven to him because of the mystic word "metamorphosis."

Once again Pascal:
He never irritates, never disappoints. He isn't borrowed from anywhere. His logical conclusiveness leaves doors open. Even if you do not agree with a single word of his, you want to read his words again and again, so as to think them over. No discovery bars his way. In him you sense the absolute equality of faith and thought.

In the *Pensées* Pascal benefits from the fact that he constantly *interrupts.* In each one, the parts can be assembled differently, but it is best to leave them unassembled.

The beginning is its essential component, and the purity of Pascal is expressed in every one of his beginnings.

"Diversity which fails to merge into unity amounts to confusion; unity independent of diversity amounts to tyranny."

Out of the enormous legacy left by antiquity, the transformations have retained the most vitality.

Their effects are still inexhaustible. They will never be exhausted.

He who learns of them early is never lost—not even today. Of all the miracles, this is the only one which has remained credible.

When he says that he does not believe in anything but transformation, this means that he practices a kind of slipping away, fully aware that he himself will not succeed in eluding death—but others, someday others.

V

Death and Transformation

17.

"The Profession of the Poet"

Translated by Lucas Zwirner

Among the words that have long lain in helpless exhaustion, shunned and hidden away, words that one made a mockery of oneself by using, words that were so drained of meaning that they shriveled and became ugly warnings—among these one finds the word "poet." And any person who still took up the activity of writing, which continued to exist as always, called himself "someone who writes."

One might have thought that writing meant abandoning false claims, setting new standards, becoming stricter with oneself, and above all avoiding everything that leads to spurious success. In reality, the opposite occurred. The same people who mercilessly attacked the word "poet" developed their own style of sensationalism. They pathetically proclaimed that literature was dead and printed their small-minded idea on expensive paper, as if this claim were somehow worth considering. Naturally, their particular case soon drowned in its own ridiculousness, but other people—people who weren't yet barren enough to wear themselves out with proclamations, and who instead penned

bitter if intelligent books—soon gained the reputation of "people who write." They did what poets had done before them:
they wrote the same book again and again instead of remaining silent. And regardless of how imperfect and deserving of
death mankind seemed to them, one task still remained for men:
to applaud those who write. Anyone who didn't want to do
that, anyone who had grown tired of the endlessly repeated out-
pourings, was damned twice: once as a human—humans were
already lost—and then as someone who refuses to acknowledge
the endless obsession with death—the writer's obsession with
death—as the only obsession that has any value whatsoever.

Because of all this, I'm no less suspicious of those who *merely*
write than I am of those who self-indulgently continue to call
themselves poets. I see no difference between the two; they re-
semble each other like drops of water, and they consider the recognition they once received an irrevocable right.

In truth, nobody today can be a poet if he doesn't seriously
doubt his right to be one. Anyone who fails to recognize the
condition this world is in can hardly have anything to say about
it. The perilous state of the world, once the primary concern
of religion, has been pushed into the realm of human affairs,
and those who aren't poets watch the world's destruction (more
than once rehearsed) with calm composure. There are even
some among them who have calculated the world's prospects
and profit from its decline, making it their profession, fatten-
ing themselves upon it. Prophecies have lost all value ever since
we entrusted them to machines; the more we chip away at ourselves, the more we place our trust in lifeless objects and the less
control we have over what happens to us. Our growing power
over everything—lifeless as well as living—and especially over
ourselves, has become a countervailing force that we only ap-

pear to be in control of. Hundreds, even thousands of things might be said about this, but they are all well-known. That's the most surprising thing about this loss of control: its every detail has become a daily news item, a wicked banality. No one needs me to repeat it all. Today, I have undertaken something else, something more modest.

Given the current state of the world, it might be worthwhile to think about whether there's still some way a poet (or what we have until now considered a poet) could make himself useful. After all, despite the fatal blows that the word "poet" has suffered due to poets themselves, some part of the word's claim still remains. Whatever literature is, it is certainly not less than the people who cling to it still: it isn't dead. But what might the lives of its representatives look like today, and what do they have to tell us?

By chance, I recently stumbled upon a note by a writer whose name I can't provide because nobody knows who he is. This anonymous note is dated August 23, 1939, a week before the outbreak of the Second World War. It reads: "It's all over now. If I were really a poet, I'd be able to prevent the war." Today we think this is silly, now that we know what has happened. What arrogance! What could a single man have prevented? And why, of all men, a poet? Can we imagine anything more unrealistic? And what distinguishes this sentence from the bombast of those who deliberately used their own sentences to incite the war?

First, I read the note with irritation, and then with increasing irritation I wrote it out. Here, I told myself, is what I find most repulsive about this word "poet"—an ambition that stands in blatant contradiction to what a poet might actually be capable of accomplishing. In short, the note was an example of the silly babble that discredits the word "poet" and fills us all with mistrust the moment we see someone who claims that title pound his chest and tell everyone about all the great things he's going to do.

But then, in the days that followed, I noticed to my surprise that the sentence wouldn't leave me alone—it was stuck in my head, I returned to it, rearranged it, pushed it away, pulled it back in again, as if it depended on me, and me alone, to make sense of it. The beginning of the note was strange: "It's all over now." An expression of absolute and hopeless defeat at a time when victories were expected. While everything was geared toward victory, this sentence already gave voice to the desolation of defeat, as if it were unavoidable. On further inspection, the main part of the note—"If I were really a poet, I'd be able to prevent the war"—seemed to express precisely the opposite of empty babble: namely, a confession of utter failure. But more than that, it conveyed a sense of responsibility, and—this is the astonishing thing—it did so in a situation that had nothing to do with responsibility in the proper sense of the term.

Here, I realized, is someone who evidently means what he says because he says it in silence, and in saying it he accuses himself. He doesn't assert his claims; he relinquishes them. In his despair over what is now inevitable, he convicts *himself* and *not* those who actually caused the situation—people whose identities he certainly knows, because he would be more optimistic about the future if he'd remained ignorant of them. Thus, only one source of my original irritation remains: the idea this person had about what a poet is, or should be, and the fact that he considered himself a poet up until the moment when, with the outbreak of war, everything collapsed.

It is precisely this irrational claim of responsibility that gives me pause and impresses me. Still, it seems appropriate to add that it was through words—the conscious and habitual employment of abused words—that a situation arose in which war became inevitable. If so much can be accomplished through words, why can so little be impeded by them? It isn't so surprising that a person who occupies himself with words more than other people do would also expect more of them than others.

A poet must be a person (and maybe I was too hasty in seeing this) who holds words in especially high regard and who likes to dwell among them, maybe even more than he likes to dwell among humans; a person who, though he surrenders himself to both words and men, trusts words more. He may even drag lonely words down from their lofty heights in order to reintroduce them into the world with great force. He investigates words and touches them; strokes, scratches, pets, and paints them; and even after playing all his private games with them, remains able to cower before words in awe. Even when he seems to misuse a word (which he often does), he does so only out of love.

Behind all this play, there's a force that even he doesn't always understand, one that is most often weak but sometimes so overpowering that it tears him apart. It is the desire to be responsible for everything meaningful in words and to make himself, and himself alone, answerable for their failure.

But what good is it—this act of taking fictive responsibility for others? Isn't it lacking real power precisely because of its falseness? I believe that even the most limited minds take more seriously what a man imposes on himself than what others force upon him. And we are never closer to an event, we never have a more intimate relationship to an event, than when we feel responsible for it. If the word "poet" has been emptied of meaning for some time now, it's because people have attached a certain kind of frivolousness to it—poetry was something that withdrew from the world in order to smooth the way for

itself. And the clear connection between arrogance and aes-
thetics, right at the beginning of one of the darkest periods of
mankind's history (which poets didn't recognize even when it
was already upon them), wasn't capable of inspiring much respect. The poets' misguided trust in things, their misjudgment
of reality (which they approached with contempt and without
insight), their denial of every connection to reality, their inner
disconnect from everything *real* that was happening around
them—since there weren't many facts in the language they were
using—owing to all of this, we can easily understand why eyes
that looked closer and harder than most turned away from so
much blindness in horror.

Against all this, we have to remember that sentences like the
one that obsessed me still exist. As long as there are some sentences (and there are certainly more than one) that take the responsibility for words upon themselves, and in the event of total
collapse feel this responsibility to the utmost, we still have the
right to hold on to a word—*poet*—that has always been used to
describe the authors of the works that define our species. Without these works we wouldn't know what we amount to. They
nourish and sustain us no less than our daily bread, though
theirs is a different nourishment. And if nothing else were left
us, if we didn't even know how completely these works have
shaped us, then, searching in vain for something in our time that
equals them, we would still find one option available: if we were
very strict in judging our age, and even more so in judging ourselves, we could admit that we have no poets today, and yet
ardently continue to wish that we did.

This sounds very grand, and it has little significance if we
don't clarify what a poet has to offer us today that would merit
the title.

First and foremost, I would say that a poet preserves metamorphosis—he preserves metamorphosis in two different ways. On the one hand, the poet would make the literary legacy of mankind, which is rich in metamorphoses, his own. We are only today beginning to understand how rich this legacy is, now that nearly all the texts of earlier cultures have been deciphered. Up until well into the nineteenth century, anyone who was concerned with this truest and most enigmatic aspect of mankind— the power of metamorphosis—was limited to two examples from antiquity. The later one, Ovid's *Metamorphoses*, provides a nearly systematic collection of all the well-known mythic, "higher" metamorphoses. And the second, earlier work, *The Odyssey*, is concerned with the adventurous metamorphoses of one mortal, Odysseus. The apex of all his metamorphoses is reached when he returns home as a beggar, which is the lowest rank imaginable. No subsequent poet has achieved, let alone improved upon, the completeness and perfection of his disguise. It would be ridiculous of me to try to treat the influence of these two works on European culture before, and especially after, the Renaissance. Ovid's *Metamorphoses* appears in the writings of Ariosto and Shakespeare, as well as in the works of countless others, and it would be foolish to think that it has ceased to have an effect on us moderns. We still encounter Odysseus today: he is the first character to have entered the core of world literature, and it would be hard to name more than a handful of other characters who have had as great an impact.

Though Odysseus was the first of these omnipresent characters, he is by no means the oldest; one older has been found. It has scarcely been one hundred years since the Mesopotamian *Epic of Gilgamesh* was discovered. The epic begins with the metamorphosis of Enkidu—a man in a state of nature who lived with animals—into a civilized and cultured man, a theme that concerns us today as we now have concrete and precise accounts of children who were raised by wolves. The epic ends with Enkidu dying, leaving his friend Gilgamesh alone, preparing for a monstrous confrontation with death—the only confrontation that doesn't leave modern man with a bitter aftertaste of self-deception.

Here I offer a piece of evidence from my own life as an unlikely example: no work of literature, literally not a single one, has been as critical in determining my path as that four-thousand-year-old epic that no one knew about just over a century ago. I first encountered it at the age of seventeen, and I haven't forgotten it since. I have returned to it like a bible, and in addition to the effect it had on me personally, it has also filled me with anticipation for something as yet unknown to our culture. It is impossible for me to consider the canon that has been passed down to us and nourished us as final. And even if it turns out that no written work of the same importance is ever created again, there still remains the enormous reservoir of orally transmitted works by earlier peoples.

There is no end in them to the metamorphoses that concern us here. We could spend a lifetime contemplating and reconstructing them, and that life would not have been badly spent. Tribes often made up of fewer than one hundred people have left behind riches that we surely don't deserve. We are to blame for their extinction, and they continue to die out because of our carelessness. They preserved their myths until the end, and the paradox is that hardly anything in existence has proved more useful, hardly anything fills us with as much hope, as these early, unparalleled poems by people who have been hunted, damned, and plundered by us until they collapsed into misery and bitterness. They—the people we scorned for their simple culture, and who we blindly and mercilessly exterminated—have left behind an inexhaustible intellectual legacy. We cannot thank the scholars enough for saving it. The preservation of this work, its resurrection within our lives, is the poet's task.

I have portrayed poets as conservators of past metamorphoses, but they are conservators in another way as well. In a world so invested in achievement and specialization, a world that recognizes nothing but the very pinnacle of success, which it approaches as a type of logical consequence; in a world that turns all its strength toward the cold solitude of the peak and disregards and erases anything beneath it—the multitude, the real—because it doesn't contribute to the peak; in a world where metamorphosis is increasingly forbidden because it contradicts the sole purpose of production, which recklessly multiplies the means of its self-destruction and strangles everything innate in men that might oppose it—in such a world, which one might like to describe as the blindest of all worlds, it seems of cardinal importance that there are still some of us who, in spite of this world, continue to practice the art of metamorphosis.

This, I think, is the actual task of the poet. A poet should try, no matter the cost, to preserve a gift that once was inherent but now has atrophied, and he should do so in order to keep open the doors between people—himself and others. He must be capable of becoming everyone: the smallest, the most naive, the most powerless. But this desire to experience others from within can never be determined by the goals that compose what we call our normal or official lives. This desire would have to be completely free from any hope of success or achievement; it would have to constitute its own desire: the desire for metamorphosis.

An always-open ear would be necessary. But that alone isn't enough. Most people today can barely express themselves in language. Increasingly, they repeat the same clichés from newspapers and other mass media without actually meaning anything at all. Only through metamorphosis in the most extreme sense of the word—which is the sense I'm using here—would it be possible to feel what a man is behind his words, to grasp the continued existence of what is alive. This is a mysterious process, one which is hardly ever explored, and yet it is the only true path to other people. I have tried in various ways to give a name to this process—it is roughly what we used to call "empathy"—and I am using this formidable word "metamorphosis" for reasons I don't have time to get into here. But whatever we call this process, no one would deny that something real and very precious is at stake. In this ongoing practice, in this compelling experience of the full range of humanity—especially that part of humanity that draws the least attention to itself—in this restless practice not withered or crippled by any system, I see the poet's actual profession. It is conceivable, even likely, that only a sliver of this experience makes its way into his work. How one judges this work—which again belongs to the world of prestige and the pinnacle—is not our concern. Today we are interested in grasping what a poet would be, if a poet existed, not in judging the work that a poet leaves behind.

If I disregard everything that has to do with success, if I actively mistrust it, I do so because it comes with a danger that is left to each person to know for himself. The drive toward success, like success itself, has a constricting effect. Someone whose sole concern is achievement considers everything that doesn't help him attain his goal as deadweight. He throws it all away, and so becomes more efficient. It doesn't worry him that he may be throwing away the best in himself because he regards achievement as more important. He swings himself ever higher, from place to place, and measures the distance he has covered. Position is all; it is determined from outside himself, and he doesn't create it. He has no part in it. He sees it and

strives toward it. But however useful and important these efforts may be in many areas of life, for the poet, as we would like
him to be, they are utterly destructive.

Because above all else, the poet must make more and more
space within himself: space for knowledge—knowledge that
he doesn't acquire for any specific goal—and space for people,
whom he experiences and incorporates through the process of
metamorphosis. As far as knowledge itself is concerned, he can
acquire it only through the clean and honest processes that determine all systems of knowledge. But among the many different branches, which may lie far apart, he is guided not by any
conscious rule, but instead by an inexplicable hunger. Given that
he simultaneously opens himself up to people of vastly different
experience and understands them through the oldest of presci-
entific methods—metamorphosis—given that he is thereby in
a constant state of inner turmoil that never abates because he
can define for it no goal—he does not collect people; he does
not systematically set them side by side; he merely encounters
them and incorporates them as they come and as they are—and
given the sudden jolts of feeling caused by these encounters, it
is likely that sudden swerves in direction toward new branches
of knowledge will occur.

I know how disconcerting this prescription might seem. It
will inevitably be criticized. It sounds as if the poet aims solely
at chaos and at being at odds with himself. For now, I have little
to put forward against this charge—it is a very substantial one
indeed. The poet is closest to the world when he carries this
chaos inside of himself, yet—and this is the assumption we began with—he feels responsible for it. He does not approve of
it. He does not feel good carrying it. He does not feel powerful
or expansive because he has room for so much that is loose and

opposed. He hates this chaos. He hates it, but he doesn't abandon the hope that he may overcome it for others and thus for himself.

If a poet wants to say anything meaningful about the world, he must not push the world away from himself or seek in any way to avoid it. Despite the best of plans and intentions, the world is more chaotic than ever, and this chaos is pushing it with increasing speed toward self-destruction. The poet must carry this chaos as such—not smoothed and polished ad usum Delphini—but in such a manner that he does not fall under its spell. Through his experiences, he must oppose it from within and set the force of his hope against it.

But what is this hope? And why is this hope worth something only when it feeds on metamorphoses—earlier metamorphoses born out of the excitement of his readings, or contemporary metamorphoses, which he appropriates for the modern world through his openness? On the one hand, the violence of these characters occupies him, and they never relinquish the space they have claimed within him. They act through him, as though they were the sum total of his being. They compose at least the principal part of his being, and since they live in him, conscious and articulated, they are his resistance against death. One property of orally transmitted myths is that they demand to be retold. But their continued existence has its roots in their cultural specificity, so it is also characteristic of them not to change. Thus, it's possible to discover what their vitality consists of in each individual telling, and perhaps we have looked too infrequently at what enables them to be retold and passed along. It might be possible to describe what happens to someone who encounters a myth for the first time, but a complete description from me would be impossible, and a partial description would be pointless. I want to note only one thing: the feeling of certainty and incontestability imparted by myths, which is to say: *that was how it was; it could not have been any other way.* Whatever it is that myths communicate—however implausible the events would appear in any other context—in each individual retelling of the myth, our experience of it is free from doubt, and the myth assumes one unmistakable form.

This reservoir of certainty has been passed down to us, but has been abused for the strangest purposes. We know the political forms of this abuse all too well. These inferior uses deform, dilute, and tear at this certainty as they grasp and clutch at myths until they finally break. The abuses in the name of science are of a completely different nature. I will name only one obvious example: whatever we think about the truth of psychoanalysis, it has derived a good part of its power from the word "Oedipus." The serious critique of psychoanalysis, which has only just begun, takes aim at precisely this word.

We can explain the aversion to myths in our time through the many abuses that have accompanied them. We feel that they are lies because we know only abuses, so we cast them both aside. What they have to give us by way of metamorphosis appears untrustworthy, and we recognize only those wonders in them that have been made real through technological innovations. We fail to give myths their due as the original sources of all our ingenuity.

But beyond all specific cases, what constitutes the core of myths are the metamorphoses they contain. It is through these metamorphoses that man created himself. Through them he made the world his own; through them he shares a bond with the world. It's easy to see that he owes his own power to metamorphosis, but he owes to it something better still—his compassion.

It's important not to shy away from a word that seems deficient to those who study the humanities. Compassion—and this is also a product of specialization—is increasingly being relegated to the realm of religion, which has assigned it names and overseen its operation. Compassion is being kept far away from the objective decisions of our daily lives, with the result that these decisions are becoming more technical.

I have said that a poet can be only someone who takes responsibility upon himself, even if he can do little to prove that he in fact has through his actions. His is a responsibility for life—life which is destroying itself—and we should not be ashamed to say that the responsibility is nourished by compassion. This responsibility is worthless when proclaimed as an undefined or general feeling. Rather, it must serve as a call for actual metamorphosis in every living individual. Through myth, through past literature, the poet learns and rehearses this metamorphosis. The poet is nothing if he does not ceaselessly apply myth to the world around him. The thousandfold life that enters him, though by all appearances it remains separate from him in all its manifestations, does not collapse into a conceptual category. Instead, this life gives him the strength to stand against death and thereby becomes something universal.

The poet's task cannot be to deliver mankind unto death. The poet, who opens himself to everyone, will experience with dismay the growing power of death in many people. He will grapple with death and never capitulate even if his efforts appear in vain. With pride he will withstand the envoys of emptiness that proliferate in our literature, and he will fight them with his own weapons. He will live by a law that has not been made for him but is his own. And it is this:

Let him push no one into nothingness who would gladly dwell in nothingness. Let him search for nothingness only in order to find the way out of nothingness and show that way to everyone. Let him remain in sorrow and despair so as to know how to pull others out of sorrow and despair, and not begrudge creatures their happiness, even though they claw and maim and tear one another apart.

18.

From *Das Buch gegen Tod*
[*The Book Against Death*]

Translated by Peter Filkins

1945

The fact that the gods can die makes death more brazen.

The cities die, and people dig in deeper.

The souls of the dead are in others, namely those left behind, and there they slowly die out entirely.

Whatever you have ever thought about death is no longer valid. In a single monstrous leap it has attained a power of contagion like never before. Now it really is all-powerful, now it is the true God.

1946

It is said that for many people death is a release, and there is scarcely a person who has not at some point wished for it. It is the ultimate symbol of failure: whoever fails on a grand scale comforts himself by thinking it possible to fail even more, and he reaches for that monstrous dark cloak that covers us all equally. But if death did not exist, then we could not fail at anything; every new attempt would rectify weaknesses, shortcomings, and sins. Unlimited time would lead to unlimited courage. From an early age we are taught that, here at least, everything in the known world ends. Limits and narrow straits everywhere, and soon a last, painful strait that we cannot extend. Everyone looks down this narrow strait; whatever might come after it is seen as inevitable; all must bow to it, regardless of their plans or means. A soul may feel as expansive as it likes, but it will be squeezed until it suffocates at a point it cannot determine. What does determine it, that is a matter for the powers that be and not the single soul itself. The slavery of death is the core of all slavery, and if this slavery were not accepted, no one could wish for it.

The shortness of life makes us behave badly. Now it remains to be seen whether possibly the length of life might not make us behave badly as well.

Only the really dumb can hope for grace, for there is none to be had, but rather only gods who like to kill.

1947

I would love to study the faces in heaven. Otherwise I'd know of no reason to want to show up there. The faces in hell I already know well, as I wear them all at various times myself.

———

It is the hours in which one is alone that amount to the difference between death and life.

That the letters of the alphabet still mean something; that they still have their form and weight and the power to manifest something in this destroyed landscape of belief rife with bodies; that they still remain signs rather than having disintegrated like life itself; that they have not grown invisible out of shame, and every good sentence that they are forced to compose still holds potential; that an innocent man does not hang the moment any are crossed out on this page—or could it be that they are even more damned than we are and haven't a clue?

1949

The thought that torments him is that perhaps everyone dies *too late*, and that our death really spells death only when it is delayed, and that each has the chance to live on if he were to die *at the right moment*, though nobody knows when that might be.

1950

I swear that my life is not all that important to me. I swear that the life of the one I love is not all that important to me. I swear that my work is not all that important to me. I swear that I am prepared to disappear without a trace, such that nobody would even know, if only it would mean there would be no war. I am prepared for this bargain. To which authority do I make my appeal? Is God not even available for this?

———

It's not the dead we fear, it's all those who will come after us.

1951

We carry the most important thing around inside ourselves for forty or fifty years before we risk articulating it. Therefore there is no way to measure all that is lost with those who die too early. Everyone dies early.

He asks himself whether he can manage to succeed at composing readable notes in which the following words never appear: God, Death, Crowd, Metamorphosis, Love, and Fear.

He only wants to be kissed by very old ravens.

1952

We do not die of sadness—out of sadness we live on.

I am waiting for the *sensible* death of a person I have known, and I know that such a thing does not exist; it is always senseless.

Can any language be made viable that does not know the word "death"?

1953

A terrible peacefulness comes over you as more and more die around you. You become totally passive and no longer fight back, becoming a pacifist in the war on death, turning the other cheek toward it and toward others as well. From this, out of this frailty and fatigue, religion mints its coin.

Oh, the comforts of those who believe, those who can deny everything, who can take comfort in the idea of seeing their loved ones again, a privilege that in fact will never be granted them! What wouldn't we give to live in this placid, civilized world, where the dead simply *wander off*! Where we have simply to *call* in order—at least briefly—to see them and hear them, before we are with them once again for good. Where they can be angry with us, such that we try to appease them, where they are hungry and are thirsty and freeze and worry about those left behind. My desire for this world of belief is sometimes so fierce that I can think of nothing else. I see then the shadow of Odysseus and wish that mine stood inside his. I draw its image in empty space, and a subtle voice says straightaway: Believe, and you will have it, whenever you want!—but it is this voice that brings me to my senses. I cannot *ransom* my dead. I cannot allow anyone to negotiate anything between them and me. If they are *captured*, and should they let me know they are, then I will do anything to free them. If they have *resigned themselves*, then I have time to fall into this awful submission/submissiveness, and the time still allotted me, the time of such rebellion, is the most precious thing that I have. If they are *nowhere*, then I do not want any kind of fata morgana to hide them, for here every lie as well as every fiction ceases, since here, and only here, I want the naked truth.

1954

We never know ahead of time what will be the most precious thing to those who are left behind, meaning that perhaps someone will press some old pair of worn-out shoes to their lips long after all your papers have been burned.

1955

So long as there is death, humility is not possible.

A nightshirt from which one never again awakens.

1956

With the growing knowledge that we sit atop a heap of dead humans and animals, and that our sense of ourselves is genuinely nourished by the sum total we have survived, with this rapidly realized knowledge it becomes certainly much more difficult to come to any kind of solution about which we do not feel ashamed. It is impossible to turn away from life, whose value and prospects we always feel. But it is also impossible to not experience the death of other creatures whose value and prospects are no less than our own.

The bliss of simply withdrawing into the distance, something that traditional religions feed upon, can no longer be our bliss.

The Hereafter is within us: a grave realization, but it is trapped within us. This is the great and irreparable fissure of modern humans. For within us is also the mass grave of all creatures.

1957

The heartbeat of those who have died too early. Likewise does his own heart beat, as all of theirs did, through the night.

I, the witness of the two greatest wars humankind has ever known, have experienced both as an onlooker. I wasn't in any army, nor could I have ever been, nor will I ever be. With all the strength of my soul—and it is a strong and powerful soul—I have opposed war. To make it no longer possible is the acknowledged goal of my entire life, which I cannot abandon. But such an attitude, which pervades humankind entirely, is not meant to lessen my understanding of war from the inside out. Every indictment made from *outside* of it is pointless. Better people than myself have failed at this. I must have the strength to shove my hand into war's mouth and gullet entirely and mercilessly yank out its intestines. Whoever is overcome with disgust even before it opens its mouth, it's better that he stands out of the way and sings songs. Oh, I would have loved to sing songs, and far be it from me to condemn those who have given in to them. But I have decided to oppose war and death, to not kill, to destroy its magic aura, to chase away its priests, and to remind people what they can be without war and without death. Everything that I have tried to do thus far was in preparation for this decisive moment. It has opened its mouth before, and I've stuck my fist in it. I cannot pull it back out until I have grabbed hold of its intestines and all its innards.

1959

Sometimes it seems to me as if taking things in stride has become an end in itself. I'm thinking about the goals with which
I began, about the confidence that I had that I would achieve
something real. As I have worked toward those goals, the world
has become weighed down by a thousandfold destruction. This
destruction is *contained*, but does that make any difference?

And what is this obsession that drives me to address every
kind of destruction as if I had been named the world's protector? What am I myself but a helpless creature who suffers the
death of one close friend after another, who cannot keep his
own loved ones alive, shipwreck occurring left and right, as well
as pitiful wailing!

To whom am I of any use, whom do I serve with this fierce
defiance?

Nothing is left but this defiance. New people slide away, new
words and conversations slip one's mind, only the latest remain
alive, and when will they be destroyed as well? Nothing will be
left, and I will still be standing here—a child who has stood on his
own feet for the first time—and with all my might yelling: No!

1962

There the dead live on as clouds and inseminate the women
as rain.

There the living fast and feed the dead.

Might not returning be even sadder than disappearing?

———

With every hour spent alone, with every sentence that you draft, you win back a piece of your life. There never was a person who could so easily be made happy. Especially someone who writes without ceasing—and, moreover, never anyone who has failed so persistently and senselessly amid such happiness.

Write until your eyes close, or the pencil falls from your hand; write without wasting a second or thinking about what and how it should sound; write from a feeling of untapped life that has become so huge that it is like a massive mountain gathering inside of you; write without setting up a hundred different plans and restrictions, and with the risk that it will not last, and the risk that it will fall to pieces; write because you are still breathing and because your heart, which is probably already diseased, still beats; write until *something* from the mighty mountain of your life is carried away, since an entire nation of giants could not carry it *all* away; write until your eyes close forever; write until you choke to death.

1963

Those who are unbroken, how do they manage it? Those who remain unshaken, what are they made of? Once it's over, what do they breathe? When it is dead quiet, what do they hear? When the fallen do not rise again, how do they go on? How do they find the words? What wind blows across their lashes? Who penetrates the ear of the dead? Who whispers the name of those who have wandered off? When the sun no longer strikes their eyes, where do they find light?

We are familiar with all those we have known who have died; it's the living we do not recognize.

1965

I wanted solitude. Now I have it. But do I want it now?

There is only solitude in the face of life. In the face of the dead there is no solitude. They are always there.

1966

There ought to be a court that would absolve us of death, if we answered all of its questions honestly.

What point is there in the unspeakable victims, the blood of animals, the torment and guilt—given that we also die?

Misery is what He knows. How miserable God must be in knowing everything.

He stood before his most precious dead and said: God is good. He repeated it over and over, a thousand, a hundred thousand times: still the dead did not rise.

God is good, he still keeps saying, and the dead don't even reappear in his dreams.

1967

These people who smile at death have a death wish. What else are they saying except that any resistance mustered against it is in all cases too little?

And what if God has withdrawn from creation out of shame at the existence of death?

1968

A good man asked me for directions. "I don't dare tell you" was my answer. He looked at me kindly and was astonished. But he said nothing and seemed satisfied with this answer. Uncertain, he walked on, and from the way he walked it was clear he would not ask anyone else. Sadly, I watched him go. Should I have told him the truth? I knew that he must die, since no matter which way I might have pointed, death awaited him. If he had known that, he could have not moved from the spot, for his salvation lay only in standing still.

"Don't move," I called after him. He heard me, but since I had refused to answer him, he didn't dare stand still and kept on. "Don't move," I called out louder, and he walked faster. Then I hollered it, guilt consuming me, and he began to run.

1970

At the burial the coffin was lost. So the bereaved were shoveled quickly into the grave. The deceased appeared out of nowhere and threw a handful of dirt at all those lying in his grave.

Ban obituaries. Only allow the news of a death to be carried from house to house, apartment to apartment.

1971

It could indeed come to pass that someday I may submit to death. I ask anyone who hears that I have to forgive me.

———————

You have watched the fly that panicked amid the heat of your lamp and fell to the desk on which you write as if it were badly wounded or burned. It lay there on its side, a wing looking as if it were mutilated, two of its legs stuck together, incapable of moving. It lay there awhile and twitched. Slowly it spun itself around, but as if it were in its final throes. I had no idea how I could help it. It appeared to me that it was in great pain, and the only thing I could do was not to cause it any anxiety by disturbing it.

Suddenly it spread its wings as if to fly. I felt as I gaped at it that it would take off, and though it didn't do so right away, it tried to, trembling a little as it did. Then it flew off and disappeared, circling past my pencils.

I was overwhelmed with happiness and would have been delighted to let it know how I felt.

The only letters I would like to write would be those to my dead.

I would be prepared to do nothing else but to write letters to my dead.

1972

What one still has plans for at the end is very important. It's the measure of the injustice of his death.

When one knows how wrong everything is, when one is capable of appreciating the extent of its wrongness, then and only then is stubbornness the best: the constant pacing of the tiger behind its bars in order not to miss the single brief instant of its rescue.

1973

I would not know how to count them, all of my dead. If I tried, I would forget half of them. There are so many, and they are everywhere, I have scattered the dead across the entire Earth. Thus the entire planet is my home. There's hardly a country I need make my own, the dead having taken care of it for me.

Only within his scattered and contradictory sentences is it possible for a person to keep himself together, to entirely become something without losing the most important thing, to replicate oneself, to breathe, to experience his own gestures, to adopt his own accent, to practice wearing different masks, to fear his own truths, to puff up his lies into truths, to piss off death, and once rejuvenated, to disappear.

1975

This indestructible feeling of lasting, not to be reduced by death, by despair, by any passion for the other better ones (Kafka, Walser): I cannot come to grips with it, I can only record it with revulsion.

However, it is true that only here at my desk, before the leaves of the trees, whose movement has stirred me for twenty years, I am myself, for only here does the feeling of a terribly wonderful sense of certainty remain intact, which perhaps I *must* have in order not to lay down my arms before death.

I think it is possible that we really live off the dead.

I dare not think what we would be without them.

————

Goethe configured his life as landscape. Now he is a part of the earth, but with birds flying above.

1976

Each must grapple with death anew.
There are no rules that are handed down.

He forgot to die, that's how satisfied he was with himself. However, he made sure that others didn't forget it.

To hope that you alone will be the one remaining, that's a deadly sin.

It is useless, it is senseless, it is also despicable to think of people as utterly lost.
There is only one possibility: until you draw your last breath, to hope for a way out not yet known to us.
It does not matter what one calls this hope, so long as it exists.

1977

Whoever has opened himself up too early to the experience of death can never close himself off; it is a wound that turns into a lung through which one breathes.

Death and love are always set side by side, but they share only one thing: parting.

1978

The *very last* book he reads: unimaginable.

There is no such thing as a dignified death. There are only deaths forgotten by others. They, too, are undignified.

I'm curious about the *last* conversation. With whom will it be?

1979

To write without a compass. I have always had the needle inside me, always pointing to magnetic north: The End.

Once dead, one is never alone anymore.

It is difficult to believe in the transmigration of souls. Would it not be much harder to believe that one never returns?

Of what value is a past, upon which you expend so much effort, if there is no future? Or can you finally rid yourself of the image of this *river* of time and get it out of your head?
   Think of time as a room full of winds that blow hither and yon, and without a river.

1980

He clapped his hands and death was there. It was the only thing on which he could rely.

———

There is nothing more *specific* than death. Yet everything that is said about it is so general.

It is as if I must always *paint* the same thing, my Mont Sainte-Victoire.

1981

And if death did not exist, where would the pain of loss be? Is this the only thing that can be said for death: that we need this greatest of pains, and that without it we would not be worthy of being called human beings?

Reincarnation had to be enough for the animals. They never got as far as resurrection.

1982

His experience for ages: whenever his railings against death increase, death takes another near and dear one away from him.
    Does he anticipate what awaits him or is it his punishment? Who does the punishing?

He smashed his coffin to pieces and chased off the mourners, gnashing his teeth at them.

He shed tears for a friend whose name he had forgotten.

Today I found myself again aboard the *Titanic* and aware of what the band really played as it went down.

———————

Any opposition to death can appear to be only about your own death. That would be too little. That would be nothing at all. How can I make it obvious enough and beyond any doubt that what I am opposed to here is not the brevity of life as a *consequence* of death—which poisons every thought—but rather death *itself*.

Death is our cancer, it infects everything, it *cuts into* every life, it is everywhere and always possible. You *reckon* with it, even when you least expect to.

What's astonishing is that we live as if we had nothing to do with death. This duality: that we encounter it everywhere and nevertheless behave as if we can avoid it, that everyone recognizes its power and yet some deny it (since we build houses, make plans, give assurances)—this duality is a kind of fundamental falseness at the heart of existence.

They suspect that you are *afraid* of death and don't want to believe that you *hate* death. What terrible readers!

1983

People who live like flies, for a single day—would that at last be infuriating enough?

The butterfly—a ghost of the caterpillar.

1984

A full supply of dead, something to *rue*.

———————

I think of my miserable dealings and my inner life, as well as the fact that the older I get the more powerfully and strongly I love others, preoccupied as I am not with my own death, but constantly with that of my loved ones. I realize that I am less and less objective and *never* indifferent about my next of kin, and that I despise everything that does not breathe, think, and learn.

I also realize that I do not want to see *others*, that every new person I encounter upsets me in my deepest depths, that I cannot protect myself from feeling upset through either disgust or scorn, that I am completely at the mercy of another (even if he doesn't know it), that for his sake I can find no peace, nor sleep, nor dream, nor breathe—that each new person is for me the epitome of all that is vital, the most vital, which I compare with Goethe's more practical (more courteous) and more comfortable peace, which he *deserved* more than any other—and I don't know which I prefer. I am as much ashamed of his peace as I am of my naked soul, and would like to be like him and yet not like him, though one thing I know for certain: the death that he escaped I have depicted better than he.

He felt terror, but he concealed it. Both of us grew old. His work stands, I have sacrificed mine to terror, and by now there is hardly anything of me left within it—do I even know if I'd like to trade places with him?

Why do you deny the thought of another life, be it an earlier one or a later one, and why do you loathe the idea of the soul's journey?

Are you addicted only to this tangible desk at which you write? What of this child, this woman? Can you grant no one at all the chance to hope for another life? Is there no room for unexpected realizations and encounters? Are the dead completely dead to you and you alone?

No, it's only because of the idea of seeing someone who has died again that I loathe all notions of the soul's journey.

1985

And yet I curse death. I can't help it. And if I go blind as a result, I can't help it. I have to strike back at death. If I were to accept it, I would be a murderer.

The hardest thing for you? A last will and testament. To write one would spell capitulation.

Yesterday they buried him. Today he gets up and crows on the dung heap.

1986

He died in his sleep. In which dream?

He would like to die while writing; before he's entirely finished, he'd like to complete a sentence and then exhale before the next sentence, and die exactly in between the two.

1987

Upon his dead horse, he rides onward.

———

He forgot the dead, and they were alive once again.

1990

He who will hear nothing of death has the most religion of all.

Since they no longer believe in the devil, people have become dangerous.
  Man no longer sees the devil: he has swallowed him whole.

What I will leave behind nags at me. Thoughts are not possessions. Thoughts must spring up and they must be able to conceal themselves. Thoughts shift their weight. Thoughts burn bright and fade. Thoughts moan and are pummeled with silence. How can a thought be left behind?

If it were still possible to entirely disappear without a trace, really without a single trace—would you not opt for that?
  What has there been that is more ridiculous than you?
  Who has hated death so from his earliest youth?
  Who has managed throughout his life, his long life, to lose the most precious and most devoted people he knew? Who lived on and continued to lose others? Who recognized, finally and irrefutably recognized, that survival is the core of every wretched power? Who has indeed abhorred this kind of power, and nevertheless has grown older and older and is finally old? Who never once had a God before whom he could justify himself, and lived on without any such justification?
  Who is convinced in his innermost self that because of his understanding of power he will live on, even when he is no longer alive, a kind of Ixion lashed to a fiery wheel for eternity?

———

Knowledge *orphaned* — how unspeakably sad.

The most beautiful thing about *longing* is the word for it.

1991

Wouldn't it be more appropriate if nothing remained of a life, nothing at all? If death meant that everything attached to the image we have of someone would disappear on the spot? Would it not be more considerate of those who will follow? For perhaps everything of us that remains behind is a burdensome demand upon them. Perhaps humankind is therefore not free, namely because too much of the dead remains within us, and many refuse to ever let go of any of it.

When he says that he believes in nothing but metamorphosis, that means he works at nothing else but the chance to escape, knowing full well he has not yet escaped death, but someone else will, someday someone else.

After the rain he went out in search of snails. He talked to them, they did not creep away from him. He held them in his hand, observed them, and laid them to the side where no bird could see them.
     When he died, all the snails from the neighborhood gathered together to form his funeral cortege.

All who missed out on life. All who were never loved. All who could not love. All who could not watch over a child. All who never traveled to other countries. All who never knew the many different kinds of animals. All who never heard a foreign language. All who were never astonished by faith. All who did not wrestle with death. All who were not overcome by the need to know. All who were not allowed to forget how much they knew. All who never staggered home. All who never said no. All whose stomach never made them feel ashamed. All who did not dream of the end of murder. All who let their memories be stolen. All who never succumbed to their pride. All not ashamed of the honors conferred. All who did not shrink away, who could not disappear. All who could not lie unless it was for a good cause. All who did not tremble before the lightning bolt of truth. All who did not hunger for dead gods. All who were not comfortable with them, and whose talk they could not understand a word of. All who did not free any slaves. All who did not drown in compassion, who were ashamed that they had never killed anyone. All who did not allow themselves to be plundered out of gratitude. All who refused to vacate the Earth. All who could never forget what an enemy is. All who could never be freed from their honest ways. All who never gave too little. All who did not let themselves be deceived, and all who let themselves forget how badly they were deceived. All who were not beheaded by their own hubris, all who did not smile knowingly. All who did not laugh magnanimously. All who missed out on life.

Slowly he loses one after another, the letters of the alphabet. Which remain? Which does he slur? Which is the last that he slurs?

Metastases: today the Greek word cited more than any other.
    Metamorphoses should replace it.

———

He plucks people from his meditations, in which he continually carries them around. At all times he has these people inside him. He could populate a city with them. He chooses to keep them in the dungeons of his memory. Sometimes he would like to see one, so he yanks him out and cooks him like a fish.

1992

He *knows* too little to die. Perhaps in the very next moment he might know the most important thing of all.

One loves the dead because of their failings. That's why there are no dead angels.

Nothing more outrageous than the idea of a *last* person. For whom would that person die?

He no longer breathed and kept on reading.

1993

The ninety-year-old develops his plan for a new Proust. He plans to begin tomorrow.

We leave nothing behind. We leave sentences that are falsely written and even more falsely understood.

However, if it is all pointless, if eighty-eight years really has amounted to nothing worthwhile, when every hour of every day, every month, and every year comes to absolutely nothing—then why do you constantly keep writing about what vexes you? Are not these sentences meant to be read by someone who through them comes to his senses, takes them in hand, considers them, thinks about them, and has done with them?

1994

It is time for me to sort matters out again within myself. Without writing I am nothing. I sense how my life dissolves into dead, dull speculation when I no longer write about what is on my mind. I will try to change that.

Copyright acknowledgments